John Gurda is a Milwaukee-born writer, researcher, and photographer. Since 1972 he has
authored several books and more than a dozen
smaller publications, most of them concerning
Milwaukee's neighborhoods and ethnic
groups. Gurda holds a B.A. in English from
Boston College and an M.A. in Cultural Geography from the University of Wisconsin-
Milwaukee. *The Quiet Company* is his first
history of a single organization.

The Quiet Company

A
Modern
History of
Northwestern
Mutual
Life

John Gurda

Published by The Northwestern Mutual Life Insurance Company

CONTENTS

PHOTO SECTIONS

Introduction

Life insurance is a simple business. A mutual company, in particular, is basically a cooperative, a group of people who pool their resources to soften the economic impact of life's one guarantee: that it will end. In numbers sufficiently large, the law of averages comes into play. Mortality rates for given age groups are predictable, and premium rates for given levels of protection are easily calculated. The company's management acts as an intermediary, calculating the rates, paying the claims, investing the funds held to meet future obligations. A balance is struck with each policy every year. If death claims and operating expenses are lower than expected, and if investment earnings are higher, the difference is returned to the membership in the form of dividends.

But the simplicity is deceptive. Mutual companies, like all cooperatives, assume lives of their own. They vary widely in personality, contracts offered, and methods of operation. They are, more importantly, manufacturers of a product. Life insurance can't be eaten, worn, driven, or hung on the wall. It is a piece of paper, a promise, but it is sold with all the fervor of any tangible. The agents who sell it hope to profit by meeting a consumer need. The companies who manufacture it have marketing strategies and sales goals. The members are customers; the dynamic is competition. Mutual companies may be cooperatives, but they operate by the same economic rules that govern computer manufacturers and auto parts suppliers. Life insurance is a business.

Northwestern Mutual is a particularly simple member of a deceptively simple industry. It is based in Milwaukee, a city better known for beer and bratwurst than for life insurance. Its headquarters complex consists of two buildings, the tallest only sixteen stories high. Its home office telephone listing occupies precisely one line in the Milwaukee directory. The company has no branch sales offices. Northwestern has been, until recently, a specialist in individual life insurance, and its product line is one of the industry's simplest. It is one of the last firms whose policies are sold exclusively through independent general agencies.

On March 2, 1982, Northwestern celebrated the completion of its 125th year in the business. It is the oldest major life insurance company west of the Appalachians. The name itself is an antique, the legacy of a time when "Northwest" meant "Midwest" and Washington and Oregon were sparsely settled frontier territories. But Northwestern thrived in isolation, becoming one of those companies whose financial reports omit the last six zeroes as a matter of course. In 1982 its assets totaled $13.3 billion, making Northwestern the tenth largest insurance firm in the nation.

Its size notwithstanding, the company has maintained an insistence on quality and efficiency throughout its history. Its operating expenses are 20 to 30 percent lower than its nearest competitor's. Its products are consistently rated as among the best values in the industry, regardless of the measures used. And its continued reliance on nineteenth-century values has given the company a reputation for corporate integrity and fairness to all policyowners. In a 1983 *Fortune* survey, competitors and outside analysts identified Northwestern as the most respected of the leading American life insurers.

In 1957, the company's centennial year, Northwestern University published *Northwestern Mutual Life: A Century of Trusteeship,* by economists Harold Williamson and Orange Smalley. The book followed earlier histories completed in 1908 and 1933 by company counsel Henry Tyrrell. *The Quiet Company* is the latest addition to that series. It summarizes the formative events of the first ninety years and describes the decade following World War II in more general terms than the authors of 1957 could, given their proximity to the events at hand. The book's focus, however, is on the years between 1957 and 1982, easily the most challenging period in the histories of both the company and the industry.

The Quiet Company is not an attempt to unravel actuarial mysteries, evaluate accounting procedures, or explain annuity tables. It is determinedly non-technical, the work of an outsider and a generalist. The book is about the adaptations a major institution in a major industry has made in a time of pervasive change. It focuses on character, on the participation of thousands of individuals in a corporate identity, on the bending of that character in the stiffening winds of change.

The Quiet Company was commissioned by The Quiet Company. It is not an exposé. There have been, at the same time, no direct or indirect attempts by anyone in the company to censor its contents. At the project's beginning Francis Ferguson, then Northwestern's chief executive, told the author, "Be honest. Be factual. I don't think we have much to hide." The book was written in that spirit. It is the author's hope that it will give outsiders some insight into an unusual company, and insiders an overview of events that may at times have seemed unmanageably complex.

CHAPTER ONE

The First
Ninety Years:
A Review

The history of Northwestern Mutual Life begins in Catskill, New York, a sleepy little town on the Hudson River, just 100 miles above New York City. The Catskill Mountains are best remembered as the home of Rip Van Winkle, but the town itself produced two insurance men who were anything but sleepy: John C. Johnston, founder of Northwestern Mutual, and Henry B. Hyde, founder of the Equitable. Hyde became one of the industry's great success stories, but Johnston's career, despite some remarkable achievements, ended far less happily.

Little is known of Johnston's years in Catskill, but enough to confirm the impression that he was a man of boundless energy and a short attention span. At one time or another, he taught in the village school, operated a planing mill and a door factory, made and sold "invalid chairs," and served as head of the local militia. His involvement with the militia earned Johnston the title "General," which was more than honorary, but not much more. The peacetime American militia trained only occasionally, and many units spent more time marching in parades than practicing military skills.

Johnston was 68 years old in 1850, but he was still three careers away from retirement. In 1850 he and his son moved down the Hudson to New York City. Henry B. Hyde and his father either accompanied the Johnstons or followed a short time later. All four men were soon working for the Mutual Life Insurance Company of New York, the younger Hyde as a clerk and the other three as agents. Mutual Life is among the nation's oldest major insurance firms, but it had been in business for only seven years when the entourage from Catskill arrived.

Johnston enjoyed spectacular success in his new field. Within three years he and his son had the most productive life insurance agency in the country's largest city. Johnston also controlled the proxy votes of the people he insured, and he swayed the 1853 election of Frederick Winston as company president. Surprisingly, Johnston quit as soon as the election was over. The Mutual Life board, probably relieved at his decision, gave him $30,000 (the value of his future commissions) and a $5000 paid-up policy, but the trustees also extracted a pledge from Johnston to stay out of the life insurance business.

No one said, "Go west, old man," but the unpredictable patriarch, at 72, took his small fortune and moved to Wisconsin in 1854, this time taking his grandson. At the time he arrived, the state was only six years old. The pioneer period was over, but Wisconsin's 500,000 residents were scattered thinly across the southern third of the state. There was one railroad, and travel on the surface roads was slow going at best. Transplanted New Yorkers like Johnston made up nearly one-fourth of Wisconsin's population — the largest contingent from any state or country. Unlike Johnston, most were farmers who had followed the westward movement of wheat culture. By 1860 Wisconsin was in second place among the wheat-producing states.

Johnston became a farmer, but hardly a typical one. At a time when the size of the average Wisconsin farm was 114 acres, Johnston owned almost 3000 — a total of nearly five square miles. His farm was located a few miles northwest of Janesville in Rock County, then and now one of the state's most productive farming districts. While his neighbors specialized in wheat, Johnston concentrated on cattle. He owned 260 head, and he apparently wanted to go into the breeding business on a large scale. Wisconsin was a few decades away from becoming America's Dairyland; it is likely that Johnston's herd consisted of beef cattle. He employed up to thirty men at times, and they harvested feed crops that, in one year, included 360 tons of hay and 10,000 bushels of corn. The sprawling estate was centered around one of the largest brick houses in Wisconsin. An 1856 Rock County observer expressed surprise at the newcomer's progress: "The General has only been in the State about *two years*, and intends to break 400 acres more the present season — making altogether, under improvement, 1,240 acres; and we may reasonably anticipate that when he 'gets the hang of the country,' he will be considerable of a farmer."

Johnston could certainly have lived out his life as a member of the landed gentry. Even if his breeding schemes had proved unsuccessful, he had an abundance of good land to support cash crops like wheat. But the impetuous New Yorker apparently failed to "get the hang of the country." By 1857 he had found something else to do. Remembering, perhaps, the life he had left in New York City, the 75-year-old wanderer founded a life insurance company.

Life insurance was not a new idea in the United States. The first successful venture — the Presbyterian Ministers Fund — was established in 1759, and a number of stock companies appeared in the first decades of the nineteenth century. But it wasn't until the 1840s — a time of rapid economic expansion — that the industry blossomed. Of the largest American companies now writing life insurance, a dozen were founded in the decade following 1842. All were mutual companies, whose policyholders shared in the earnings, and all were located in the older commercial centers of the East.

It was unlikely that a major company would arise in the wilds of Wisconsin in 1857, and that is an understatement. Life insurance, according to theory, is the natural by-product of a mature economy, one in which there is enough surplus capital for people to need protection and to pay premiums. Wisconsin's economy was anything but mature in 1857. Both capital and labor were exceedingly scarce. Most of the state was unsettled, and many farmers were still making the transition from subsistence crops to market agriculture. The long-term financial security of life insurance was not the first thing on their minds.

If John C. Johnston knew anything about economic theory, he ignored it. Against all odds, he founded a company that became a giant in the field. Of the ten largest life insurance companies in the United States, Northwestern Mutual is the only one born west of Philadelphia.

Johnston's first task was to recruit a board to sponsor a charter petition before the state legislature. He was a newcomer, but that was a small handicap in so young a society. His position as a large landholder gave him access to Wisconsin's leading citizens, and by early 1857 he had persuaded thirty-six of them to lend their names to his effort. They included merchants, bankers, and lawyers from across the southern portion of the state. Twelve were, like Johnston, natives of New York, and another ten had migrated from the New England states. Significantly, a third were involved in politics. The charter members included a United States senator, the Wisconsin state treasurer, two assemblymen, and a state judge. One of the assemblymen, David Noggle of Janesville, introduced a bill to incorporate "The Mutual Life Insurance Company of the State of Wisconsin." On March 2, 1857, it was passed without debate.

The company was required to obtain commitments for $200,000 of insurance before it could issue its first policy. Working out of a small office in Janesville, Johnston traveled across southern Wisconsin in search of prospects. Progress was slowed by a financial panic in late 1857, and he was obliged to seek help. He recruited Hiram G. Wilson to solicit for the company in Milwaukee. That, as it turned out, was a strategic error of major dimensions.

It was clear from the start that Johnston was introducing a carbon copy of his former employer — Mutual Life of New York. The new company's charter was a barely edited version of the New York firm's, and its products (ordinary life policies) and premiums were the same. Even details like the company's name and the size of its board were borrowed from Mutual Life.

It was also clear that the company was Johnston's personal project. After agreeing to sign the charter petition, the members of the original board had little interest in Mutual Life of Wisconsin. Only eleven of the thirty-six bothered to take out policies, and three of these failed to pay the first premium. Within a year, almost half of the original board had been replaced. Johnston was one of the replacements, although he never served as president — perhaps in belated recognition of his pledge to stay away from life insurance.

Johnston's position was clear in a proposal he made to the board in October, 1858. Stating that he had "got up this company at his own risk and charge," Johnston asked that he be made general agent (assisted by his grandson) at a salary of $2000 a year, and he requested a paid-up $5000 insurance policy. He also asked that his grandson receive, at the time of Johnston's death, 5 percent of the premiums collected by the company up to that point — in addition to a salary. The trustees made Johnston their agent and agreed to give him the $5000 policy but, showing uncharacteristic resolve, they refused to pay his grandson more than an annual salary. Johnston was 76 at the time, and the 5 percent finally amounted to less than $2000, but the board might have feared that he would live forever.

On November 25, 1858, with the $200,000 insurance minimum met, Mutual Life of Wisconsin issued its first policies. Policy Number l went to Johnston, who had solicited more than half of the first insurance. The company was finally in business, but it was breathing very slowly. It had taken almost two years to meet the $200,000 requirement. (The founders of Mutual Life of New York had sold five times as much in nine months.) There was constant turnover on the board. When a $100 loan came due, the trustees borrowed another $100 to pay it off. The company's first president was named, fittingly, Sleeper.

All of this changed quickly, and it changed, in large part, because of the geographic rivalries of the day. Wisconsin society was still fluid in the 1850s, and the state was growing with remarkable speed. Every village, it seemed, had dreams of becoming a metropolis. A railroad depot or a post office could mean the difference between success and failure. The competition for settlers, businesses, and government favors was intense. Janesville itself, the company's home, was built on a foundation of three rival settlements. Nearby Whitewater wanted a share of the young insurance company, and the trustees agreed to give Whitewater three seats on the board (including the vice-presidency) and an agency that could make its own loans and investments.

But the real competition was from Milwaukee, another community that had begun as three rival settlements. Natural advantages and aggressive promotion had made Milwaukee the largest city in the state by 1850. Ten years later its population was 45,000 — twentieth in the nation and nearly six times the size of its nearest competitor in Wisconsin. Milwaukee was the commercial center, the financial center, the rail center, and it was soon to become the insurance center as well.

There were four Milwaukeeans on the original board of trustees, but they were among the inactive members. According to Amherst Kellogg, the company's first secretary, the credit for Milwaukee's ultimate control goes to Hiram G. Wilson, the agent recruited by Johnston to solicit for the company in Milwaukee. After working as an artist and a sewing machine salesman, he must have seen life insurance as a way to prosperity. Wilson had, wrote Kellogg, "unbounded faith in the future of the business and of the Company, and a contagious enthusiasm in presenting them both; which combined to make him a fit receiver of the old prophet General's mantle which he was soon to let fall." Two of Wilson's clients were doctors who later became company medical examiners. More importantly, his "contagious enthusiasm" was soon shared by a group of prominent Milwaukeeans. The young company's focus shifted steadily from Janesville to Milwaukee.

The Milwaukee forces began to move almost as soon as Mutual Life of Wisconsin was officially in business. On December 18, 1858, just three weeks after the first policies were issued, four Milwaukeeans were elected to the board, including S.S. Daggett, a fire insurance executive; H. L. Palmer, a lawyer; and E. B. Wolcott, a prominent physician. All three played major roles in the next stage of development. A few days after the election, sales reports showed that, within a month, twenty-six policies had been written in Milwaukee (presumably by Wilson), against fourteen in Whitewater and only seven in Janesville. The tide had turned.

The final scene was played at the March 7, 1859, board meeting. The Milwaukee trustees had prevailed upon the legislature to strike "in the City of Janesville" from the company's charter a few weeks before. On March 7 they offered a resolution "that from and after the close of this meeting, the office of the Company be located in the City of Milwaukee." There were only twelve trustees at the meeting. Five from Milwaukee voted in the affirmative. Six of the Janesville trustees, perhaps tired of the company's slow progress, perhaps tired of Johnston, followed suit. One negative vote was recorded — that of John C. Johnston.

Why were prominent Milwaukeeans so attracted to a fledgling insurance company? It offered, first of all, a chance for increased income and enhanced prestige. As a mutual company, it required absolutely no financial investment from its promoters. Most importantly, it could serve as a vehicle for the accumulation of capital. Wisconsin was remarkably cash-poor in 1859. There was no national currency at the time, and hard coin was in short supply. (Immigrants who brought gold from their homelands were welcomed with open arms.) Local banks issued notes that were hard to redeem at even a fraction of their face values, but they became the medium of exchange. In 1859 the entire supply of state bank notes circulating in Wisconsin amounted to only nine dollars per person. The opportunities for investment were abundant, but capital was scarce. Stimulated by Hiram Wilson and encouraged by the success of the eastern companies, the Milwaukee faction on the board saw Mutual Life of Wisconsin as a means to build their city, their state, and their own reputations.

When the five Milwaukee trustees left for home on March 8, they took with them a small black trunk (since lost) containing the company's entire inventory of books, records, and office supplies. Janesville quickly forgot both the company and its founder. A standard 1879 history of Rock County declared, "Janesville's record as an insurance mart is unenviable." It mentioned "a party by the name of Johnson" who had started a life insurance company that died "for lack of sufficient policyholders to keep it alive."

Mutual Life of Wisconsin's first home in Milwaukee was Hiram Wilson's office, on the southwest corner of Broadway and Wisconsin Avenue. Although the company began a new life there, it had some old business to finish. Johnston was still under contract as general agent, but he was no longer on speaking terms with the board. On March 11, 1859, at what must have been an unbearably tense meeting, Johnston agreed to surrender his contract in exchange for $700 and a new $5000 policy. He later moved to Madison, where he died on March 23, 1860, at the age of 78.

John C. Johnston was a remarkable man. He squeezed several lifetimes into one, and began his most active years at a time when lesser figures were nodding by the fire. Although he lost custody of the infant he had conceived, Johnston's contribution to life insurance should not be underestimated. Through the company he founded, he had an enormous impact on thousands of lives. Without him, eastern companies might have monopolized the industry. Without him, there might be no home office on East Wisconsin Avenue and no agencies serving every state in the nation. Without him, among other things, you wouldn't be reading this book. The idea of life insurance was "one vagrant seed carried westward by an aging zealot," in the words of former vice-president Laflin Jones, and it bore abundant fruit.

At the same time, Johnston's contribution should not be exaggerated. He was a convincing visionary and a gifted promoter, but the company might well have died with its founder. Until the Milwaukee trustees took over, there was no one to put the operation on a sound business footing. None of the early board members displayed much knowledge of (or interest in) life insurance, and Johnston himself was devoted exclusively to sales. In his mid-seventies at the time of incorporation, he was hardly the person to nurture the company patiently during its formative years. The men who carried Mutual Life of Wisconsin out of its infancy were far less colorful than Johnston, but they were ultimately more effective.

A Second Beginning

Milwaukee was a large city in 1859, but "large" should be understood in the context of its time. With 45,000 residents, the city was smaller than some of its modern-day suburbs. Gravel roads were the rule, and pigs still roamed the streets. The first horse-drawn trolley was still in the planning stages. Most of the downtown area was residential, and the business district consisted of small clusters of buildings at Wisconsin Avenue and the Milwaukee River. The city was already dominated by transplanted Europeans. In 1850, just four years after Milwaukee was chartered, 64 percent of its population was foreign-born, and most of the immigrants were from Germany.

Political and economic control of the young city, however, was firmly in the hands of the Yankees, those New Yorkers and New Englanders who had begun to arrive in the 1830s. Adapting with relative ease to the rigors and rewards of the frontier, they had promoted the railroads, banks, grain elevators, mills, and harbor facilities that made Milwaukee the state's leading city. By mid-century, they had developed their own neighborhood — Yankee Hill. Situated on the high ground between the river and Lake Michigan, Yankee Hill was where the leaders lived.

It was from this group that Mutual Life of Wisconsin's new officers were drawn. Their names might have been found on the passenger list of the *Mayflower*: Samuel Slater Daggett (president), Erastus B. Wolcott (vice-president), Amherst Willoughby Kellogg (secretary), and Hiram G. Wilson (general agent). All had come to Milwaukee from the East, all were residents of Yankee Hill, and nearly all had achieved some distinction in life before entering the insurance field. They saw potential in the company, potential they were determined to realize.

Potential does not insure instant prosperity, and the company got off to a very modest beginning in its new home. Kellogg, the only home office employee in the first year (at a $600 annual salary), had to close the office when he went to the bank. Wolcott (who doubled as medical examiner) and Henry Palmer (the company attorney) were paid for their services in premium credits. The 1859 annual meeting was postponed for lack of a quorum, even though Milwaukeeans already had a working majority on the board. The entire company —trustees, employees, and all 137 policyholders — was less than 10 percent the size of its present clerical force. And the company was not without competition. When Mutual Life of Wisconsin advertised in the 1860 Milwaukee city directory, it was listed with nine other companies. All were headquartered in the East, and all but one were listed in larger type.

There was the very real fear that even a few death claims would wipe out the company. Daggett and his colleagues must have felt some panic in late 1859, when a cow and a passenger train collided near Johnson's Creek, Wisconsin. Fourteen people were killed in the resulting wreck, including two insured by the company. The claims amounted to $3500, which was $1500 more than Mutual Life of Wisconsin had on hand. Daggett, however, turned a potential embarrassment into a public relations coup. On his own signature, he borrowed enough money to settle the claims immediately, and he issued a leaflet calling attention to both the train wreck and "the importance of *timely life insurance*." Sales increased rapidly. Immediate settlement was a genuine service, but it was not the company's standard policy. When John C. Johnston died in 1860, the company took four years to pay off his claim.

One of Mutual Life's earliest decisions had a profound effect on the company's future. In 1859 the board established an executive committee of five trustees (including the president and vice-president) with full power to make decisions between the quarterly board meetings. By entrusting authority to a group instead of to the chief executive, the board set a precedent for the committee system that is still, despite some recent modifications, a company trademark.

Daggett, Kellogg, and Wilson were the trio guiding the company in its day-to-day operations. Daggett had spent a decade as head of a mutual fire insurance company, and he brought invaluable experience to the new concern. Kellogg, a Phi Beta Kappa at Wesleyan, knew very little about insurance, but he learned quickly. In 1860 he traveled to New York City to seek advice from some of the industry's leaders. (They included Frederick Winston, whom John C. Johnston had elevated to the presidency of Mutual Life of New York in 1853; and Henry B. Hyde, who had left Mutual Life to found the Equitable in 1859.) Wilson was also new to the insurance field, but he was an extremely productive general agent. Within a year of the company's move, he had recruited agents in "all the principal towns" of Wisconsin, and he was moving the field into Minnesota. Sales were the overriding concern in the early years, and the company's salaries confirmed it. By 1863 Wilson was earning $2500 a year, plus commissions. Daggett, who did not work full-time, was paid $1200, and Kellogg, who often worked eighty-hour weeks, earned $1600.

Wilson and his agents had only three products to sell in 1860 — ordinary life, limited payment, and endowment policies. All contained provisions that seem harsh by today's standards. There was no guaranteed cash value. Any policy could be canceled at any time for late premium payment or false statements in the application. Sailors, railroad workers, and single women were not insured. No policies were issued in large sections of the deep South, the West, and the Mississippi and Missouri River valleys. These regions were considered "unhealthful" for reasons ranging from Indian attacks to outbreaks of yellow fever and malaria. The company was based in Milwaukee, but beer drinkers were considered bad risks — they were taking "the first step to intemperance." Many of these provisions were liberalized in the next ten years, but they were the industry standard at the time.

By 1865 Mutual Life of Wisconsin was a definite contender, with general agencies scattered throughout the Midwest. The number of policyholders increased from 350 in 1860 to 4297 in 1865 — a remarkable gain in five years — and assets topped the $500,000 mark. Milwaukee newspapers boasted that the home-town company was "side by side" with the eastern giants.

It was becoming obvious that the company had outgrown its name. In 1865, after lengthy discussion, John Johnston's dream was rechristened "The Northwestern Mutual Life Insurance Company." (The region defined by the Northwest Ordinance of 1787 included the territory "north and west of the Ohio River" — now the states of Ohio, Indiana, Michigan, Illinois, and Wisconsin. By 1865 "Northwest" referred to all of the states in the present Midwest.) A new name meant new stationery, new policy forms, and new sales pamphlets. Secretary Kellogg farmed out the tedious work of folding and bundling to the ladies of Summerfield Methodist Church (on Yankee Hill), who used the proceeds to help pay off the church mortgage.

As the company expanded, it outgrew a succession of home offices as well as its name. In 1862 Mutual Life of Wisconsin moved from Wilson's old office to the Iron Block on Water and Wisconsin — the heart of Milwaukee's business district. Three years later the company moved back up the street to the first building it owned, near the northeast corner of Broadway and Wisconsin. Just two years later, in 1867, celebrated architect E.T. Mix submitted plans for a new home office on the northwest corner of the intersection. The company had twelve employees at the time. After a series of annoying delays, the picturesque stone building was completed in 1870. All four home offices of the period were no more than a block apart. The east side of the downtown area was the city's most fashionable commercial district, and it was within walking distance of the executives' homes on Yankee Hill.

Although Northwestern Mutual quickly became a regional company, it remained, on the investment side, very much a local institution. Beginning with the first loan in 1860, urban real estate, particularly in Milwaukee, was the heart of the investment portfolio. The city was growing rapidly, and capital was scarce enough to command the surprisingly modern interest rate of 10 percent. The field was gradually expanded to include the entire Midwest, but mortgage loans remained the investment of choice for the rest of the century. The company, as always, proceeded cautiously. In 1863 it took the Executive Committee two pages of resolutions to demand payment from a tardy borrower.

The emphasis on mortgages was suspended briefly during the Civil War. In a conscious effort to aid the Union, Northwestern had purchased $100,000 of federal bonds by 1867. Daggett was the first chairman of the Milwaukee County Republican unit, and both he and Kellogg were avid supporters of Abraham Lincoln. In 1860 they closed the office to attend the Republican national convention in Chicago, at which Lincoln was nominated. After the final vote, wrote Kellogg, "even so conservative a man as President Daggett, with many others, danced up and down with the contagious enthusiasm of the hour."

In 1868 Northwestern formally adopted the banyan tree as its corporate symbol. The banyan is an Indonesian fig tree with an unusual growth habit. Vine-like shoots descend from its branches to take root in the soil, forming new trunks and broadening the tree's crown. The company's motto, accordingly, was "We Spread to Protect."

By 1868, the last year of Daggett's tenure, Northwestern Mutual had indeed spread impressively. Ranked by insurance in force, the company was twenty-fifth in the nation in 1860 (when there were barely 40 competitors) and fourteenth in 1865. Three years later, when there were 113 companies, Northwestern was closing in on eighth place, a goal it reached in 1870. The company had general agencies in thirty states from New Hampshire to California, and in

1869 it contracted with two agents to prospect in New York, the home of the industry's giants. David was going to meet Goliath.

Why the phenomenal success? Northwestern Mutual was well-managed, first of all. Despite the company's rapid growth, the rock-ribbed Yankees at the helm proceeded with a cautious attention to detail that became a Northwestern hallmark. But they had one basic factor in their favor — geography. It is difficult to exaggerate the importance of the company's Midwestern roots. In the mid-1800s, the "Old Northwest" was the fastest-growing region in the United States, and it offered unique opportunities for life insurance. The region's population was younger than the national average, and mortality rates were consequently lower. Its economy was booming, offering an abundance of investment outlets. It was growing out of its dependence on the East, and home-grown institutions could make a strong appeal to local pride.

In 1867 Northwestern took time out to celebrate its success with a banquet at Milwaukee's elegant Newhall House. (Agents were included, a practice which has been followed annually every since.) Following a dinner of oyster stew, roast partridge, and venison steaks, board member Henry L. Palmer spoke of the company's progress:

> There is no locality in the Union more favorable for life insurance, none more healthy and none where investments of capital are so profitable . . . . Our Life Insurance Company is a *Northwestern* institution. We realize that we have no need to bind ourselves down to the East for everything we want; we can do our own banking, can manufacture our own goods, we can build our own railroads and we can do our own life insurance.

His remarks were greeted with thunderous applause.

Growing Pains

Samuel S. Daggett died in 1868 after a lingering illness, and a power struggle developed in the effort to name his successor. Although Northwestern continued to grow, internal strife hampered its progress for the next five years.

The central figure in the struggle was Heber Smith. Born in a town called Bastard, Ontario, Smith had become a traveling agent for the company in 1862. He displayed such talent that he was named superintendent of agencies in 1867. Smith saw things from an agent's point of view. Throughout the history of American life insurance, agents have at times felt that company management was insensitive to the market and less than appreciative of the field force. Smith voiced these concerns, and he played such a large role in the company's affairs that Northwestern was widely known as "Smith's Company" during his tenure.

In the 1869 board election, Smith and his allies adopted a strategy identical to John C. Johnston's when he was a power at Mutual Life of New York. They gathered thousands of proxy votes from policyholders, enabling them to assure the election of Lester Sexton, a Milwaukee merchant and banker, as president. He defeated S.D. Hastings, Wisconsin state treasurer. It was a measure of Northwestern's importance that a prominent politician could not only want the position, but also lose badly in the contest for it.

Sexton died two months after taking office, and the board met again to elect John H. Van Dyke, a highly successful lawyer and businessman. He had not actively sought the presidency, considering the pay too low. Van Dyke had to resign briefly before the board agreed to his demands for a $10,000 salary. Smith himself became vice-president, and it was clear that he nursed higher ambitions.

Northwestern was not entirely "Smith's Company" in 1869. Some board members remained neutral, and a faction led by banker Charles Ilsley actively opposed the efforts of "the agents-employees of the company to obtain complete control of the company's affairs by means of proxies." The situation was aggravated in 1870, when Ilsley's father, Edward, the company's actuary, made a serious mistake in the calculation of dividends. Elizur Wright, the most respected figure in the industry, was called in to straighten things out. He looked beyond the immediate issue and convinced the Executive Committee to lower the rate of reserve (assumed interest rate on investments) from 4.5 to 4 percent. The new standard guaranteed greater safety by increasing the reserve, but it meant that there would be no dividend in 1870. High dividends had been one of Northwestern's major selling points, and agents did not greet the change with enthusiasm. Bowing to pressure from the field, Northwestern dismissed the senior Ilsley and hired its first trained actuary in 1871.

After losing their board seats in the 1871 election, Charles Ilsley
and three of his allies took their case to the policyowners and the
public. A war of words followed. There were petitions, advertisements, cartoons, and mass mailings, generating a great deal of bad
publicity for the company. Smith had some impressive backers. A
letter supporting the agents' position was published in the *Milwaukee
Sentinel* over the names of dozens of prominent Milwaukeeans,
including Harrison Ludington (the mayor), Frederick Pabst, and
Joseph Schlitz. The Ilsley forces were routed in the 1872 election, and
Smith got a raise.

A central issue remained unresolved. The company's informal
investment policy had been to favor loan applicants who were policyholders, assuming the investment was sound. The agency forces,
hoping to increase sales and commissions, proposed that Northwestern
require all applicants to buy insurance and, further, that loan activity
in each state reflect sales volume. President Van Dyke and a majority
of the board disagreed, arguing that the investment side and the
insurance side should be absolutely separate. In the 1874 election, the
Smith faction reacted by retiring Van Dyke from the board, thus
ending his presidency.

In the election for president that followed, Heber Smith
appeared to be a front-runner. Proxy votes, however, could not be
used in the election of officers, and the board had grown increasingly
restive under Smith's manipulations. They chose Henry L. Palmer,
company attorney, much to the surprise of both Smith and Palmer
himself. They stripped Smith of his vice-presidency and hired Matthew Keenan to replace him as superintendent of agencies. By the end
of 1874 Smith had resigned from the board. The most serious power
struggle in the company's history was over.

A New Conservatism

With the election of Henry Palmer, Northwestern Mutual
entered a period of calm administration that lasted for decades.
Another ex-New Yorker who lived on Yankee Hill, Palmer had
moved to Milwaukee at the age of 30, reportedly for relief of his
asthma. He was one of the five Milwaukeeans who had carried the
little black trunk from Janesville in 1859, and he had served as legal
counsel and an active board member since that time. Palmer, an
ardent Democrat, was elected to the state senate in 1867, where he

played a key role in reducing a proposed 3 percent tax on Northwestern's premium income to 1 percent. He also served as an assemblyman, city attorney, school board president, and 1863 Democratic candidate for governor. (He was soundly beaten.) Elected a county judge in 1873, Palmer resigned to lead Northwestern. He stayed for a record thirty-four years.

Northwestern Mutual had held its own during the years of internal strife. Its investment performance, in particular, was excellent. The Midwest was still growing rapidly, and earnings on urban mortgage loans (40 percent of them in Wisconsin) gave Northwestern the industry's highest return on investments in 1870 and 1872. But the Panic of 1873 ushered in a depression second only to the 1929 collapse in severity. Like all depressions, its full impact was felt gradually. The company's new business fell off sharply after 1876. Policy lapse rates rose just as sharply, and Northwestern, for the only time in its history, had a negative cash flow in 1878. Real estate foreclosures amounted to 15.6 percent of the mortgage account in 1880 (higher than the second peak in 1939). Northwestern found itself with a great deal of property on its hands. Unwilling to act as a landlord, the company sold the "distressed" real estate as fast as it could, and the investment managers turned increasingly to the bond market.

As survival became an issue, Northwestern, under Palmer, adopted a policy of retrenchment. The company resisted new products and raised its underwriting standards considerably. Agents were withdrawn from California and sections of the South. Women were no longer insured. Most significantly, an Inquiry Department was established in 1878 to investigate the "moral hazard" and medical condition of existing policyholders. Two special detectives ferreted out clients who were intemperate or in ill health. If the premium payments of those under suspicion were even slightly late, Northwestern canceled their policies.

The same retrenchment applied to the agency force. Some dissatisfaction lingered from the Heber Smith years, and his successor, Matthew Keenan, responded by more or less cleaning house. He weakened the general agency system by recruiting agents who were placed under contract to the company. In 1879, 460 of Northwestern's 600 agents reported directly to the home office. Relations with the rebuilt field force were cordial. Agents still came to the annual meetings and still suggested candidates for the board, but there were no power struggles. In 1877 the Association of Agents was organized.

Unique in the industry, it became a vital means of communication between the home office and the field.

A central issue of the Smith period was resolved in 1878. Although prospective borrowers were not required to purchase life insurance, most mortgage loans were still made through Northwestern's general sales agencies. In 1878, after months of discussion, the company hired its first salaried loan agents, whose sole responsibility was to seek out quality mortgage investments in their assigned territories. Northwestern's sales and lending operations were finally separate.

When the clouds of the depression lifted in 1882, it was clear that Northwestern had weathered the storm rather well. A dozen companies had closed their doors, but Northwestern remained healthy. It ranked seventh by insurance in force in 1882, its dividends were among the industry's highest (35 percent of premiums), and its policy reserve was exceptionally large. By adopting the conservative course, Northwestern could boast that it was "the strongest of the ten largest companies in the United States."

From Personality to Character

The next quarter-century was the most prosperous period the young company had ever experienced. The annual volume of new business increased more than 500 percent between 1882 and 1907, and insurance in force jumped from $83.4 million to $881.6 million. The life insurance industry was growing even faster than the booming national economy, and the focus shifted from survival to maintaining a share of the market. The "Big Three" — Equitable, Mutual Life of New York, and New York Life — set a standard of intense, even ruthless, competition. Smaller companies had to work hard to stay in sight of the leaders.

The insurance fad of the time was the tontine or semi-tontine plan. Named for Lorenzo Tonti, an Italian banker who used the scheme to raise money for the court of France in the 1600s, tontine insurance was a sort of longevity lottery. Policyholders received a death benefit, but all dividends were deferred for ten, fifteen, or twenty years. There was no cash value. Forfeited premiums and the dividends of deceased persons were divided among the lucky people who survived to the end of the term, and consumers were led to expect small fortunes. The semi-tontine plan was different only in that it guaranteed a modest cash value. Introduced by Equitable in 1871, semi-tontine insurance became enormously popular in the 1880s.

In the feverish competition of the time, the largest companies often paid commissions of 100 percent or more on first-year premiums. Agents, in turn, customarily rebated a portion of their commissions to new policyholders. Raids on rival agency forces were common, and "twisting" (replacement of one company's policy with another's) became an epidemic. Expenses soared as the huge tontine surpluses were plowed back into marketing. Volume, not service, was the desired goal.

In this heady atmosphere, Northwestern proceeded with caution. The company was in the right location to serve the growing western states, but it wanted to expand to the east as well. One of its first priorities was to enlarge and improve the field force. Northwestern returned to the general agency system in the 1880s, and by 1907 there were 91 general agents and nearly 4000 sales agents. As in earlier years, a large percentage of the agents (perhaps half) worked only part-time. Rural agents, in particular, were often schoolteachers or grocers or bank officers who represented Northwestern as a sideline.

The general agents were responsible for sales training and advertising, but the company's role in both areas began to expand. The first elementary training manuals were issued in the 1890s, and *Field Notes* appeared in 1901. Introduced as an experiment, *Field Notes* endured as a vital link between the company and its agents. National print advertising was stepped up at the same time. Magazines like *Harpers* carried "Over Their Own Signatures," a series of ads featuring prominent clients extolling the virtues of Northwestern Mutual Life.

It was during Henry Palmer's administration that Northwestern agents developed their enduring reputation as highly skilled and intensely loyal representatives of the company. Their attitude, in the view of some competitors, bordered on pietism. One president of the Metropolitan reportedly said, "You can tell an Equitable agent by his checkered vest, a Prudential agent by his kit, and a Northwestern Mutual agent by his halo."

The company modified its old products and introduced some new ones to meet the competition. The provisions of ordinary life contracts were liberalized. Travel and job restrictions were lifted after the first two years. Settlement options were expanded. In 1883, after prolonged debate, Northwestern began to offer semi-tontine insurance. The company had trained its agents to dismiss the semi-tontine plan as unproven and unsound, but they quickly learned to tell the other side of the story. Within ten years semi-tontine policies made up more than 60 percent of the company's insurance in force.

Although Northwestern jumped on the bandwagon, it remained one of the industry's most conservative members. While other companies were paying 100 percent, Northwestern limited first-year commissions to 50 percent for even its most productive agents. While others were expanding overseas, Northwestern remained steadfastly in "healthy" areas of the United States. While others were relaxing their underwriting rules, Northwestern was raising its standards. Medical Department rejections became more frequent, leading to regular protests from the field. Reflecting the easy prejudice of the times, Northwestern stopped insuring blacks in 1902, and would issue policies only to "educated" Indians. The company's intolerance of intemperance grew stronger, and the Inquiry Department expanded its campaign to seek out dubious risks.

The same policy of caution applied to the company's investments. Stung by its foreclosure experience after the 1873 panic, Northwestern gradually moved away from real estate. Mortgages accounted for 84 percent of the company's invested assets in 1890 and only 50 percent in 1907. Within the mortgage portfolio, urban loans (which peaked in 1902) were steadily replaced by loans on Midwestern farms. In every case, the company's loan agents and lawyers made a meticulous check of the property and its title before recommending a loan.

As mortgage loans declined, policy loans and bond investments increased. In 1893 Wisconsin authorized Northwestern to lend up to 90 percent of a policy's cash value at 6 percent interest. The company found some ready takers. The policy loan account grew from $79,000 in 1894 to $1.9 million in 1895. The bond portfolio was six times that large in the same year. Government bonds were dominant until 1900, when railroad securities became the investment of choice. In 1907, when bonds made up nearly one-third of the company's investments, 90 percent were in railroads.

Holding the line on expenses, risks, and investments, Northwestern resisted the growth-at-all-costs thinking that pervaded the industry in the late nineteenth century. The company's philosophy was summarized neatly in the 1888 annual statement: "The ambition of the Northwestern has been less to be large than to be safe; its aim is to rank first in benefits to policyholders rather than first in size."

Its Midwestern modesty aside, Northwestern was growing much faster than most of its competitors. The home office on Broadway and Wisconsin was soon overcrowded. In 1885 the board approved plans for an elegant six-story structure on the "northwestern" corner of Broadway and Michigan. Predictably, the new location was only one block south of the company's headquarters, and only a few doors from its first office in Milwaukee. It had been the site of the Newhall House, the prestigious hotel where Northwestern held its first large annual meeting in 1867. (The hotel was destroyed by a disastrous fire in 1883.) Construction proceeded rapidly, and the company moved into its building in the summer of 1886, occupying only the second floor and renting out the remaining space. At the time of its completion, the new home office was one of the largest buildings in downtown Milwaukee.

The company's clerical employees worked five days a week and a half-day on Saturday. Nearly all were men. (The first woman, Frances Madden, began her job in the Collection Department in 1880.) Stiff collars and dark ties were the work clothes of the day, and the clerks labored at desks that filled open rooms the size of auditoriums. Much of the work was mind-numbing by modern standards. Policy information had to be retrieved from a massive card file, and from 1869 to 1891 every single policy application had to be copied by hand. Employees were judged by their penmanship rather than their typing speed. The first modern conveniences began to appear in the late 1800s — a telephone in 1880, a typewriter in 1887 — but the company was decades away from the automation it now takes for granted.

By 1908 there were 60 telephones and 100 typewriters. The home office staff had grown to 422 people, including 64 women. Northwestern had taken over all six floors of its home office, and it was renting floor space in the building next door.

The company's growth at home mirrored its growth in the nation. By 1899 its assets ($115 million) were larger than the entire assessed valuation of the city of Milwaukee. By 1907 Northwestern's insurance in force ranked it sixth among the nation's life companies, and it had the second highest earning rate in the industry. It had entered the 1882-1907 period as a Midwestern upstart, selling and investing primarily in its home region. When the era ended, Northwestern was a national power.

Much of the credit for the company's strong showing goes to Henry Palmer. The former politician proved to be an excellent executive — diligent, decisive, and well-organized. Palmer was not the easiest man to work for. Henry F. Tyrrell, the company's first legal counsel, wrote, "During office hours he was a martinet. He was an indefatigable worker himself, and he expected — and required — others to be the same. In the office Judge Palmer often appeared autocratic, cold and self-centered." He did, however, slip away twice daily to a nearby saloon, where he drank one shot of straight whiskey and returned to the office. The Inquiry Department apparently overlooked the "moral hazard" posed by these visits.

Palmer may not have had the love of his subordinates, but he had their earnest respect. As the years passed, that respect turned to veneration. In 1899, on Palmer's twenty-fifth anniversary as president, a ceremony was held to mark the event. Alonzo Kimball, the Chicago general agent, addressed the leader: "Sir, the Northwestern is bone of your bone, and flesh of your flesh. In every fibre and sinew are marks of your unerring counsel and masterly guidance . . . ." He was not exaggerating. Palmer had inherited a young company and guided it to maturity. Through depression and tumultuous growth, he gave Northwestern a distinctive role to play. He took four principles — simple products, low expenses, high risk standards, and cautious investments — and made them commandments. When Palmer arrived, Northwestern had a personality. When he left, it had a character, and that character has endured to the present.

The First Consumerists

As the company matured, Palmer himself aged. He was 81 years old in 1900, three years older than founder John C. Johnston at his death. He wanted to retire. Events of the next few years, however, led to a full-scale investigation of life insurance. The industry got its first strong taste of consumerism, and the patriarch decided to stay with his company in its hour of need.

It was the age of the tycoon. For decades American corporations had operated in a relatively free environment. Too many businesses developed a weak sense of ethics and a bulldozer approach to growth. They displayed a greed and an arrogance that earned them a reputation as public enemies. The inevitable reaction began in the late nineteenth century and quickly gathered steam. Muckraking authors like Lincoln Steffens and Upton Sinclair found a ready market for their exposés of corporate injustice. Trust-busting Teddy Roosevelt

became president in 1901. Reform movements attracted large follow-
ings, and distrust of wealth became epidemic. The captains of capital
met with almost unreasoning suspicion.

Railroads, utilities, and banking syndicates were among the
reformers' targets. Life insurance might have escaped close scrutiny,
but events at the Equitable made that impossible. Henry B. Hyde, the
company's founder and Johnston's old associate, died in 1899. With
the passing of the patriarch, the Equitable was soon embroiled in a
serious power struggle. The squabble began to make the newspapers,
and an internal investigation only created more strife. At the same
time, muckrakers were turning their guns toward the life insurance
industry. The public outcry for an investigation mounted.

In 1905 the New York state legislature set up a committee to
look into the life insurance business. Chaired by Senator William
Armstrong, the committee focused its attention on the Big Three:
Equitable, Mutual Life of New York, and New York Life. The three
companies held the majority of the industry's assets. (Northwestern,
in sixth place, had less than half their average holdings.) The committee's counsel was Charles Evans Hughes, a brilliant lawyer who
later became chief justice of the U.S. Supreme Court. Under his
patient questioning, the Armstrong Committee uncovered a cesspool
of abuses: dictatorship, bribery, nepotism, diversion of funds,
extravagent salaries, and illegal investments. The findings were
trumpeted in the New York press, and there was a rash of resignations
and lawsuits. After four months of hearings, the committee released
its report in 1906 and proposed a long series of reforms. Among them
were the abolition of semi-tontine insurance, permanent limits on
sales volume and expenses, more democratic management, and curbs
on political activity. Over the outcries of the industry, the legislature
passed them.

While the ink on the Armstrong Committee report was drying,
Wisconsin launched an investigation of its own. Robert La Follette
had been elected governor in 1900, and the Progressive faction he led
was among the most prominent reform movements in the nation. La
Follette had long campaigned against "the menace of the machine" in
both politics and business. In 1905 insurance premiums paid by
Wisconsin residents were four times larger than the state budget.
Northwestern, of course, was the state's largest insurer. Early in 1906,
as he was about to leave for the U.S. Senate, La Follette asked the
legislature to set up its own Armstrong Committee.

There were fears that the investigation would turn into a political sideshow. Progressives dominated the committee, and many of Northwestern's officers and trustees were "stalwart" Republicans who had watched with keen resentment as the La Follette forces took over their party. The fears proved groundless. In hearings that lasted more than two months, the atmosphere was businesslike and restrained. Before the inquiry was half-over, the *Milwaukee Sentinel*, a virulently anti-Progressive paper, announced that Northwestern had been completely exonerated. The company bought 2000 extra copies of the edition and mailed them across the country.

The final report (totaling more than 4000 pages) was not so laudatory. The committee found that Northwestern's management was self-perpetuating, and that twisting and rebating were common sales techniques. There were harsh words for the Inquiry Department's practice of ferreting out alcoholics and drug abusers who had insured with the company. The committee also criticized staff members who made loans to clients. Semi-tontine policyholders could not borrow against their cash values, and many officers and employees loaned them money personally at higher-than-average interest rates. Between 1900 and 1905, more than $1 million in private loans were made. Another area of criticism concerned real estate investments. The committee was surprised to find that, in 1905, Northwestern had only 14 farm loans in Wisconsin outside Milwaukee County, against 2800 in Minnesota and 2100 in Iowa. Company officials defended the practice, but the committee felt that Northwestern should play a larger role in its home state.

Northwestern did not emerge from the inquiry as a white knight, but the disclosures were pale in comparison with the New York committee's. The Wisconsin panel found Northwestern paternalistic, perhaps, but not corrupt. There had been no diversion of funds, no influence-buying. The company was praised for its sound accounting procedures and its cautious investment stance. Palmer was treated as an elder statesman. The committee chairman reported that the president had turned down his board's offer of a raise from $25,000 to $100,000, and said, "His conservatism has ruled the Northwestern, and to that is due one of the great reasons for the success of that company."

There were no resignations and no lawsuits, but there was a spate of legislation. Seventy-two insurance bills were introduced in 1907 alone. The ones that passed required more open elections, a limit on premiums, more liberal policy provisions, stricter fiscal reporting, some compulsory investments, and curbs on salaries and other expenses. The industry was appalled by the severity of the measures, and twenty-three out-of-state companies withdrew from Wisconsin. Northwestern could have exploited the situation but, to the relief of its competitors, the company responded with dignity and restraint. Wisconsin agents were reminded that the out-of-state insurers were still perfectly solvent, and their clients received every encouragement to keep existing policies in force.

Only Wisconsin and New Jersey (home of Prudential) followed New York's lead in mounting full-scale investigations, but the rules of business changed across the nation. The less workable laws were dropped or amended, and the industry learned to operate in a new climate. (The competition returned to Wisconsin in 1915.) Although the reforms were bitter medicine for the life insurance industry, they did cure some flagrant abuses. More importantly, they made the principles of trusteeship a matter of law. Insurance became better and cheaper, and public confidence in the industry returned.

Growth and Tension

Henry Palmer was 89 years old in the spring of 1908. With the investigation over and its reform measures passed, he finally felt free to step down from the post he had held since 1874. His hand-picked successor was George C. Markham, who had been a board member since 1895 and a vice-president since 1901. Like his mentor, Markham was a Yankee from New York. Like Palmer and John Van Dyke, he was a lawyer. Like almost every executive since John C. Johnston, he was an able but cantankerous leader. Henry Tyrrell gave a somewhat restrained description of Markham's character:

> He was a man of strong convictions, and he was not always diplomatic in their expression. Because inflexible in his opinions, he appeared arbitrary at times, but when business proceeded unruffled, he was a kind, considerate gentleman. The arbitrary rules required by modern methods often irked him, and there were times when he was disregardful perhaps of those exact amenities which are expected from a diffusion of responsibilities in a cor-

poration . . . . While he remained in office, as its titular head, there was no room for doubt as to who was President of the Company.

This autocrat guided Northwestern during another decade of prosperity. The twin forces of industrialization and immigration were making the United States a nation of city-dwellers. As the cities grew, real income rose, and life insurance companies found new markets. While the country's population increased 7 percent between 1908 and 1918, its total insurance in force more than doubled.

The insurance industry expanded, but the rules of the game had changed. Semi-tontine insurance was gone, a victim of its own excesses. Increasing longevity and falling interest rates had made it impossible to fulfill the extravagant promises of the semi-tontine companies. (According to one Northwestern agent, the rate books were "sworn by" at the time of a sale and "sworn at" when they proved too optimistic.) Cutthroat marketing practices had drawn the attention of public officials, and semi-tontine insurance was a casualty of the new regulatory climate.

With their main product gone and new expense limits imposed, the largest companies learned to fly with clipped wings. Ordinary life policies regained their central place, and some companies began to experiment with new products: group plans, disability income insurance, and double indemnity. Northwestern, as always, took the conservative course. The company dropped some of its plans and introduced two new ones late in the period: a convertible term policy and a paid-up-at-65 endowment contract. Business insurance, especially partnership and key-employee policies, became more important after 1909, and Northwestern emerged as a leader in the field. But simplicity remained the company's keynote.

With the marketplace changing and commission rates cut by government decree, many companies had to rebuild their agency forces. Northwestern, by contrast, had always had a moderate commission schedule, and it retained a core of productive career agents who could easily adapt to changing conditions. By 1915 there were 90 general agents and 5925 sales agents (40 percent of them full-time). The company was in an excellent position to expand, and new business increased steadily.

There were problems in the field, however. Precisely because there were so many long-term agents, leadership had become somewhat fossilized. The Association of Agents was dominated by a small group of general agents who were not representative of the entire sales force. Northwestern's district agents (who developed sub-territories within areas served by general agencies) and special agents (the bulk of the sales force) grew disenchanted with the leadership of the existing organization. In approximately 1906 they established their own association.

The company's management did little to help matters. Markham was an investment specialist, and his tenure was not one of the high points in relations between home office and field. Some agents were openly hostile to the management, criticizing the executives for a lack of "sales-mindedness." Others felt that Northwestern was run by a clique of general agents. One of these, Bernard Rose, attacked Northwestern with the zeal of a crusader. He detailed his charges in a book called *The Northwestern Unmasked.* A few years later, his anger still rising but his imagination apparently failing, Rose published *The Northwestern More Completely Unmasked.* Nothing came of the charges but some unfavorable publicity.

If Northwestern was sometimes less than solicitious in dealing with its agents, the company did pay more attention to its customers after the public inquiries of 1905-1906. The Wisconsin investigators had criticized the management staff's lack of accountability to the policyholders. In 1907, accordingly, the board established the Policyholders Examining Committee, a group of three Northwestern insureds who were asked to evaluate everything from accounting practices to management performance every year. In 1909 it became a five-member committee. New examiners were chosen annually from lists of prominent clients provided by the general agents, and committee membership was often a prelude to board membership.

The company grew despite the occasional rancor between home office and field. Northwestern's insurance in force topped the $1 billion mark in 1909, and new business averaged well over $100 million a year. The increasing volume meant a larger home office staff. Like a snail outgrowing its shell, the company was soon too large for its headquarters on Broadway. In 1910 Northwestern purchased an entire city block at the east end of Wisconsin Avenue between Cass and Van Buren Streets. In fifty-one years the company had never moved more than one block from the intersection of Broadway and Wisconsin. Now it was moving a grand total of four blocks away, but the break with the past was not traumatic. The new site was at the top of Yankee Hill, overlooking Lake Michigan and only a stone's throw from Henry Palmer's old house.

Construction began in 1912. Work crews soon uncovered a zone of extremely wet soil that lives on in Northwestern folklore as "Lake Emily." A large spring on the site (apparently a source of drinking water for early Milwaukeeans) had been buried under tons of landfill by nineteenth-century developers. Northwestern's builders drove thousands of wooden pilings to solve the foundation problem, and the home office was ready for occupancy in 1914. At the dedication ceremonies, George Markham said, "We of today think we are building permanently for the future. So thought our predecessors." The company was already looking ahead. The northern half of the block was kept open for future expansion.

Northwestern's new home office was a powerful symbol of its determined conservatism. At a time when architects were designing early forms of the skyscraper, the company went in the opposite direction. The new building was an updated version of a Roman temple, a mass of granite dominated by stately Corinthian columns. Although the building's style, sometimes referred to as the "academic reaction," had ancient roots, its technology was modern. Structural steel, electric lighting, pneumatic mail tubes, and forced-air ventilation — all recent innovations — were included in the design. Solid and symmetrical, the home office dominated the east end of Milwaukee's downtown until 1973, when it was literally overshadowed by the forty-two-story First Wisconsin Center.

The new building symbolized a reverence for the past but, in the view of at least one traditionalist, it also marked a departure from the personalism of Northwestern's earlier years. Company historian Henry Tyrrell, writing in 1933, looked back wistfully at the Palmer era:

> In those days the executive officers knew all the junior officers, the heads of the departments and most of the clerical employees by their first names; they were acquainted with the circumstances in life of each other; their families fraternized, and the Home Office of the Northwestern, even while the Company was forging ahead splendidly, seemed to be a happy fraternity house under whose roof everyone was an interested co-worker . . . .

When the Northwestern entered its present Home Office building, it conformed to the inevitable. It put aside childish things and donned the trappings of bigger business. Northwestern officers and employees fell into their respective lines of duty with military precision. Personalities became submerged in duty . . . . The company had reached the point where its service was dispensed with the regularity of clockwork. It had to go on, regardless of persons and personal ambitions.

There were 562 home office employees in 1914, 140 more than in 1906. They may have worked with "military precision," but the company did its best to soften the impersonality of its new surroundings. A free lunch was offered for the first time in 1915. (There were separate dining rooms for men and women, smoking was forbidden, and all meals were served by waitresses.) Lounges and game rooms were available for employee use. The first salary ranges were established in 1912, and a pension plan was adopted in 1915. Although Northwestern was a leader in identifying the welfare of its employees with the welfare of the company, there was an added reason for its benevolence. Industrial expansion had practically wiped out unemployment, and the company was competing for workers.

George Markham presided over Northwestern from a new suite of offices, but he didn't have long to enjoy them. Markham was primarily concerned with investments. Under his guidance, Northwestern became the industry's leading holder of farm mortgages. By 1918 the company had invested nearly $140 million in farmland, two-thirds of it in the Midwest (but very little in Wisconsin). One such investment hastened Markham's resignation. In 1917 he authorized the purchase of a block of farm mortgages in northern Wisconsin and upper Michigan. The board became suspicious when it learned that the seller was a brokerage firm headed by Markham's son, that the properties may have been overvalued, and that Markham had acted without consulting the board's Finance Committee. The president argued that he was simply responding to criticism that Northwestern invested too little in its home state. An investigation turned up no evidence of misconduct, but many board members had apparently tired of Markham's imperious manner over the years. They pressed for his resignation, and Markham, at 75, was unwilling to fight the tide. In the week before Christmas, 1918, he stepped down and retired to his daughter's home in Pasadena, where he died in 1930.

A Specialty Company

The board wasted little time in naming Markham's successor. The clear choice was William D. Van Dyke. He had been active in the company for fifteen years, first as a board member and then as a vice-president. On January 29, 1919, less than six weeks after Markham's departure, Van Dyke got the ultimate promotion. As both a lawyer and an investment specialist, he continued a long company tradition. Van Dyke was 62 years old when he became president, but his involvement with Northwestern actually went back to his teenage years. His father, John H., had been president between 1869 and 1874, when Heber Smith and his agent allies were making life uncomfortable for Northwestern's executives.

Like others before and since his time, William Van Dyke lived and breathed Northwestern. According to Henry Tyrrell, "He was a zealot in its behalf. He could not have been more fervent had his obsession been a religious one." He delegated authority very sparingly. He took no vacations. He was often the first to arrive and the last to leave. Van Dyke's only outside interest was the flower garden at his home on Prospect Avenue, a short walk up the lakeshore from the home office.

When this austere figure took office, World War I had been over for barely two months. In 1917, the year American troops entered the conflict, most insurance companies had adopted war risk clauses requiring prohibitively high premiums for servicemen. (Northwestern charged an extra $50 per $1000 of insurance annually, more than most competitors.) In response, the federal government set up its own insurance program, providing policies of up to $10,000 for the men in its armed forces. The government's action provided, in George Markham's last words as president, "the incalculable benefit of national endorsement" of life insurance. Public awareness grew, and the industry was on the threshold of yet another boom.

The American economy as a whole entered what some were calling a "new era" in the 1920s. It was a time of stable prices, rising productivity, and dizzying speculation. Once again, the life insurance industry outperformed the economy. More insurance was sold in the 1919-1929 period than in the industry's entire previous history. Insurance in force and assets nearly tripled. The nation's per capita coverage increased from $340 to $800. In Van Dyke's first year as president, Northwestern's new business more than doubled, and sales averaged $325 million yearly for the next decade.

The Twenties were in some ways a throwback to the semitontine era of forty years earlier. The growing demand for insurance encouraged old companies to expand and new ones to enter the field. Competition became intense. But the Armstrong investigation and subsequent reforms had put an end to cutthroat marketing practices. To gain a competitive edge, the most vigorous companies turned instead to product diversification. "Industrial" companies (which specialized in small, low-cost policies for blue-collar families) stepped up their sales of ordinary insurance, and the ordinary companies began to offer group and disability income coverage, double indemnity benefits, and then-exotic policies like health and accident plans. The day of the "department store" insurance company had dawned.

Northwestern, under Van Dyke, would have none of it. The company wanted to maintain its position as sixth largest in the nation (by insurance in force), but not at the expense of its principles. Despite pressure from many agents and some trustees, Van Dyke refused to be drawn into the deep waters of diversification. Northwestern introduced a few modest variations on its existing plans and continued its growth in the business insurance field, but Van Dyke and his advisors resisted any significant change.

Their resistance had one far-reaching effect: Northwestern became, by default, a specialty company. As its competitors ventured out into new territory, Northwestern stuck with the level-premium individual coverage it had offered since the beginning. The company found itself increasingly on the defensive, as cries of "fogeyism" and "behind the times" began to reach the home office. Northwestern countered by projecting the image of a dignified loner, not one to follow the leader, not one to risk its policyholders' welfare in the pursuit of volume. The executives continually admonished the agents to remember that "It takes courage to say 'No.'" In 1926 the company printed "The Northwestern Credo" in several trade journals, underlining its emphasis on simple, select-risk insurance. Its image in the industry was fixed.

Although he sided with tradition, Van Dyke fought more than a holding action during his tenure. Much of his energy was absorbed in solving the investment "problem" of the Twenties: what to do with more than $1 million of new money every week. Mortgages remained the largest area of investment, with a steady shift back to urban loans, especially on Chicago properties. Railroad securities still made up most of the bond portfolio, but public utility bonds grew in importance. Policy loans, the third largest area of investment, carried a standard 6 percent interest rate throughout the Twenties. Many policyholders complained that 6 percent was exorbitantly high, and they urged the company to vary its interest rate according to local economic conditions. Van Dyke replied that a variable loan rate "would obviously be un-mutual, unworkable, impractical and would result in unjust discrimination."

Authority clearly emanated from the president's office, but some of Van Dyke's subordinates made important contributions. One of them was Michael Cleary, who became vice-president for insurance in 1919. He had been Wisconsin's insurance commissioner since 1915 and was the newly elected head of the National Association of Insurance Commissioners when he joined Northwestern. When it became clear that Van Dyke intended to retain control of insurance matters, Cleary found an outlet for his energies in field relations.

During the Markham years, agency morale had reached a low point — a distinct disadvantage in a highly competitive market. Cleary initiated several changes that made the field force more cohesive and more efficient. The country was divided into three large sales regions: east, central, and west. More district agents were recruited to develop territories too large for general agents to serve effectively. A correspondence course was introduced to train new agents. A publicity committee (headed by Cleary) was established to coordinate advertising. As a result of these and other efforts, Northwestern's agents emerged as leaders in the "selling to needs" movement. Life insurance was an increasingly sophisticated business. Agents had to be financial counselors and estate planners as well as salespersons, and Northwestern's field force made the transition with relative ease.

As the company's sales increased, so did its home office staff. When Northwestern moved to the top of Yankee Hill in 1914, some optimists had predicted that the company would have ample space for the next fifty years. They were wrong by more than three decades. Plans for a new building just north of the home office were approved in 1927, and construction was completed in 1932. The addition was plainer and more functional than the original building, but it had its share of marble and bronze. Although the structure was eight stories tall, it was designed to support sixteen more — a fact that presented serious problems fifty years later. With the completion of the new building, Northwestern moved another step away from the "happy fraternity house" eulogized by Henry Tyrrell. The company's executives stayed in the south building. The addition became, in Tyrrell's words, "a complete work-room for the mechanics of the business."

Hard Times

Depressions have always been a part of the American economy's up-and-down cycle, but the collapse that began in October, 1929, has earned a place as The Depression. The foundations of prosperity proved insubstantial, and the "new era" ended more quickly than it had begun. The nation's average personal income was cut in half between 1929 and 1932. Farm prices plummeted. Thousands of businesses closed their doors. Practically the only thing going up was the unemployment rate, which peaked at nearly 30 percent.

William Van Dyke was 73 years old when the stock market crashed. His administrative style imposed a heavy burden on his energies, and now the burden increased. Although he could do little to improve conditions, Van Dyke found less and less time for his flowers. Nearly all of his waking hours were spent at the office, and he finally wore himself out. After a leave of absence and a trip to Panama failed to renew his strength, Van Dyke died on June 7, 1932.

In the politicking that followed Van Dyke's death, Northwestern was without a president for more than four months. The two major candidates were Frederick Walker, vice-president for bonds and acting president, and Michael Cleary. Walker seemed to be the natural choice for a time, but the general agents joined several trustees in rallying support for Cleary. On October 18, finally, in a close but dignified election, Cleary became Northwestern's ninth president.

Cleary had distinguished himself in the insurance field before joining Northwestern, but his early career gave no hint that he would end up as president of a major company. The son of Irish immigrants, Cleary was born and raised on an Iowa County farm in southwestern Wisconsin. After earning a law degree from the University of Wisconsin in 1901, he began his practice in Blanchardville, a small town not far from his birthplace. He soon won a seat in the state assembly, and it was there that his interest in insurance was awakened. Cleary served on the committee that drafted the flood of insurance bills following the 1906 investigation of Northwestern.

If William Van Dyke was the company's Hoover, Michael Cleary was its Roosevelt. The comparison might have galled him (he was an ardent Republican), but Cleary did represent a sharp break with the past. He was an Irish Catholic in a perennial stronghold of white Anglo-Saxon Protestants. He was an informal man following a procession of leaders who might be described as courteous but cool. Under Cleary, trustees stopped wearing swallowtail coats to board meetings and officers started calling each other by their first names. He was the first president since 1880 who was still in his fifties (55 in 1932). Most importantly, he was the first leader since John Johnston himself whose particular area of interest was not investment but sales.

Cleary's tenure began in the darkest hours of a dark time. The Depression was nearing its low point and, like all businesses, the life insurance industry was reeling. Lapse and surrender rates had soared, and the demand for policy loans was almost overwhelming. By March of 1933, nearly one-third of Northwestern's policyholders had borrowed against their cash reserves. The total loan account reached $250 million — a quarter of the company's assets.

Anticipating further demands, Cleary arranged for a $3 million loan from a New York bank. (The company was still solvent, but it had no desire to liquidate assets in a depressed market.) The loan wasn't necessary. Franklin Roosevelt took office in March, and he immediately closed the nation's banks, ending a panic of withdrawals. The states quickly followed suit by imposing moratoriums on insurance policy loans.

Roosevelt's "First 100 Days" had begun, and they resulted in a torrent of legislation that would fundamentally alter the fabric of American society. Cleary, meanwhile, was meeting with the Executive Committee virtually every day of the week. The loan moratorium had ended one crisis, but there were others ahead, including some that took years to develop. New business declined dramatically. The face value of insurance sold in 1933 — $191 million — made it the worst year since 1918. Investments turned sour. By 1938 one-third of Northwestern's bonds were in bankrupt railroads. By 1939 the company had become, through foreclosure, the owner of nearly 1000 square miles of farmland. Northwestern proved to be a good landlord. In a manner befitting its Midwestern roots, the company made sure that outbuildings were painted, new fences were strung, marginal soils were improved, and techniques like contour plowing were introduced.

The Depression's impact on life insurance was severe but not catastrophic. The high lapse and surrender rates were counterbalanced by sales of new insurance to people who discovered a sudden need for long-term protection. After 1934, in fact, the industry showed a modest rate of growth. Perhaps the brightest spot was employment. While most industries were ordering massive lay-offs, life insurance companies were hiring more clerks to process the steady volume of surrenders, loan requests, and foreclosures. The agency forces also grew, as the unemployed turned to new fields in order to survive. By the mid-Thirties, Northwestern had 7100 agents (more than half part-time) and 1391 clerical employees. The first number is an all-time record; the second wasn't equaled until the 1960s.

Northwestern could do little more than react to the flow of events, but the company did change perceptibly under Cleary. Like Roosevelt, he exuded confidence in a time of doubt, and his personal style was refreshing. William Van Dyke had played his hand close to his chest, unwilling to share power with anyone. Cleary, by contrast, was a delegator. He had abiding faith in the competence of his officers, and he allowed them a great deal of latitude. He was also a shrewd judge of talent. Two men he hired in 1933 — Edmund Fitzgerald as executive vice-president and Grant Hill as director of agencies — played major roles in the following decades.

The general agents found no reason to regret their support of Cleary. Relations between the home office and the field continued to improve. Grant Hill brought some of the brightest young agents into the home office to assist him, a practice followed by every agency executive since his time. Several returned to the field as general agents. National advertising efforts were revived. In 1934 Northwestern placed ads in seven national magazines, including two farm publications. (Farmers were the largest occupational class among the company's policyholders.) Agent training received more attention. The "short course" was introduced in 1935, and the company relied on the American College of Life Underwriters for advanced education. By 1938, 10 percent of the nation's Chartered Life Underwriters (CLUs) were Northwestern agents — the highest proportion in the industry.

The agents had long agitated for a wider variety of products, and Cleary was a sympathetic listener. In 1933, after a lapse of fifty-eight years, Northwestern began to insure women again, but their coverage was limited to half of what men could purchase. Policies on children (over the age of ten) were offered for the first time. Other new products included a family income plan (whole life with a term rider), single-premium annuities, and an age-55 retirement endowment. Northwestern became more competitive, but the company did not abandon its basic principles in expanding the product line. It remained a specialist, offering select-risk coverage on the lives of individuals.

Despite the Depression, agency-company relations were marked by a spirit of cooperation that had not existed in thirty years. In the home office, however, just the opposite was taking place. The company's headquarters had been a male domain before 1910, but in 1930 women outnumbered men by a margin of three to one. The balance shifted back during the Depression, when the company gave priority in hiring to unemployed men who were supporting families. Despite the free lunch and the paid vacations, there were problems. The new employees found it hard to feed their children on a single woman's salary. The company's personnel policies were chaotic. Every department acted independently, and workers with the same jobs often received different salaries. Transfers and promotions hung suspended in red tape.

A grassroots union was organized in 1937. Its representatives presented management with demands for increased salaries, Saturdays off, and more coherent job classifications. Cleary agreed to negotiate. Nearly all the demands were met, and a Personnel Department was established. Its first director was Louise Newman, who became Northwestern's first woman officer in 1951.

Relations between the company and the union were consistently courteous. (The organization's first president, William Minehan, later became the company secretary.) The union remained independent until 1945, when it became a local of the Associated Unions of America. The clerical employees on the bargaining team were joined by professional negotiators with ample knowledge and years of experience.

Northwestern's union was one of thousands organized after passage of the Wagner Act in 1935. The law gave a new legitimacy to the American labor movement. A host of other New Deal measures had a direct impact on life insurance during the Roosevelt era. By 1935 Northwestern's state legislative counsel was spending so much time in Washington that another full-time state lobbyist was hired.

One of the major innovations of 1935 was the Social Security Act. The industry had found much to praise in servicemen's life insurance, the bank moratorium, and other federal actions, but the guaranteed income of Social Security struck too close to home. Some executives denounced it as "the first step to socialism." Michael Cleary indulged in wishful thinking: "The idea of social security through legislative decree and political machinery has not clicked with the American public; and anyone who thinks it has should look at the record." But Social Security met a need for low-cost, bare-bones protection that the industry had been unwilling to provide. As it turned out, the act benefited the life companies regardless of their fears. Thousands of Americans purchased insurance products to supplement their Social Security benefits.

Another development late in the Depression brought back memories of the Armstrong Committee. Roosevelt had long suspected that capital-heavy corporations like insurance companies were sabotaging his plans for economic recovery. He asked Congress to investigate "the concentration of economic power." In hearings that began in 1939, the Temporary National Economic Committee grilled insurance executives about company size, price-fixing, investment practices, lapse rates, and net-cost statistics. In contrast to the Armstrong hearings, writers for the scandal sheets found little to report. The TNEC expressed fears that the huge scale of the industry could lead to abuses, but it found that, on the whole, America's insurance companies were managed soundly and responsibly. Northwestern, in particular, emerged with a blue ribbon. The committee praised the company's scrupulous sense of ethics, its below-average lapse rate, its encouragement of competition, and its low net-cost insurance.

The TNEC and other federal actions had one long-term effect on Northwestern. Since its founding, the company had maintained a Midwestern provincialism. Stubbornly, almost defiantly, it had declared its independence from the Eastern giants and gone its own way on matters affecting the entire industry. During the Depression, when problems and proposed solutions became truly national in scope, the company's isolationism began to end. Northwestern participated fully in national business organizations like the Chamber of Commerce and the Conference Board, and it moved one step closer to membership in the insurance industry's trade associations.

The War Years

The Depression was followed (and ended, many would argue) by America's involvement in World War II. When Europe became a battlefield in 1939, the United States launched a program of rearmament that boosted industrial production to record levels. By the time Pearl Harbor was bombed in 1941, national income had regained its pre-1929 heights and unemployment was disappearing. The nation jumped from the pained idleness of the Depression to the anxious activity of wartime.

Although it was not a time for aggressive marketing, life insurance companies shared in the restrained prosperity of the war years. Sales showed a modest increase and, thanks to a steady decline in lapse and surrender rates, insurance in force grew even more impressively. By 1945 Americans held policies with an aggregate face value of $155 billion — an increase of 55 percent from the 1935 level.

World War II presented the industry with a serious labor shortage. The armed forces became the nation's largest "employer" and, for those who stayed home, factory jobs were abundant. At Northwestern's home office, women quickly regained their pre-Depression dominance. In the field, the number of agents dropped to 3633 in 1943 — almost half the 1932 level. Northwestern had dismissed some because of low productivity, but many had joined the armed forces or found other jobs. The company was forced to assist the general agents in their recruiting efforts. Beginning in 1943, Northwestern advanced up to $200 per month for each new agent placed under contract by its general agents.

A reduced agency force contributed to a sluggish increase in sales, but the company did grow dramatically in one area: pension trusts. Social Security, union pressures, and significant tax advantages had focused attention on employer-sponsored retirement plans, and Northwestern entered the field in approximately 1938. Concentrating on smaller firms, the company offered a variety of endowment and annuity contracts, each individual, each requiring a medical examination. Between 1943 and 1945 pension trusts accounted for nearly a third of Northwestern's new premium income.

The greatest change during the period was in the area of investments. The role of the federal government, under the strong will of Roosevelt and the necessity of war, continued to expand. The impact on life insurance investments was profound. The government placed a ceiling on interest rates and entered the home, farm, and industrial loan markets on a large scale. With the prime rate at 1.5 percent and the federal presence in the marketplace growing, insurance companies were forced to develop new investment strategies.

Until the Depression eased, Northwestern could do little more than manage its "distressed" farms and reorganize its bankrupt railroads. When assets began to grow again in the late Thirties, the company turned to new investments, including industrial stocks and bonds, and government securities. In 1933 Northwestern had the industry's second largest mortgage account and the smallest portfolio of stocks and bonds. By 1947 the company was second lowest in mortgages and third highest in stocks and bonds. Foreshadowing more recent events, Northwestern purchased its first industrial bonds from oil companies, and made one of its largest loans to a cargo ship firm.

Despite the adjustments, investment earnings continued to decline — a problem that was shared by the entire industry. Northwestern's premium rates were calculated, in part, on the basis of a 3 percent rate of return. As the wartime economy pushed investment yields below the 3.5 percent mark, the company's margin of safety began to erode. Lowering the reserve rate was an obvious solution, but it would have required a corresponding increase in insurance premiums. Some of the company's officers, concerned about the effect on sales, favored a modest drop in the rate to 2.5 percent. Cleary, in the conservative Northwestern tradition, decided on a new level of 2 percent.

The decision, made in 1946, involved a great deal of agonizing for Cleary. His entire administration had been a time of stress, and the end of the war in 1945, as welcome as it was, involved a whole new series of adjustments. Cleary had slowed down his pace after a heart attack in 1943, but there was little time for rest in his position. On February 20, 1947, the day before a planned Arizona vacation, Cleary suffered a second, fatal heart attack.

Michael Cleary guided Northwestern during the most distinctly abnormal period in American history since the Civil War. During his tenure the United States, at staggering human cost, survived an economic collapse and won a global armed conflict. It was a roller coaster ride, with more downs than ups. Under Cleary, Northwestern hung on, and it left the period with its principles and its prosperity intact.

The company paid a price for its conservatism. By resisting changes that would have resulted in greater diversity and greater volume, Northwestern failed to keep pace with some of its competitors. Measured by insurance in force, the company's rank in the industry dropped from sixth in 1918 to seventh in 1932 and eighth in 1946. But the decision to remain an individual, select-risk insurer had been made with an eye to safety rather than size. Other yardsticks became more important. By the time Cleary's tenure ended, his company was near the top in earnings and persistency rates, and near the bottom in operating expenses and net cost. Northwestern's self-image as a standard of excellence was confirmed.

Northwestern Mutual
1857-1947

John C. Johnston, schoolteacher, industrialist, part-time militiaman, insurance agent, farmer and, in 1857, founder of Northwestern Mutual Life.

Samuel Daggett, 1859-1868   *John Van Dyke, 1869-1874*
George Markham, 1908-1919   *William Van Dyke, 1919-1932*

Presidents

Henry Palmer, president from 1874 to 1908. In his thirty-four years at the helm, Palmer guided Northwestern from adolescence to maturity, from personality to character.

Upper Left: *Modest beginnings — the company's first headquarters in Janesville, 1857.*

Upper Right: *The first Milwaukee home office constructed for Northwestern, 1870.*

Lower: *The home office from 1886 to 1914.*

Top: *A group of Iowa agents in 1894.*
Bottom: *The 1890 annual meeting of agents, held on the home office roof.*

Top: *720 E. Wisconsin Avenue under construction, 1913.*

Bottom: *The finished product in 1914 — a Roman temple adapted to business use.*

Top: *The South Bend (Indiana) general agency staff takes time out for a picnic.*

Bottom: *An agents' annual meeting at the home office in the early 1900s.*

Agency Department Officers — 1894

First row, left to right: *Alonzo Kimball, Willard Merrill (superintendent of agencies), and Henry Norris.*

Second row, left to right: *George Copeland, W. J. Doolittle, and Mather Kimball.*

Top: *The Cashier's Department in 1894.*

Bottom: *The restaurant staff in approximately 1915, ready to serve the free lunch that has been a Northwestern institution for nearly seventy years.*

Top: *There were rules against smoking, but Dr. John Fisher (right), the company's medical director, and an agent friend lit up cigars to celebrate Fisher's fiftieth anniversary at the home office in 1935.*

Bottom: *Laflin Jones (left) and Edmund Fitzgerald acted as umpires at a New England agents' celebration just before World War II.*

Michael Cleary, president from 1932 to 1947, testifying before the Temporary National Economic Committee in 1939.

CHAPTER TWO

Affluence, Anxiety, and Northwestern Mutual

1947-1957

Nothing was the same after World War II. Nothing is the same after any major war but, following V-J Day, the pace of change quickened and the scale of change increased to dimensions that startled many observers. The balance of world power shifted fundamentally and, with the advent of nuclear weapons, became a balance of terror. The American economy performed as if every other boom period had been a rehearsal. American society began a long series of wrenching changes. It was the beginning of the "super" era: superhighways and supermarkets, supercharged cars and supersonic aircraft, superstars and superpowers.

The post-war years are all one piece. The foundations of contemporary society — Cold War, consumer culture, social upheaval, and inflation — were all laid in the period following 1945. The war itself stands out as a benchmark, a watershed, a border separating one way of life from another.

The new world, one that blended affluence and anxiety, did not emerge as soon as Japan surrendered. No one was sure what to expect in peacetime. The Depression was still a fresh memory, and there were widespread fears that the full employment of the war years was only a fluke, an artificial lull in the continuing hard times.

The pessimists were wrong. It took a few years for American industries to switch from military to civilian goods, but production soared when the transition was complete. The gross national product (the total value of goods produced and services rendered in a given year) jumped from $212.3 billion in 1945 to $506 billion in 1960 — an increase of 138 percent. Unemployment became a fading memory, and there was a serious labor shortage. In 1952 Edmund Fitzgerald, Michael Cleary's successor as Northwestern Mutual's president, said, "Like all employers, we are shorthanded and could use about 10 percent more people."

Consumer demand fueled the expansion of the economy. The steady incomes and material shortages of the war years had left millions of Americans with sizable savings and nothing to buy. When the war ended, the luxuries of the Thirties became necessities. By 1960 75 percent of all households owned a car, 87 percent a television, 86 percent a refrigerator, and 75 percent a washing machine. Home use of electricity tripled during the 1950s.

When savings were depleted, incomes rose to supply more buying power. The median family income increased 64 percent between 1947 and 1957 — from $3031 to $4971. When income failed to keep pace with expectations, credit was easily available. Short-term consumer loans totaled $8.4 billion in 1946 and $45 billion in 1958, a rise of 436 percent.

The basic consumer purchase, then as now, was a home. A pent-up demand for housing led to the biggest building boom in the nation's history. The number of housing starts soared from 150,000 in 1944 to 1.4 million in 1950. Suburban communities grew like mushrooms after a rain. By 1958, 85 percent of the 13 million new homes built in the previous decade were in the suburbs.

The suburban boom was accompanied by a baby boom. More than 3.4 million children were born in 1946 — the biggest one-year gain in American history. Large families became a national norm, as births passed the four million mark in 1954 and stayed above that level until 1965. The number of babies born exceeded the present population of Minnesota every year for a decade. The baby boom created, among other things, a new source of consumer demand. In 1955, $100 million was spent on Davy Crockett gear alone.

Millions of Americans thought they had found the American dream: a new home in the suburbs, a car in the garage, all the modern appliances, and three or four children playing in the family room. Church attendance rose dramatically, and "togetherness" became a national norm. In 1960 Adlai Stevenson said, "The engine of social progress has run out of the fuel of discontent."

Business leaders thought they had found a perpetual motion machine. More people meant increasing demand, demand created jobs, jobs created income, and income carried demand to new heights. A prominent sociologist proclaimed, "The problems of the industrial revolution have been solved." As growth rates outstripped projections year after year, some observers were almost grateful for periodic slowdowns.

There was a darker side to America's prosperity. Millions in the underclass never experienced the "barbecued bliss" of the suburbs. By the late Fifties, one-third of all prescriptions included tranquilizers. Social critics lampooned the conformity and materialism of American culture. And there was an enemy that became more familiar in the following decades: inflation. The cost of living rose 14.4 percent in 1947 and increased 6 percent annually until 1952. Columnists chided Harry Truman for predicting, in 1950, that inflation would boost the GNP past the $1 trillion mark and family income past the $12,000 mark by the year 2000. He was short by twenty-nine years on the first count, twenty-seven on the second.

Inflation tapered off after 1952, slowing to an average annual rate of 1.3 percent for the rest of the decade. Another source of anxiety refused to go away: the Cold War. An ironic reversal of roles took place in the years after 1945. The Soviet Union and mainland China, both American allies during the war, became adversaries. Germany and Japan became allies. The United States, under Harry Truman, adopted a policy of "containment," taking whatever steps were considered necessary to curb the expansion of Communist influence. The Truman Doctrine led to American involvement in Greece, Turkey, French Indochina (later Vietnam, Laos, and Cambodia), the Berlin airlift, and the Korean War (1950-53).

It was a frail peace that followed World War II, and the threat of a nuclear holocaust kept the world on edge. The Soviet Union developed its first atomic bomb in 1949; both superpowers had the hydrogen bomb by 1953. Ironically, the arms build-up played a vital role in America's peacetime prosperity, as military public works projects kept hundreds of factories humming. But the nuclear stalemate had a profound impact on the national psychology. Americans were not yet numbed by the presence of weapons that could literally wipe out life on earth, and the post-war generation developed what one historian called "a special awareness of impermanence."

The life insurance industry reflected the prevailing fears. In 1951 one of the trade associations proposed a pool to share the risk of fatalities in case of a nuclear attack on American cities. Northwestern microfilmed its records in the late Forties and transferred a complete set of films to a vault in a safe rural area. In 1951 Northwestern reassured its policyowners that no state had more than 11 percent of the company's investments.

A 1947 ad for Northwestern's retirement products summarized the nation's worries:

> Somewhere in this United States there's a man who loves the woods, probably millions of him. He's fed up with atom bombs — power politics — the exasperating ebb and flow of materials and prices — the claims and counter-claims of pressure groups — the dire predictions.

The ad could have been written yesterday. Throughout the post-war period, affluence has been counterbalanced by anxiety.

Shifting Currents, Steady Course

Northwestern entered the new era under the leadership of a new president — Edmund Fitzgerald. He was a home office veteran with fifteen years of experience. In 1928, when Fitzgerald was a rising executive at what became the First Wisconsin Bank, Michael Cleary recruited him to help in the Community Fund drive. A friendship developed, and Cleary kept Fitzgerald in mind when he became president. In 1932, over lunch at the Milwaukee Club (two blocks west of the home office), he convinced Fitzgerald to join Northwestern as his executive vice-president. Fifteen years later, when the Board of Trustees elected him to the presidency, Fitzgerald celebrated with a dinner at the Milwaukee Club. The election was held on April 23, 1947, less than two months after Fitzgerald's fifty-third birthday. He was the youngest man to head the company since John Van Dyke took office in 1869.

A third-generation Milwaukeean, Fitzgerald was descended from a line of Great Lakes sailors. His grandfather and all six great-uncles had captained ships that sailed the inland seas, and a drydock firm owned by his grandfather and then his father had earned the family a prominent place in Milwaukee society. Fitzgerald maintained a lifelong interest in the Great Lakes, but his career led in other directions. A 1916 Phi Beta Kappa graduate of Yale, he served as a soldier, foundry worker, promotional writer, company secretary, and banker before joining Northwestern.

Fitzgerald continued the informal tone set by Michael Cleary. A man of great style, he combined Ivy League poise with a deft common touch. Approachable, gregarious, and yet clearly in command, Fitzgerald remains one of the best-loved leaders in Northwestern history. "I do try for a measure of relaxation and detachment," he said. "A laugh here and there, an occasional wisecrack or a bad pun can help a lot. To me the accouterments of office are not as important as its opportunities for setting a tone of pleasant informality."

Fitzgerald's central task was the same as the nation's: rebuilding. The Depression and war years had been a prolonged period of stagnation, even atrophy, for Northwestern and its competitors. The company's annual sales had fallen steadily from $380 million in 1929 to $265 million in 1944. Insurance in force had grown less than 14 percent during the same fifteen years. The number of full-time agents had declined from 3382 in 1932 to 2127 in 1946. Investment yields had been moving downward since the 1920s, skidding to 3.01 percent in 1947. Northwestern and its competitors were like out-of-shape athletes, forced to wait on the sidelines until normal play resumed.

The end of the war meant the end of the wait. The nation's new-found affluence and anxiety produced the most remarkable period of growth the industry has ever known. To put it simply, more people had more to protect and more money to pay for protection. Large families, higher incomes, the surge in home ownership, and dreams of a college education for the kids provided natural markets for life insurance. Uncertainty about the years ahead heightened the desire for economic security. In 1946, the first full year after the war, insurance sales increased 48 percent, the beginning of a crescendo that has yet to peak. In the fifteen or twenty years that followed the war, marketing conditions for life insurance were probably closer to ideal than they ever have been.

Northwestern shared in the general prosperity. New sales for 1946 ($471 million) represented a 47 percent increase over 1945, the highest rate of gain since 1919. The company's agents broke their own sales records in most years, and Northwestern's insurance in force increased by nearly two-thirds between 1947 and 1957.

Although Northwestern became more affluent, it also found reason for new anxiety. The growth of competition was nothing short of phenomenal. The number of life companies in the United States increased from 473 in 1945 to 1273 in 1957. Nearly all were stock companies seeking to emulate the success of the established giants. A peak was reached in 1955, when 216 new companies were formed: an average rate of four per week.

Even more importantly, the industry was diversifying as fast as it grew. Life companies branched out into the health and accident fields. By 1957 property and casualty companies were acquiring their own life affiliates. An article in *Best's Review*, a leading trade journal, asked, "Will everybody be multiple-line?" The companies that continued to concentrate on life insurance broadened their offerings dramatically. Disability income and accidental death policies found new markets. "Special" policies with premium discounts for size and "classified" insurance on substandard risks were offered by scores of companies. "Combination" plans used both term and whole life coverage to provide maximum protection for young families.

The most dramatic growth, however, was in the area of group insurance. Fringe benefits became a basic part of employee compensation in the 1940s, and group term insurance became a basic part of the benefit package. In 1945 one-fourth of the nation's non-farm workers had group life coverage, and group sales accounted for 8 percent of the industry's new business. In 1957 half of the labor force was covered, and group plans made up 22 percent of new sales.

The post-war trends were a basic challenge to Northwestern's identity. As rapid growth and diversification became industry norms, the company found itself increasingly on the defensive — a position that, in some ways, it has never really left. Like William Van Dyke in the 1920s, Edmund Fitzgerald found it necessary to constantly reaffirm Northwestern's commitment to simple, select-risk insurance on individual lives. In a 1948 speech to the eastern region's agents, he summarized both the trends and his company's response:

> Somebody is going into group, somebody else into substandard; another thinks that disability insurance may be all right if you can calculate the premium; others are going into Texas — and then another western division is being opened . . . . We have no intention of following them in the foreseeable future.

Northwestern could have rebuilt rapidly and joined its counterparts in the quest for volume. The company could have added dozens of new territories, recruited a host of new agents, and introduced a full line of new products. It did not, and the reasons for its refusal were a mixture of tradition and economics. Northwestern's "all time number one consideration," in Fitzgerald's words, was the low net cost of its products — their premiums minus dividends and cash values. It was cost, consistent with quality, that gave the company its competitive edge. Maintaining that position was Northwestern's first commandment, and all the rules that followed — cautious underwriting, simplicity of operations, sound investments, lean salary and commission structures — were corollaries of the first.

Investment yields, a major component of dividends, were depressed in the post-war years. Operating costs were rising rapidly at the same time. Development of group, health, and other new products would have cost, in Fitzgerald's estimate, an additional $15 to $20 million. Geographic and field expansion might have been even more expensive. As a result, the aggressive pursuit of new customers and the welfare of existing clients were diametrically opposed. Rapid growth meant lower dividends (and higher net cost); higher dividends meant slower growth. Given Northwestern's insistence on net-cost superiority, there was no agonizing over the decision. Looking back in 1957, Fitzgerald said, "We believed seriously that the present policyholder who was the victim of controlled and lower interest rates . . . should not at the same time be assessed the cost of an expansion of sales activity."

Fitzgerald took the decision one step further. Northwestern not only refused to expand and diversify, but the company also became extremely cost-conscious in its existing operations. Departmental budgeting and staff expansion were watched closely. New programs were developed to boost the productivity of the existing field force. Even executive salaries were affected. As other companies raised their top pay scales rapidly in the post-war boom, Fitzgerald held the line. (The president himself, independently wealthy, never earned more than $60,000 annually from Northwestern — roughly $170,000 in 1982 dollars.) Most importantly, the company's cost-consciousness led it into the computer age, a process that is described in the next chapter.

Although Northwestern's refusal to follow the leaders was a business decision, it was entirely in keeping with Fitzgerald's character. Specialization quickly assumed a moral dimension. In speech after speech, interview after interview, Fitzgerald worked and reworked the theme of individualism. Northwestern, in his view, was a company that offered "a specialized service superlatively well," attracting "discerning persons" who wanted the "prestige" of a "rather unique enterprise." If the president came dangerously close to elitism in some of his public views, they were beliefs sincerely held. Fitzgerald's Northwestern was the industry's aristocrat: well-bred, dignified, classically simple, devoted to quality without thought of compromise. No president before or since his time has lavished comparable eloquence on the delineation of Northwestern's character.

Despite Fitzgerald's impassioned defense of the company's narrow role, Northwestern did not return to the nineteenth century. Market conditions dictated significant changes in plans and standards. New products were designed to meet the needs of the fastest-growing segment of the American public: married couples with young children. A revised family income policy (whole life with a term rider) was introduced in 1950 and met with instant success. The lower age limit on insureds was dropped from $9\frac{1}{2}$ to $4\frac{1}{2}$ in 1951, and to one month in 1956.

Other products were introduced purely to meet the competition. Northwestern entered the classified field in 1956, explaining that it wanted to protect policyowners who had become uninsurable. Most applicants were newcomers, however, and substandard risks brought in 9 percent of Northwestern's new business for the next decade. A more novel approach to the competition was Quantity Earned Savings, adopted in 1957. QES was a response to the discounts many companies offered to the buyers of exceptionally large policies. Northwestern applied the same principle across the board, grading down premiums on policies as small as $5000. Just as importantly, QES was applied in "the mutual way;" dividends on old policies were graded up to insure fair treatment for all policyowners.

Despite the changes, permanent products — whole life and endowment contracts — remained Northwestern's stock in trade. They accounted for nearly 80 percent of the company's new business (face value) during the Fitzgerald years. Term insurance — the remaining 20 percent — was sometimes viewed as the black sheep in Northwestern's family of products. It had an acknowledged place in the company, but it was decidedly subordinate to permanent insurance. As "the trend to term" accelerated after the war (rising from 16 percent of Northwestern's new business in 1947 to 24 percent in 1957), Fitzgerald expressed concern. He praised the agents whenever there was a temporary decrease in term sales, explaining that non-permanent products lacked "the creation of that new capital or that deferred spending in the form of savings which is a part of ordinary insurance."

The market for all of Northwestern's products grew more sharply defined in the post-war years. American business managers had begun to use the tools of the social sciences — particularly the survey — in an effort to increase sales and efficiency. Life insurance surveys showed something that agents had known for years: insurance ownership and policy size rose in direct proportion to a person's income. Northwestern policyholders had always been a diverse group, ranging from corporate presidents to clerks and from doctors to farmers. That diversity remained after the war, but there was a new emphasis on the upwardly mobile prospects who were swelling the ranks of the middle class. In 1951 Northwestern reported that 55 percent of its policyowners earned at least $5000 a year (the U.S. average was 17 percent); 55 percent were professionals, managers, or self-employed persons (vs. 18 percent); and 56 percent were insured for at least $10,000 (vs. 18 percent).

The new emphasis was reflected in the company's advertising campaign. Northwestern had always been a reluctant advertiser, preferring to rely on word of mouth and the skill of its agents. In 1948, however, a new series of ads began to appear in *Time*, *Newsweek*, and the *Saturday Evening Post*. They featured photographs of prominent Northwestern clients taken by the renowned Yousuf Karsh of Ottawa, Ontario. Practically every subject was an executive or a professional, and each portrait appeared alongside a testimonial to the central importance of life insurance. The campaign made a strong appeal to the aspirations of the new middle class, but it wasn't the company's first attempt to identify itself with the elite. In the 1890s Northwestern had published a series of pamphlets called *Over Their Own Signatures*, each filled with ringing endorsements of the company by well-known policyowners.

The self-imposed limits on Northwestern's products and market were, of course, limits on growth. Between 1947 and 1957 the nation's insurance in force grew 152 percent; Northwestern's increased only 64.5 percent. Income growth was even slower. Throughout the industry, the size of the average policy increased at the same time premium rates were falling. Improved mortality, younger buyers, and more term sales were reponsible for the lower rates. The premium per $1000 on all Northwestern insurance sold fell from $40.36 in 1947 to $26.52 in 1957. Annual sales volume increased 79 percent, but premium income rose only 17 percent.

There was also a steady decline in the company's pension trust business. Northwestern was neither in nor out of the pension field. The company had imposed stricter and stricter limits on the number of lives it would insure in a single trust, and the decline reflected a desire to lessen Northwestern's dependence on the field. Much of the business was captured by competitors who were more than willing to write policies on a group basis.

By the end of the period, Northwestern had slipped a notch in the industry rankings, from fifth to sixth in assets, and from eighth to ninth in insurance in force. Although the company grew more slowly than its competitors, "slow" was a relative term in the post-war insurance industry. Northwestern sold more insurance in 1957 ($886 million) than the company had had on its books in 1907, the year of its fiftieth anniversary.

Fitzgerald made it clear that Northwestern's growth rate was a matter of choice, that the company's goal was "to improve rather than enlarge." In the new era of mass production and mass consumption, he saw Northwestern as a guardian of older values. Speaking to the Association of Agents in 1957, Fitzgerald restated the theme of individualism:

> To me that sentiment understates the response which you will continue to receive when you make that person aware that you bring not a bag of samples, not a suit of clothes on the rack, not a row of prefabricated houses, but a perception of things he is seeking in his own life . . . something of value.

The Career Company

For the people selling the policies — Northwestern's agents — the 1947-1957 period was a time of steady improvement and occasional frustration. Because Fitzgerald was reluctant to invest in expansion, Northwestern's growth was the result of more sales per agent rather than more agents. Personal production records soared.

The size of the field force actually declined from 4054 agents in 1947 to 3883 in 1957. During the same period, however, the ratio of full-time agents rose from 50 to 63 percent of the force. Northwestern became increasingly "the career company."

The agents' performance was exemplary. They continued their domination of both the National Quality Award and the Million Dollar Round Table — the industry's two major symbols of success. In 1955 nearly a third of full-time Northwestern agents earned the Quality Award (which recognized superior persistency rates), compared with less than 6 percent of all the nation's career agents. And Northwestern continued to have more life members of the Round Table (agents producing at least $1 million in sales for three consecutive years) than any of its competitors.

Joe Thompson, Jr., a veteran Nashville agent, recalled his first Round Table meeting in 1954:

> It was like another Northwestern meeting. Several of the top speakers were Northwestern agents. Every fourth or fifth person you saw was a Northwestern agent you'd seen at the home office meeting. I'm not saying we were the only ones there, but that impressed me.

The agents compiled sales records that are impressive even by today's standards. Alfred Ostheimer, a Philadelphia agent, led the field in sales for five consecutive years after the war. Between 1941, his first year with Northwestern, and 1952, Ostheimer averaged sales of $3.9 million on 1393 lives every year. His cumulative sales volume was nearly twice that of the second-ranked agent, leading Grant Hill, director of agencies, to call him a "one-man insurance company." Jack Meeks, a Columbus (Ohio) agent who led Northwestern from 1953 to 1957, had average sales of $3.75 million on 488 lives. Both Ostheimer and Meeks were pension specialists; they regularly made hundreds of sales through one corporate client. Far more typical was Aaron Finkbiner, Jr., who was the volume leader (pension trusts excluded) in 1954 and 1956. Working out of the Philadelphia agency headed by his father, Finkbiner averaged sales of $2.2 million on 116 lives in his two award-winning years.

Much of the success was the result of training. As agents for other companies became Jacks and Jills of all trades, Northwestern agents honed the skills they needed to represent a specialist. In 1945 the company offered a refresher course for agents who were returning from World War II. It was the beginning of perhaps the most sophisticated training program in the industry. By 1947 an agent could advance from a compulsory short course to the thirteen-week Reporting Program, and then go on to intermediate and advanced courses. The company also introduced the Career School, an in-service program patterned after the refresher courses, and held regional seminars on a variety of specific topics. Hundreds of Northwestern agents became experts on business insurance, taxes, and estate planning. The company was a firm believer in the Chartered Life Underwriter movement, offering agents every encouragement to continue studies on their own. By 1956, 16 percent of Northwestern's full-time agents were CLUs, compared with 3 percent for the industry as a whole.

The director of Northwestern's educational programs was Harold Gardiner, a strong-willed figure who had joined the company as a part-time agent during his college years. World War II interrupted his career, and he served with distinction as an artillery commander in Europe, rising to the rank of colonel. Gardiner came to the home office after the war to develop educational courses. "The Colonel," as he was known to nearly everyone, ran the programs with military precision and a scrupulous sense of decorum. If agents attending the Career School told off-color jokes or used profane language in his presence, Gardiner was not reluctant to send them home. The training division was his exclusive domain for more than twenty years.

Despite their sales records, their high level of skill, and the prosperous climate, the 1947-1957 period had its darker moments for the agents. Northwestern's long-standing conservatism became an irritant in a time of dramatic change. It was the agents who knew clients and prospects best, and it was they who felt the most intense pressure from competitors. Many perceived the home office as a bastion of the status quo, and some suspected that the company's emphasis on excellence was a disguise for complacency.

The Special Agents Association, a free-standing organization since the district agents split off in 1931, was the largest and most vocal advocate for the agents' interests. Response to its requests for new products and policy revisions was often slow in coming. Northwestern was, for example, the very last of the top 100 companies to insure substandard risks. The problems were aggravated by the attitudes of some home office personnel. Fitzgerald was popular in the field, but a few of his insurance executives were apparently less than sensitive to the needs of people who considered themselves, with reason, the foundation of the company's success.

The result was a near-mutiny in 1953. Alleging the "inaccessibility of key Home Office officials" and "the apparent lack of awareness of the extent of the problems," the Special Agents Association adopted a resolution outlining its concerns and demanding a meeting with Fitzgerald. The group also announced its intention, if the meeting failed, to bring the issues to both the board and the Policyholders Examining Committee. (The agents were miffed that the 1952 committee had found field relations "excellent.") The special agents' resolution contained the strongest criticism of management since the World War I era.

The home office added fuel to the fire, sending letters to the general agents about the actions of their sales representatives and enclosing the statements of special agents who disagreed with the majority. Tempers flared for a time but, after a series of meetings in New York, Chicago, and Milwaukee, the dispute was settled in 1954.

The company made several changes that have set the tone for agent-home office relations since that time. An annual fall meeting was arranged for company officers and agent representatives to review Northwestern's policies, projects, and proposed changes. (Under insurance vice-president Robert Dineen, the management presentations were almost choreographed, with elaborate audio-visual programs and painstakingly prepared speeches.) An office of Insurance Services and Planning was established to develop and coordinate, for the first time, Northwestern's marketing efforts. Its head was Laflin Jones, who had come to the company in 1929, assisted by Ralph Harkness, a California agent whose proposed solutions to the 1953 crisis had caught Fitzgerald's eye. One of the new department's first projects was publication of *Your Milwaukee Letter,* which offered a quick, concise view of home office developments for the agents. (It became *FieldNews* in 1971.) Finally, Robert Templin, later vice-president for agencies, assumed responsibility for liaison with the Special Agents Association. The result of all the changes was, in the words of the association's special committee report, "a new period of mutual cooperation and understanding of respective problems."

Another problem persisted throughout the period: recruitment. Northwestern agents were among the most successful in the industry, but the allure of other fields was overpowering for many prospects.

An agent's first year is typically the most difficult, and dozens of other occupations offered high salaries without a "break-in" period.

Although Fitzgerald was decidedly non-expansionist, Northwestern took several steps to enlarge and improve its field force. College recruiting was accelerated. A new office in the Agency Department developed contacts with college placement officers, professors, and graduating seniors. The ratio of college graduates in the field force rose steadily, a definite indication of the company's growing emphasis on professionalism.

Northwestern added several new sales territories at the same time, particularly below the Mason-Dixon line. The South began to truly rise again after World War II, shedding the "poor relation" image it had borne since Reconstruction days. Northwestern re-entered Alabama in 1950, South Carolina in 1952, and Florida and Texas in 1957 — all after an absence of at least fifty years.

The district agency system also received more attention during the Fitzgerald years. District agents had always been non-urban specialists, developing territories too remote to be served effectively by general agencies. They were like player-coaches, prospecting for their own clients and supervising their own sales workers ("soliciting agents") at the same time. The standard contract, however, made it profitable for them to recruit failures; they received all of the renewal commissions earned by agents who left the company.

The problem was remedied after World War II. As a leader of the District Agents Association, Deal Tompkins chaired a study committee that recommended greater emphasis on the district agents' management role. The home office, accordingly, introduced a system of development fees in 1947 (revised in 1954) that rewarded them for recruiting and retaining effective salespersons. The number of district agents rose from a low of 212 in 1953 to 245 in 1957. Tompkins himself, based in Charleston, West Virginia, headed the company's most productive district agency for fifteen years during and after the war. As Charleston's district agent and later as its general agent, he enjoyed legendary success in both sales and recruiting.

Home office liaison with the district agents was the responsibility of Benjamin Bigelow "Big" Snow, a district agent himself in Massachusetts before coming to Milwaukee in 1948. (The Agency Department seemed to attract people with distinctive names; two of Big Snow's co-workers were Glenn Miller and Ralph Waldo Emerson.) Snow played key roles in the revision of recruiting fees and the introduction of metropolitan district agents, both 1954 developments. Reflecting the nation's suburban growth, metropolitan district agents were assigned to serve the mushrooming population on the outskirts of major cities.

Dollars for Main Street

Rebuilding the investment departments was one of Fitzgerald's highest priorities. As described earlier, the company entered the period on a low note. Federal actions during wartime had driven interest rates down, and low-yielding government bonds became the only investment outlet that was both practical and patriotic. By 1945 31.4 percent of Northwestern's assets were invested in United States bonds (well below the 46 percent industry average). At the same time, corporations began to refund (pay off) their own bonds on a large scale, retiring old debts and issuing new securities at the rock-bottom interest rates prevailing. In 1957 Edmund Fitzgerald recalled his exasperation at the events of the Forties: "A lot of fine investments with good rates were called and refunded and paid out, and all we could do was to loan the Government the money at $2\frac{1}{2}$ percent."

The result was a steady decline in Northwestern's rate of return, which fell to 3.01 percent in 1947. In the same year, the reserve rate (guaranteed rate of interest) was dropped, just in time, from 3 percent to 2 percent. The dividend rate was cut more sharply in 1948 than it had been since the Depression. The last move was extremely unpopular with the agents, but Fitzgerald defended it as necessary to keep Northwestern "conservative and strong."

It would be an understatement to say that the economy improved in the late 1940s. Reflecting the general prosperity, Northwestern's assets rose from $2.16 billion in 1947 to $3.73 billion in 1957, an increase of 73 percent. By 1953 premiums were coming in at the rate of $1 million every day. The demand for capital reached an all-time high, and Northwestern's investment portfolio was completely transformed.

Since the company's earliest days, there had been two major investment categories: mortgages and bonds. They had become the responsibility of two separate departments shortly after World War I, leading to a spirited intramural rivalry. For decades the department heads competed for the favor (and the funds) of the company's Finance Committee. Fitzgerald's investment executives were Howard

Tobin (mortgages) and Donald Slichter (bonds). Tobin was a high-spirited Chicago Irishman with sound business judgment and impressive political skills. Slichter, a native Wisconsinite, was softer-spoken but just as astute. Although their personal relationship was amicable, the departmental rivalry continued. Fitzgerald was a willing referee. Gravely concerned about the company's dividend performance and net-cost standing, he gave both men every encouragement to raise Northwestern's investment yield.

Northwestern's mortgage loans had always followed the boom-and-bust cycle of the American real estate industry. They formed the heart of the investment portfolio in the 1860s, only to fall after the panic of 1873. They rose again through the late 1920s, when the Depression gutted the industry. The third rise mirrored the housing boom that began after World War II. Between 1947 and 1957 residential loans jumped from less than 3 percent of assets to nearly 19 percent.

The growth in the account surprised even insiders. The author of Northwestern's 1951 annual report stated confidently, "The phenomenal growth in this field during post-war years has about run its course." The writer was wrong, of course. Between 1945 and 1960 the company financed the construction of 120,030 single-family homes and 840 apartment buildings — enough to house all the residents of a major city. To complement the houses, Northwestern's "city loan" managers financed suburban amenities like shopping centers.

The nation's housing boom was fueled in part by federal guarantees on home loans. Northwestern had refused to make government-backed loans in the 1930s, a reflection of the management's political conservatism. The objections were overcome after the war. In 1952, 78 percent of all new loans were guaranteed by federal agencies.

Slichter's department was as busy as Tobin's. Federal bonds plunged from 36.2 percent of assets in 1947 to 4.8 percent in 1958. New money was invested in the nation's booming industrial sector. Northwestern's industrial bond account rose from 8.5 to 22.3 percent of assets during the period. The policyholders' dollars financed the production of lumber, the mining of ore, the extraction of oil; and the barges, railroads, lake ships, and pipelines to carry them. Northwestern money built cement plants and college dormitories, toll roads and airplanes, grain elevators and nuclear power plants. The company advertised its assets as "dollars that come back to Main Street twice" — once in the form of investments, a second time in the form of benefits.

Slichter expanded a practice he had helped to pioneer in the

1930s: direct placement. With demand for capital at record levels, Northwestern found it advantageous to negotiate directly with a borrower rather than to buy bonds at fixed terms in the public market. Interest rates were generally higher, and the company could attach stiff prepayment penalties to prevent a recurrence of the massive refunding of the Forties. Northwestern, in fact, did some refunding of its own, "rolling over" old bonds at a loss to take advantage of the higher interest rates on new issues. Many direct loans also gave Northwestern the right to purchase stock in the borrowing company, an option that became more important in later years. By 1957 direct placements accounted for 64 percent of the company's utility bonds and 91 percent of its industrial securities.

The potential for diversity grew during the period. In 1945 the Wisconsin legislature passed the "leeway provision," permitting companies to invest up to 5 percent of their assets in practically anything legal. This "basket" was supplemented by new 5 percent allowances on preferred stocks in 1947, real estate in 1953, and common stocks in 1959. Northwestern saw no need to act quickly on its new freedoms. In 1957 stocks and real estate made up only 3.8 percent of the company's investments.

Common stocks, however, had begun to compete with life insurance for the American public's savings dollar. Many consumers found the potential for quick returns attractive in comparison with the long-term values of life insurance. If someone had bought equal shares of all 500 stocks listed in Standard & Poor's Index, a dollar invested in 1947 would have been worth $4.58 in 1957. For those who lacked the time or courage to play the market alone, mutual funds offered professional management and broad-based portfolios. The total value of stocks owned by mutual funds increased from $2.5 billion in 1950 to $9.2 billion in 1957.

Life insurance companies weren't hurt as severely by the stock market as they were by the money market twenty years later, but the industry was forced to respond to the new trends. Most companies increased their holdings of common stocks. A few began to offer products like variable annuities, in which the benefits were based on stock performance. Northwestern waited until 1968 to introduce a variable annuity, and its common stock holdings (0.5 percent of assets in 1957) were less than a third of the industry average. In 1952 Donald Slichter described stocks as "volatile" and thus "obviously not a suitable source for raising funds to meet cash demands."

For the investment managers of the volatile Eighties, the 1947-1957 period may induce strong feelings of nostalgia. Policy loans averaged less than 3.7 percent of assets. At a 1952 agents' meeting, Fitzgerald boasted about a 4.13 percent loan to a paper mill. After their disastrous wartime experience, the company's investors were understandably eager to lock in higher interest rates. In the 1950s Northwestern was still buying 3 percent railroad bonds maturing in the 1990s.

Under Tobin and Slichter, the company's investment side was considerably more aggressive than its insurance side. The results were gratifying. Although the change might seem slow by current standards, Northwestern's net rate of return edged up steadily from 3.01 percent in 1947 to 3.9 percent in 1957 — one of the highest yields in the industry. In 1953, for the first time since 1925, Northwestern raised its dividend rate — a regular occurrence since that time.

Involvements and Adjustments

Although investments, agency issues, and product decisions absorbed most of his attention, Fitzgerald had a definite impact on areas less central to the company's existence. He led Northwestern to greater involvement in the outside world. At the same time, he initiated several changes in the operations of the home office.

In style, temperament, and philosophy, Edmund Fitzgerald was a direct descendant of Michael Cleary. The line between their administrations was virtually seamless, and many of the seeds planted by Cleary sprouted during the Fitzgerald years. One of these was the end of Northwestern's isolationism. Cleary had led the company to its first involvement in national issues during the Depression, but there was still a stubborn resistance to membership in the insurance associations. In the post-war years, both the American Life Convention (ALC) and the Life Insurance Association of America (LIAA) — the two major groups — stepped up their research and education efforts. Northwestern could not comfortably stand apart, and in 1950 the company joined both groups. Fitzgerald was elected president of the Life Insurance Association in 1956, thus ending the old industry joke that there were three major trade groups: the LIAA, the ALC, and Northwestern Mutual Life. Northwestern became a national company in spirit as well as in sales.

The company began to play a larger role in its home community at the same time. For most of its history, Northwestern had practiced an almost monastic isolation from the city around it. The company hired Milwaukeeans and invested in Milwaukee properties, but its public profile was extraordinarily low. Michael Cleary took the first steps toward civic involvement. Edmund Fitzgerald jumped in with both feet. A man with an enormous appetite for leadership, he devoted a great deal of time to fund drives, building campaigns, hospital boards, study committees, and a host of other activities. He expected other executives to follow suit, and Northwestern became a good example of what was later called "corporate responsibility."

"The Northwestern Mutual is a Milwaukee institution," explained Fitzgerald, "and its officers are Milwaukeeans — in my case a third generation in a city 105 years old." The Fitzgerald family had long been prominent in Milwaukee, and the president's wife, Elizabeth, was the daughter of Frank Bacon, founder of the Cutler-Hammer Corporation. As a member of the social elite, Fitzgerald might have been expected to play a role in civic affairs, but his activities went far beyond the limits of noblesse oblige. The list of Fitzgerald's civic involvements, board memberships, industry posts, and awards eventually filled six pages.

Although he continued Cleary's policies in most areas, Fitzgerald adhered somewhat less rigidly to the organizational structure he had inherited. Power at Northwestern was both concentrated and diffused. Ever since the move to Milwaukee in 1859, the company had depended on the committee system. The trustees met quarterly, the Executive Committee monthly, the Finance Committee twice weekly, and a host of staff committees shared responsibility for daily decisions. "At times I wonder," Fitzgerald told the eastern agents in 1953, "if some of us in Milwaukee have time for anything but committee meetings." The committee system was a sacred Northwestern tradition, but the president had enormous influence. Since the days of Henry Palmer, power and responsibility had been clearly centralized in the president's office. Cleary delegated more authority than his predecessors had but, when Fitzgerald took over, there were thirteen executives reporting directly to him.

In 1949 Fitzgerald underwent surgery for a detached retina. During his two-month convalescence, the Executive Committee made Louis Quarles, a Milwaukee attorney who had been a board member since 1929, Northwestern's acting president. It became abundantly clear to Quarles and others, including Fitzgerald, that the president's office was overburdened with responsibilities for direct administration. In Fitzgerald's absence, all but the most routine decisions were postponed. Northwestern began to look for help at the top.

In 1950 the company hired Robert Dineen as insurance vice-president. He had worked for the previous seven years as New York state's insurance commissioner. Dineen assumed responsibility for the Actuarial, Medical, Secretarial, and Underwriting Departments, lightening the president's workload significantly. Fitzgerald continued to delegate authority. By 1953 the only executive officers reporting to him were Grant Hill (agencies), Donald Slichter (bonds), Howard Tobin (mortgages), Philip Robinson (operations), and Dineen. All but Dineen were, like Fitzgerald himself, recruits of the Cleary era who had come to Northwestern in the early 1930s.

A simpler decision had a profound impact on the company's future. In 1947 the board voted, effective November 1, to make retirement mandatory for all employees at age 65. Throughout its history, Northwestern had been headed by men who grew old in their jobs. Henry Palmer retired at 89, George Markham stepped down at 75, William Van Dyke died in office at 76, and Michael Cleary at 70. Following a national trend, the board wanted to insure that the company would have vigorous leadership in the booming post-war economy. With retirement age set at 65, Northwestern Mutual would never again be a company of patriarchs.

Fitzgerald also had an impact on the internal culture of the home office. Despite his emphasis on the casual, he did not entirely wipe out the stuffiness that had characterized Northwestern in earlier years. Officers had their own lavatories and their own dining room. Supervisors ate "family style" with their workers in the dining rooms, like, in one officer's words, "first sergeants eating with their troops." Coffee and tobacco were strictly forbidden, and subterfuge became a highly developed art in some home office departments. An informal black market offered everything from candy bars to smoked fish.

The social patterns of the home office mirrored those of the outside world. A wave of "togetherness" washed over the land after World War II. Family life, patriotism, and "wholesome" outside involvements enjoyed a prominence they would later lose. Northwestern experienced the greatest surge of organizational activity in its history. Home office employees established a recreation committee in 1946, the Sportsmen's Club in 1948, the Women's Association in 1952 (inexplicably renamed the "Girls' Club" two years later), a stamp club in 1954, and a toastmasters club in 1956. There were fashion shows, chorus concerts, athletic teams, and art exhibits. The post-war issues of *Pillar*, a home office magazine introduced in 1941, featured photographs of babies, weddings, family Christmas celebrations, and summer vacations. In 1952 Northwestern even established the Dunworkin Den, a first-floor lounge for retired employees, and one year later introduced a retirees' publication that became *New Life News*. There was an earnest innocence afoot, and it helped to make the "home office family" more than a figure of speech.

Turning 100

In its 1955 annual report, Northwestern called attention to its upcoming centennial and announced, "A modest observance will take place." Planning for the 1957 event had begun a year earlier, and some of the Centennial Committee's ideas were anything but modest. Several members favored a "Future Fair" with lavish displays depicting America in the late twentieth century. (The proposal was scaled down to a traveling exhibit and then dropped.) Others wanted to offer a sort of Nobel Prize for contributions to the welfare of the family. (A $25,000 donation to the University of Wisconsin's scholarship fund took its place.) Perhaps the most novel idea called for the trustees to hold their 1957 meeting in Janesville and then take a stagecoach back to Milwaukee. (Not one trustee volunteered.)

The final celebration was less ambitious, but it consisted of more than the executive officers sipping tea and listening to speeches about John Johnston and Henry Palmer. On March 3, 1957 — one hundred years and one day after the company was chartered — Northwestern held a "Centennial Carnival" open house for its home office employees and their families. Nearly 7000 people attended, including — a sign of the times — more than 600 children. The event featured balloons in the lobby, sideshow barkers, a brass band, tours, refreshments, and food. The Mortgage Department raffled a puppy, and the building maintenance crew won $100 for its display. The carnival was organized by Francis Ferguson, manager of farm loans.

The biggest event of the year was centered around the annual Association of Agents meeting in July. Northwestern had commissioned the Wisconsin Idea Theatre of the University of Wisconsin to produce a full-scale musical depicting the company's history. The result was *Shadow of a Giant,* a production in the best tradition of amateur theater. In three July performances, more than 150 home office employees had the chance to display their acting, singing, and dancing skills. The show never made it to Broadway, but audiences left the Milwaukee auditorium humming songs like *The Happy Widow with $5000 (Bless the Insurance Man).*

A variety of other events marked the centennial. The company financed the publication of *Northwestern Mutual Life: A Century of Trusteeship,* a definitive tome by economists Harold Williamson and Orange Smalley. Six years in the making, it was published, appropriately, by Northwestern University Press. Laflin Jones used a lighter touch in writing *To Have Seen a Century;* his historical account was immensely popular among the company's policyholders and agents. A staff artist, William Wutke, began work on a huge mural depicting events and figures from Northwestern's past, including the cow that caused the fateful train wreck in 1859. The banyan tree was finally abandoned as a corporate symbol after years of disuse. Northwestern adopted a new logo: lines drawn from "1857" converged on an infinity symbol, with "NML" placed boldly in the center. The Secretarial Department expanded a service project begun earlier, reviewing old policies and advising their owners of possibly outdated beneficiary designations and settlement options.

Throughout the year, Northwestern's hidebound commitment to tradition appeared in ways both large and small. When the Centennial Committee suggested steam-cleaning the home office exterior to wash away more than forty years of grime, the Executive Committee vetoed the idea, explaining that its members "preferred the present patina." One of the centennial planners feared that the carnival theme of the March 3 open house would be a failure: "People have been serious for so long around here that . . . they might be afraid to be undignified." They were not, as it turned out, but the company did take its heritage seriously. It was obvious to all concerned that the Northwestern Mutual of 1957 was built on the Northwestern Mutual of the 1800s. The same principles — low net cost, modest operating expenses, simple products, cautious investments, a skilled agency force, and careful risk selection — were still applied scrupulously, and the results were impressive. In a century of operation, Northwestern had paid in benefits or held in reserve $1.30 for every dollar received in premiums — a better record than both the industry giants and the company's natural competitors.

Northwestern Mutual turned 100 in 1957, but the year was significant for another reason: it was Edmund Fitzgerald's last full year as president. He decided to step down, effective in April of 1958, to make room for new leadership. His administration had reached several milestones. In 1953 new business passed the $500 million mark and assets exceeded $3 billion for the first time. In 1954 Northwestern registered its one-millionth policyholder — by a quirk of fate, a young man from Janesville. In 1955 Catherine Cleary (a banker who happened to be Michael Cleary's daughter) became the first woman to serve on the Board of Trustees. Northwestern also began its entry into the computer age during Fitzgerald's tenure, a decision that would have a profound effect on the company in the following decades.

Most importantly, Fitzgerald's efforts to rebuild the company had been successful. The investment departments were back on solid ground. The agency force was smaller, but it was leaner, better trained, and more productive. The product line had grown modestly. The company's external outlook and internal structure were more progressive. By holding the line on expenses and expansion, Fitzgerald had preserved Northwestern's net-cost superiority.

Edmund Fitzgerald had kept the faith, and that was the central theme of his administration. In a time of rapid expansion and general change, he had continued Northwestern's progress against the current. Despite pressures and temptations to do the opposite, he had adhered to the principles of the founders. The industry's aristocrat had weathered both affluence and anxiety. At the eastern agents' meeting in January, 1958, Fitzgerald closed his last major speech as president with these words:

> We are not going to dilute The Northwestern's effort by trying to be all things to all men. We are going to continue to be THE company — if it means being the only one of its kind — where skillful and well-informed agents provide sound and serviceable life insurance at low cost to individuals who will need and understand that kind of relationship, that kind of economy and that kind of service. The others will diversify as they wish. But when ordinary life insurance is thought of Northwestern will be THE competition. What we need to do is not more things, but more of the things we are doing.

Agents
1947-1982

The Career School has long been a cornerstone of perhaps the most sophisticated agent training program in the industry.

Top: *The first Career School in 1947.* Bottom: *One of the 1982 classes.*

Northwestern Mutual Agents
1964 Million Dollar Round Table
Hollywood, Florida

For more than a century, the annual meeting of agents has offered a blend of education, socializing, and "Northwestern religion." Top photo shows the 1949 gathering in the home office auditorium.

Bottom: *Some of Northwestern's delegates to the 1964 Million Dollar Round Table meeting in Florida.*

The changing of the guard: Grant Hill (right), director of agencies since 1933, accepts a retirement gift from Robert Templin, his successor, in 1959.

Top: *Griswold Boynton, a Northwestern agent since 1931, and his wife between dances at the 1982 eastern regional meeting.*

Bottom: *A representative group of younger agents at the 1982 eastern gathering.*

The 1981 Roots and Wings run, an annual footrace between agents and home office staff that began in 1978 with a challenge from a Louisiana agent.

Top: *The company's general agents at their 1949 conference in Florida.*
Bottom: *A home office clinic for general agents in 1982.*

Dennis Tamcsin (left), who became head of the Agency Department in 1973, interviews leading district agent Gary Froid at the 1979 annual meeting.

Top: *The newly elected officers of the Association of Agents in 1957 (left to right): John Mage, John Todd, Dennis McTigue, and Lester Wilbert.*

Bottom: *Six of the Association's officers at the 1982 annual meeting (left to right): Fred Goodwin, Robert Forker, Herb Schmiedel, Hugh Thompson, Charles Ferrara, and Stephen Barlow.*

Upper Left: *Vice-president Ralph Harkness (right), an agent himself after World War II, talks with agent Bill Rankin at the 1982 western regional meeting.*

Upper Right: *James Harding, then the Portland general agent, with two of his office staff at the 1979 Roots and Wings run.*

Lower: *Home office executives and agent association leaders discuss the state of the company during the 1980 November meeting.*

CHAPTER THREE

Nearing
the Rapids
1958-1967

If time is a river, the years between 1958 and 1967 were fast, smooth water, deep in places, sliding steadily downhill toward the sound of rough water ahead. American society and all that was in it, including life insurance, entered a rapids in the late Sixties, a rapids we are still negotiating with difficulty, but the start of the period gave few signs of the turbulence downstream.

In some important ways, the period beginning in 1958 was a continuation of the patterns that emerged just after World War II. The United States certainly grew more affluent. After a brief recession in 1957-1958, the economy took off on the longest sustained recovery in American history. The gross national product increased nearly 80 percent during the decade (from $449 billion to $796 billion), and the ratio of people living in poverty was cut in half (from 22 to 11 percent). A 1965 *Time* article reflected the buoyancy of the times: "The amazing United States economy could defy even the laws of physics: what goes up need not necessarily come down."

There was similar vigor in the nation's social and political life. John F. Kennedy was elected president in 1960, and the word "charisma" was added to the American vocabulary. His New Frontier and Lyndon Johnson's Great Society inspired a faith that the country's long-standing social problems could be solved in a few years. The suburbs and the Sunbelt continued their remarkable growth. The annual number of births stayed above the four million mark until 1965, and the first wave of the baby boom entered adolescence. America's teenagers spent $12 billion a year on everything from records to lipstick. To an extent that dismayed the older generations, their tastes became the nation's tastes. Louis Prima and Keely Smith won the 1958 Grammy as best vocal group; six short years later, the same honor went to the Beatles.

As in the previous period, however, affluence was accompanied by anxiety. East Berlin was isolated behind a monstrous wall in 1961, creating a flare-up in the Cold War. The specter of a nuclear holocaust became appallingly real, and thousands of Americans built fallout shelters in their backyards. An ill-planned and poorly executed invasion of Cuba failed in the same year. In 1962 world tensions reached a new high in the showdown between Kennedy and Khrushchev over Soviet missiles in Cuba. The affluence and anxiety of the times are reflected in one ironic statistic; during the 1960s the sale of Levis and the stockpile of nuclear missiles both increased nearly 500 percent.

The sound of the rapids ahead grew louder as the period progressed. John Kennedy was murdered in 1963. It was the post-war generation's first collective brush with tragedy. The country's enduring racial problems began to reach a crisis level in 1965, when the Watts area of Los Angeles went up in smoke. Another long-smoldering fire burst into flames during the same period. There had been American "advisers" in South Vietnam as early as 1950. In 1962 the United States announced that its troops would fire if fired upon. By 1967 there were 450,000 American soldiers in Vietnam, and the war was costing $33 million a day. One of many side-effects of the war was inflation. It had been creeping along at an average annual rate of 1.2 percent since 1958, but the cost of living jumped 2.9 percent in 1966, the first turn of a sinister spiral.

For the life insurance industry, the water remained smooth until the very end of the period. A healthy population, vigorous competition, and a booming economy continued to drive premium rates down and dividend rates up. Annual sales crossed the $100 billion threshold in 1964, and insurance in force exceeded $1 trillion (a thousand billion) in 1967 — more than double the 1958 figure. The major trends established after World War II continued with few interruptions. The number of companies in the field increased from 1365 in 1958 to 1724 in 1967; stock companies took the lead from mutual firms in volume of insurance in force. Group contracts remained the fastest-growing segment of the industry, increasing from 29 to 36 percent of the nation's insurance in force during the period. Diversification was still the dominant trend. Even the experts had difficulty keeping up with the flood of mergers and acquisitions, and agents found their rate books growing heavy with the flood of new products.

Northwestern Mutual shared in the relative calm. Two presidents — Donald Slichter and Robert Dineen — guided the company during the 1958-1967 period. Both continued the patterns established during Edmund Fitzgerald's years of rebuilding; stable growth and selective change remained Northwestern's hallmarks. The company lagged behind its competitors in rate of growth, but the steady volume of new business was enough to boost Northwestern's insurance in force from $9.3 billion to $15.6 billion during the period — an increase of 68 percent. Pressures from the marketplace, communicated through the agents' associations, forced the company to continue the slow drift away from its narrow specialist role. Northwestern introduced products it had resisted for years. There was a similar shift in the investment departments, as the money managers moved away from traditional bonds and mortgages and into the area of equities.

Developments in most areas occurred at the deliberate pace Northwestern had cultivated over the years, and it wasn't until the late Sixties that the rate of change began to accelerate. The biggest event of the period, however, was nothing short of a revolution: the introduction of electronic data processing. In one decade, Northwestern saw two presidents and three generations of computers.

The Scholar and the Lawyer

When Edmund Fitzgerald stepped down from the presidency in April, 1958, he actually stepped up to a newly created position: chairman of the board. Mandatory retirement was two years away, and he described the interval as "a decompression period," a time to escape the burdens of office without abandoning his successor. Fitzgerald remained head of the powerful Executive and Finance Committees, managed Northwestern's relationship with the rest of the industry, and served as an on-call advisor.

The person considered most likely to succeed Fitzgerald was Robert Dineen, Northwestern's insurance vice-president since 1950. For several reasons, however, including the company's traditional emphasis on investments, the promotion went to Donald Slichter. He had joined the Bond Department in 1934 and had served as its head since 1949. Northwestern entered the direct placement market under Slichter, and he earned a great deal of respect for his ability to identify trends and find investment opportunities in them. Like Fitzgerald, he received a new title with his promotion: president and chief executive officer. The company was his to manage from 1958 until his own mandatory retirement in 1965.

Slichter was raised in a university family. His father was a mathematics professor who became dean of the University of Wisconsin graduate school. The Slichters lived in a neighborhood that was practically on the Madison campus; their neighbors included Frederick Jackson Turner, one of the country's most influential historians. There were four sons in the Slichter clan, and it would be hard to imagine a more accomplished group of siblings. Sumner became a distinguished professor of economics at Harvard; Allen rose to the presidency of the Pelton Steel Casting Company in Milwaukee; Louis became the director of the Institute of Geophysics at UCLA; and Donald, the youngest, was chosen to head the sixth largest life insurance company (by assets) in the country.

The college setting of his early years had a profound influence on Slichter. As Edmund Fitzgerald put it, "His whole character is touched by the atmosphere of the university." He was trained as a chemical engineer, but Slichter is best remembered as a scholar: thoughtful, temperate, a careful researcher, a man with catholic curiosities and an interest in long-term issues. He described himself as "not much of a joiner" and "that great twentieth-century oddity — a non-golfer," but Slichter was by no means an ascetic intellectual. Although he was not an extrovert in the Cleary or Fitzgerald molds, Slichter had an instinctive human touch that won him a wide circle of friends. One of his goals was to swim in Lake Michigan every month of the year — a practice that left some of his companions cold.

Slichter had not sought the presidency, and the promotion took him by surprise. One general agent described him as "innocent of knowledge of the insurance business" when he started but, with characteristic resolve, Slichter learned all he could about every aspect of the company's operations. No one was surprised when he continued to emphasize the investment aspects of insurance. He repeatedly praised life insurance as "the best all-around savings medium there is," and in speech after speech he detailed Northwestern's role in the financial markets.

What did startle some observers was Slichter's compelling

interest in the agency force. The new president later confessed that he had come into office thinking that it was easy to sell a product as good as Northwestern's, but he quickly changed his mind. Every life insurance executive extols the agency force as the company's foundation. Slichter gave substance to the rhetoric. After his retirement he said, "It was my particular obligation to see that there was very high morale in the field, and that would . . . assist and almost assure morale in the home office."

What this meant in practice was thousands of miles of travel. Slichter and his wife, Dickie, were mainstays at regional agent meetings, and other trips were far less obligatory. It was not unusual for Slichter to spend a full day as an observer at one general agency's sales meeting, talk shop over dinner with the local staff, and then take an early flight to repeat the process at the next agency. A good listener, Slichter saw himself as "a safety valve" for disaffected agents, but many veteran field people remember his visits simply as a welcome symbol of home office concern.

Back at the home office, Slichter initiated one change that improved the morale of at least a few staff members. When Slichter became head of the company, Northwestern was suddenly down to three vice-presidents: Robert Dineen (insurance), Howard Tobin (mortgages), and Peter Langmuir (Slichter's replacement as head of securities). The number was doubled in 1963, when the board named four new vice-presidents: Francis Ferguson (Tobin's successor), Robert Templin (agency), Victor Henningsen (actuary), and Laflin Jones (markets and planning). The promotions were a good indication of the talent developing at various levels in the Northwestern hierarchy. Ferguson and Templin were products of the post-war "youth movement;" both Henningsen and Jones had been with the company since the Depression.

There was an Eisenhower quality to Slichter's administration. Although he didn't play golf, Slichter managed Northwestern with a benign competence that reminded some observers of the late general. He was certainly capable of making decisions, but Slichter's approach was calm, even-handed, more deliberate than dynamic.

The tone changed significantly when Robert Dineen became president and chief executive officer in 1965. There was little mystery surrounding his election. When the board promoted Slichter in 1958, there was an informal understanding that Dineen would follow him when Slichter reached retirement age. Dineen was only three years from retirement himself in 1965. His was the shortest presidential tenure since 1869, when Lester Sexton died after two months in office.

Like John C. Johnston and several of his peers, Robert Dineen was a native New Yorker, the son of a Syracuse building contractor. Like Michael Cleary, he was both an Irish Catholic and a former state insurance commissioner. Like every Northwestern president from 1869 to 1947, he was a lawyer. If any person was ever born to be a lawyer, it was Robert Dineen. His love for litigation and legal research developed during his high school years, and he spent nearly twenty years as an insurance attorney in upstate New York. His wife, Carolyn, is a lawyer, as are all three of their grown children.

Dineen's most formative experiences were in the courtroom, where he earned a reputation as a methodical researcher and a scrappy opponent. In 1943 Governor Thomas Dewey called him to Albany to serve as New York's insurance commissioner. The New York office has long been the largest, best-staffed, and most influential in the nation; Dineen was soon playing a major role in the life insurance industry. Edmund Fitzgerald watched his career with interest and, in 1950, persuaded him to join Northwestern as vice-president for insurance.

Dineen was much closer to Harry Truman than Dwight Eisenhower in personal style. Plain-spoken, hard-working, and never one to walk away from a good fight, he soon became the most controversial Northwestern president since George Markham in the World War I era. To some, Dineen's style was a refreshing change from the subtleties of Fitzgerald and Slichter. To others, he was a bull in a china shop. Dineen remained a lawyer at heart, but his courtroom became Northwestern's committee system. Regardless of the issue, Dineen expected closely reasoned arguments from all sides, and he encouraged active, sometimes heated, debate. When he reached a decision, he fought for his viewpoint as tenaciously as if he were representing a personal client. Dineen's approach was nothing less than instinctive, but it required some adjustments on the part of his associates. Agents, in particular, were unaccustomed to a role as legal adversaries; many found the experience less than pleasant. Whatever feelings he aroused, Dineen's style had one beneficial effect. As Edmund Fitzgerald put it, "He stirred us up."

Donald Slichter looked back on the 1958-1967 years as "a period of relative calm." The feeling of calm was encouraged by the character of the two presidents. Despite dramatic differences in temperament, Slichter and Dineen had the same central goal: to keep Northwestern on an even keel. Neither felt the slightest need to tamper with the company's basic operations. Neither had the time in office or the inclination to erect monuments to himself. And both pledged allegiance to a process and to a person that gave the decade continuity: the committee system, and Edmund Fitzgerald.

Northwestern's committees had been the company's organizational mainstay for decades by 1958; their influence, if anything, expanded under Slichter and Dineen. They were the principal vehicle of communication among the various departments. They linked the home office with the agency force and the Board of Trustees. The committees gave even the junior officers a chance to contribute to major decisions, and they made one-man rule extremely unlikely. Between 1958 and 1967 Northwestern functioned practically by consensus. Dineen, a methodical record-keeper, calculated that he attended 173 home office meetings in 1967 alone, and a total of 3121 meetings during his eighteen-year career with the company.

Edmund Fitzgerald was almost as much an institution as the committee system. When he retired from the board chairmanship in 1960, he broadened his involvement in Milwaukee's civic affairs. Fitzgerald was especially interested in downtown redevelopment, and one of several projects he saw to completion was the elegant Performing Arts Center. As a promoter, fund-raiser, and public figure, he became one of the most powerful non-elected officials in the city.

Fitzgerald also remained a power in the company he had served for nearly three decades. He was a board member until 1969, and he cast a long shadow over the administrations of his successors. Both Slichter and Dineen made a conscious effort to follow the precepts and practices he had established during his tenure. When Slichter took office in 1958, he said, "Let me emphasize that, just as in the past, changes will come slowly — will come in an evolutionary rather than a revolutionary manner." Dineen, looking back from retirement, said, "You couldn't spend as many years around Fitzgerald as I did without being influenced by the way he thought. All I wanted to do was to keep on doing the things that had brought us success, and to continue to do them well." Both men were firm believers in the fiscal conservatism and simple operations that had been among Fitzgerald's cardinal rules.

Although he remained active in the company's affairs, Fitzgerald was in no sense a power behind the throne. He scrupulously avoided interfering with either Slichter or Dineen, and he rarely gave unsolicited advice. Like every good role model, he led by example rather than overt action. A large part of his influence stemmed from the fact that, to many people, he was the embodiment of Northwestern Mutual. On March 1, 1960, the company held a lavish "4:10 Party" at the Milwaukee Auditorium. It was attended by 1800 people. The nominal reason for the event was Northwestern's attainment of $4 billion in assets and $10 billion in insurance in force. It was more than a coincidence, however, that the party was held on Fitzgerald's sixty-fifth birthday.

Donald Slichter headed the company for seven years. Robert Dineen was chief executive for three, and the last year of his tenure was a period of transition between himself and Francis Ferguson, who was named president in 1967. In a long-term business like life insurance, neither Slichter nor Dineen could have been expected to lead the company in new directions. Perhaps the greatest asset of both men was their willingness to let the modest momentum of the Fitzgerald years continue. New ideas received an honest hearing, and change occurred when it was considered appropriate. Robert Dineen popularized the image of Northwestern as a "circle of success:" a superior company attracting superior agents who attract superior clients who create a superior company. Under both Slichter and Dineen, the circle remained unbroken.

Computers — A Complex Way to Stay Simple

Since its early years in Milwaukee, Northwestern had developed a reputation as conservative but independent. The company was slow to change but, when change was called for, it moved with thoroughness and speed. Computers are a good example of the latter tendency. Northwestern was not the first insurance firm to trust its fate to electronics but, in the breadth and depth of its operations, the company was a genuine pioneer.

In the early 1950s computers still had an aura of science fiction about them. The major concepts of modern computers had actually been worked out in the mid-1800s by Charles Babbage, an extraordinary English mathematician. His "analytical engine," which obsessed him for nearly forty years, included a memory, an arithmetic unit, and punch card operation. Babbage was a century ahead of his time, however, and the actual construction of his machine was too great a task for the prevailing technologies.

It wasn't until 1944 that the first digital computer was built. It was the brainchild of Howard Aiken, who conceived the idea as a Harvard doctoral student in physics. His Mark I, built with support from IBM, was electromechanical; it operated by a maze of relays that opened and closed electrically, creating a sound that one observer found similar to "a roomful of ladies knitting."

The next major step was taken in 1946, when Presper Eckert and John Mauchly built the world's first electronic computer at the University of Pennsylvania. Their ENIAC (Electronic Numerical Integrator and Calculator) used vacuum tubes, which carried electrical current in a flow of electrons rather than mechanically. The device was thousands of times faster than the Mark I, but it was also physically monstrous, weighing 30 tons and occupying 1800 square feet of space. The team that built ENIAC went into business and constructed UNIVAC I (Universal Automatic Computer), the first commercial stored-program machine. Forty-eight were built, and the first was sold to the Census Bureau in 1951. Few observers suspected that computers would become a growth industry. There was a widespread belief that a few dozen could accommodate all the nation's needs for years to come.

The first business computer was installed in Louisville in 1954, and it was in that year that Northwestern entered the electronics world. Two company employees had had some contact with computers a few years earlier. Wilfred Kraegel, an actuary who later headed the Data Processing Department, had worked with the third UNIVAC at the Pentagon during a military leave in 1951. Victor Henningsen, the head actuary, had attended a Sperry Rand — UNIVAC seminar in 1952. But the real impetus came from a one-week "executive course" at IBM's Poughkeepsie headquarters in March, 1954. Northwestern's delegates were Charles Groeschell, an actuary who had become comptroller, and William McCarter, yet another actuary. Both came back aglow with enthusiasm for the new machines. Their report to Edmund Fitzgerald and the Insurance and Agency Committee apparently struck a responsive chord.

Fitzgerald knew that home office costs had risen twice as fast as premium income since the end of the war. He was keenly interested in cutting expenses, and he was quick to see that computers could help. Within a week he appointed an Electronics Committee consisting of

Groeschell, Henningsen, and Chester Adamson, company treasurer. Few committees have had such far-reaching responsibilities, and a fortunate blend of personalities insured that its work would be thorough. Groeschell's native enthusiasm was tempered by Adamson's scrupulous concern for detail; Henningsen played a valuable role as the neutral party.

In June, 1954, the Electronics Committee appointed a working group to conduct the actual investigation of computer applications. Its members were Wil Kraegel, Will Reimer, Lewis Nagel, and Thomas Gerber. They were relieved of other responsibilities and given a great deal of freedom to study, travel, learn, and recommend. It was the kind of project many people find exhilarating.

When the investigation began, a few insurance companies had already installed computers in their home offices. Most, however, were used as glorified calculators, handling computations for individual departments. Northwestern's working group gravitated quickly to an integrated approach. They designed a system that cut across departmental lines and acted as a backbone for the company's operations. At the heart of their approach was the daily cycle. Most companies planned to process their premium bills, dividend payments, and other transactions on a monthly basis, with separate computer runs for each type of data. In the daily cycle, the computer was programmed to pass through the entire file of policies every day, extracting those that required attention. In effect, a new master file was created every twenty-four hours. The daily cycle provided faster service, greater efficiency, and broader application than any other system, and it has remained a central feature of Northwestern's data processing operations to the present day.

With its basic approach determined and approved in 1955, the working group's next task was the selection of equipment. Here a minor complication developed. One of the companies that had entered the computer field was National Cash Register, and NCR's president, Stanley "Chick" Allyn, was a Northwestern board member. To avoid any semblance of impropriety, Northwestern hired a consulting firm to help in the selection process. Six proposals were studied over a period of six months in 1956, and the final report was exhaustive. The field was developing so fast that the design features of some computers changed several times during the process, but Northwestern finally named a winner: the IBM 705.

On December 26, 1957, a semi-trailer pulled up to the home

office with "Electronic Brain" signs identifying its cargo. The computer had arrived ahead of schedule, and it took until spring for work crews to complete its new home on the northeastern corner of the second floor. (Raised floors, temperature and humidity controls, and miles of new wiring were required.) Foreshadowing later developments, the price of the equipment dropped from $1.9 million to $1.6 million between the date it was ordered and the date it was installed. Northwestern decided to buy rather than lease, thus becoming the first business in the country to own a large-scale IBM. Donald Slichter took over as president just after the computer was installed, and one of his first acts was to sign the check for the computer. With one purchase, he spent more on office equipment than Edmund Fitzgerald had during his whole tenure.

Now the work began: conversion of the company's routine operations from a manual basis to computers. It was an arduous process, involving millions of file cards and miles of magnetic tape. Most of 1958 was absorbed in training programmers, developing programs, and preparing the systems for the task ahead. The Marquette, Michigan, general agency was chosen as the "pilot" because of its small size (9000 policies). Conversion of its records was completed in June, 1959. Ninety-five general agencies remained but, buoyed by their success in the pilot project, Northwestern's data processing managers were confident that they could convert one agency every week. As complications developed, the pace came much closer to one per month by mid-1960.

Agency conversion was the most imposing task, but the computer worked in other areas as well. Northwestern's settlement option and annuity data were placed on tape by mid-1960. Computerization of the company's mortage loan files followed early in the next year. The mortgage field was still growing by leaps and bounds, and Howard Tobin and his staff felt some frustration at having to "wait in line" for the computer.

Electronic data processing caused a dramatic shift in the daily operations of the home office. Until conversion was complete, the manual and the automated systems operated simultaneously, increasing the potential for delay, confusion, and general tension. From the very beginning, however, Northwestern had taken great pains to ease both the home office staff and the agents into a new era as gently as possible. Long before the computer was ordered, mass assemblies were held in the auditorium to explain data processing and its role in the future. Two pledges were made: no one would lose a job to automation, and nearly all hiring for new jobs would be done from within. More than 300 employees took an aptitude test for the first programming class in 1957, and the computer managers chose 20. Company officers also made numerous presentations at agent meetings, introducing the system and explaining that its benefits would far outweigh its disadvantages.

There was a predictable reluctance on the part of many employees and agents to surrender control to a machine, and Northwestern made further efforts to humanize the computer. Company publicists dropped the intimidating "giant brain" imagery in favor of nicknames like "Eddie EDP" or "Ed Process." Policyowners received a brochure with a cartoon that showed a smiling console reading a policy while its four arms wrote, typed, and filed. Regular tours of the computer center were held to show the uninitiated that the machines did not work by magic. When the 705 was delivered, the IBM salesman presented Wil Kraegel with an abacus to use "just in case."

The aura of mystery surrounding the computer was enhanced by the fact that many of its operators worked at night. The daily cycle functioned as two distinct operations. For scheduled transactions (premium billings, dividend adjustments, automatic premium loans, and others), the computer automatically prepared a bill or a check or a notice on the appropriate day. Non-scheduled transactions (death claims or address changes, for example) were compiled during the day and fed into the computer at night, with the paperwork ready for mailing on the following morning. Northwestern added the night shift in mid-1960. As the volume of business increased, the programmers often worked well past midnight, sharing the building with janitors and security guards.

The computer center's schedule was interrupted with annoying frequency by equipment failure. The 705's vacuum tubes generated enormous amounts of heat and, with prolonged use, their filaments grew brittle and burned out. By April, 1960, "down time" accounted for 10 percent of the center's working hours. The problem was alleviated by the replacement of 1300 tubes, but it wasn't solved until early 1962, when an IBM 7080 was purchased. The 7080 was a second-generation machine; its design was based on transistors rather than tubes. The new computer was smaller than the 705, more reliable, and four times faster.

There was a gradual evolution in administrative structure as well as equipment. For the first seven years of its existence, Northwestern's data processing project had been managed by committees. Since virtually every department was involved, Fitzgerald and then Slichter had wanted to insure the broadest possible input and the closest possible coordination of effort. As conversion progressed, however, the computer center assumed a life of its own. In March, 1961, Data Processing became a separate department, with Wil Kraegel as its head.

Kraegel and his staff reached another milestone in 1962. On September 21, conversion of the ninety-sixth general agency was completed. The last tickler cards (with premium and dividend histories) were wheeled away to a vault, the last manual premium notice was mailed, and the last Addressograph machine clanked to a halt. After breathing a collective sigh of relief, the department added up its efforts. In a process that took more than three years, the data processing staff had placed 1.7 million policies on 15 miles of magnetic tape. Nearly 5.5 million punch cards had been used to translate the data, and the machines that punched the holes had generated 47 bushels of confetti.

Edmund Fitzgerald had envisioned the computer as a cost-cutting tool. Before conversion was complete, however, there was a shift in emphasis to include improved service as well as reduced costs. With the artificial restrictions on data lifted, the computer experts constantly generated new ideas, almost like children experimenting with a marvelously complex toy. A phrase commonly heard in the Data Processing Department was, "If we can . . . , why don't we?"

One of the earliest ideas involved premium collection. General agents had always billed their own clients and forwarded the money to Milwaukee, but the home office took over that function in the late Fifties. The general agents lost their collection fees and laid off nearly 150 employees, but centralized accounting had one distinct advantage. Premium data could be pooled with other kinds of information to provide a comprehensive master record for each policy and each agency. The result was the development of the Policy Status Card and the Agency Billing List. Both could be used to spot the early warning signs of lapse or surrender and to highlight increases in cash value. They became marketing tools as well as management aids.

In the mid-1960s, when the conversion process was over and the computer's attention could be focused on other problems, more novel ideas surfaced. The most important was the Insurance Service

Account, which merits special treatment in the next section. ISA and other innovations made it easier to sell insurance. The computer could generate proposals tailored to the age and financial needs of a prospect, saving the agent a considerable amount of time. Electronic policy issue began in 1964, with the face sheet of each new policy prepared by machine. Five steps in the issue process were condensed to one, providing the client with a one-glance summary of his or her policy. In 1965 the Data Processing Department issued breakdowns of every agent's business for the previous two years, a step many agents found useful for analysis and planning. Electronic pre-underwriting began as a pilot project in the following year. The computer was given "authority" to screen applications and begin approval of the simplest ones, shortening the delays many agents had experienced in the issuance of routine policies.

Data processing was also responsible for a number of changes in the home office. "Checkless paydays" began in 1965. Salary data were placed on tape, and funds were deposited directly in checking accounts for every employee. The computer also added a new socio-logical stratum to the home office. By the mid-Sixties Northwestern was hiring dozens of programmers from outside the company to keep pace with the growing workload. Most were young college graduates who had no particular interest in life insurance and no immediate loyalty to Northwestern. Because their skills were in great demand elsewhere, the computer center's managers sought improved wages and benefit packages in an effort to keep them. Other employees were apprehensive, and it took years for the company to assimilate its new breed of specialists.

Perhaps the computer's most important effect on the home office was also the least visible: it postponed the need for a new building. As more work was done by fewer employees, Northwestern could solve a growing space problem by remodeling rather than new construction. Beginning in the late 1950s, scores of old offices were partitioned and their space allotments cut in half. New lights and furniture, central air conditioning, and automatic elevators were installed to brighten up and modernize what Edmund Fitzgerald once called "a marble mauso-leum." In 1965, after fifty years of family-style lunches, Northwestern opened its Colonnade dining facilities. The new cafeteria offered a wide variety of foods, and self-service lunches took less time than those served by waitresses. The cafeteria was, like the computer, a sign of Northwestern's new emphasis on function and efficiency.

The dramatic progress made possible by the computer was not accomplished without some loss of the human touch. There was an inevitable decrease in the daily contact between home office and field, and many agents discovered that it is impossible to negotiate with a machine. Some policyowners found their computerized statements even less endearing than the form letters they had been receiving. A sizable number of home office employees, despite the fact that no one lost a job, found it hard to part with the procedures they had known for decades. The problems were most acute during conversion, when the natural adjustment problems involved in a new system were compounded by errors in the trial-and-error process. Even the most fervent traditionalists, however, had to admit that there was more information and better information. It was obvious to all that, whatever it lacked in humanness, the new system could accomplish much more than the old.

One minor reflection of the computer's influence appeared in the company's language. Bits and bytes, mainframes and data bases took their place alongside the mortality tables and reserve rates of tradition. Words like "dump" and "massage" took on entirely new meanings. And there was a steady increase in the use of acronyms. Capital letters used as shorthand had been a part of American life since Roosevelt's New Deal, but the computer accelerated the trend. EDP was the first home office function identified by its initials. Northwestern, like many other institutions, was in danger of drowning in alphabet soup. In 1964, at the request of bewildered agents, the company published an official *Glossary of Abbreviations.* Its 10 pages and 250 listings provided relief for those who couldn't tell a BRAP from a HOLUA, and it enabled readers to speak in a kind of code. EDP, for instance, enabled NML's SAs to use ISA in their quest for the MDRT — all, of course, with the blessing of the CEO.

By the mid-1960s data processing was an accepted fact of life at Northwestern, and its influence continued to expand. Like a vigorous plant outgrowing its container, the company's computer operations had to be continually "re-potted." The effort had begun in 1957 with barely 20 employees. By 1966 there were more than 200. In that year Northwestern accepted delivery of an IBM 360, a third-generation computer. It featured integrated circuitry composed of tiny silicon chips, which made transistors obsolete.

Although new people and new systems caused some adjustment problems, it was clear that data processing had achieved the goal

Edmund Fitzgerald set for it: cost control. Between 1958 and 1967, Northwestern's insurance in force rose from $9.3 billion to $15.6 billion, an increase of 68 percent. During the same period, thanks to the computer, the total number of home office employees rose from 1661 to 1775, an increase of only 7 percent. But the computer was much more than a labor-saving device. It brought a new dimension to Northwestern's operations, enabling the company to do more things and to do them better, whether it involved selling insurance or planning for the future.

In 1958, just after the first 705 had been installed, Donald Slichter had predicted a rosy future for the computer: "The results will, I am firmly convinced, be almost as startling as many of the inventions and developments of the past century — the steam engine, the cotton gin, the electric motor, and the internal combustion engine." He was, if anything, understating the case. The computer marked, as some writers have noted, a second industrial revolution. It extended the reach of the human mind just as the machines of the nineteenth century extended the reach of the human body. In 1957 there were 120 computers in the United States. In 1967 there were 36,000. During the same period the number of machines used by life insurance firms jumped from 16 to 800. The experiment of the 1950s became a way of life in the 1960s.

At Northwestern Mutual, the computer marked a fundamentally different way of doing things, a clean break with the past. Its application, however, owed something to the leaders of the 1800s. The simplicity that had been a Northwestern hallmark since the days of Henry Palmer made computerization possible. With relatively few products, relatively few special cases, a job that would have been a nightmare in other companies was accomplished with relative ease. As a result, Northwestern emerged with perhaps the most comprehensive and flexible system in the industry. The company's willingness to "bite the bullet," to commit itself to a system that would touch every corner of its operations, was clear evidence that Northwestern wanted to preserve its uncluttered tradition. The computer was, above all, a complex way to stay simple.

ISA and Other Attractions

The first public show of Northwestern's computer power came in 1962, when the Insurance Service Account (ISA) was introduced.

Monthly payments for everything from cars to telephone service were becoming the norm in America. Many insurance companies followed the trend to "budget-style" billing, but the price they paid was an inordinately high lapse rate. After missing one or two premium payments, thousands of clients found it easy to miss all the rest. Northwestern offered quarterly and semi-annual billing, but nearly two-thirds of its clients paid for their insurance on an annual basis. The company's procedure was less flexible than its competitors', and it was especially cumbersome for owners of multiple policies. Every policy was billed individually, requiring payments of different amounts at different times of the year.

The Insurance Service Account solved both the competitive and the administrative problems. All the policies owned by a family or business were placed in a single account. Northwestern calculated the combined annual premium, and the owner added money to his or her account (usually on a monthly basis) to pay off the total amount. The company encouraged payment by pre-authorized checks, drawn automatically on the client's bank balance. If an ISA account showed a negative balance, Northwestern charged interest on the amount due. If it got ahead, either through early ISA payments or crediting of dividends, the company paid interest on the surplus.

There had actually been a prototype of ISA in the home office nearly five years before it was offered to the public. The ever-inventive Charles Groeschell, frustrated at the red tape he encountered when he added to his own insurance portfolio, set up a small manual version of ISA for home office policyholders. (Harvey Wilmeth, then in the Mortgage Department, had envisioned a similar system in 1957.) Groeschell's experiment proved successful, and a committee was formed to develop the concept for the entire company. Headed by Laflin Jones, it had broad representation from the home office departments and, importantly, Northwestern agents. The basic idea was refined and embellished in a long series of stimulating meetings and, by 1960, it was ready for implementation. ISA was absolutely dependent on the computer, however, and the conversion process was still underway. The records of the last general agency were placed on computer tape in September, 1962. One month later, ISA was unveiled.

Agency vice-president Robert Templin was soon hailing it as "the greatest selling tool ever invented," and executives of other insurance firms were openly envious. ISA was convenient, it was flexible, and it gave a feeling of psychological unity to a client's insurance coverage. Above all, it enabled agents to use the "pennies a month" appeal. By adding a small amount to the monthly payment, or even by using dividends, a client could effortlessly add to his or her coverage. ISA was not trouble-free (and is still not, as many agents would attest), but it made a large contribution to both improved sales and better service. By 1964, 40 percent of Northwestern's new business was being placed on Insurance Service Accounts, and the home office unit handling ISA transactions had grown from three people to more than forty.

ISA was a powerful demonstration of the computer's abilities, but it was notable for another reason. It was an independent invention of the home office, perhaps the most significant since settlement options were introduced in the 1800s. Other innovations appeared between 1958 and 1967, all of them developed in response to pressures from the marketplace, which Northwestern felt through the intensive lobbying of its agent associations. The new products and policies continued the company's steady shift away from its narrow specialist role. In some instances, however, they had features that strengthened the company's image as a unique competitor.

Northwestern's refusal to offer an accidental death benefit had long been a sore point in discussions between home office and field. Often called "double indemnity" because it paid twice a policy's face value in the event of accidental death, the benefit had been an industry mainstay since the World War I years. At Northwestern, however, president after president had refused to even consider it, usually dismissing the benefit as a form of casualty insurance. Edmund Fitzgerald followed the party line, but he knew that many agents found the company's position embarrassing. When actuary Victor Henningsen began to lead a campaign for the benefit, Fitzgerald allowed him to explore the issue and design a product. The president preferred it to come after he had stepped down, however, and Northwestern's version of double indemnity didn't appear until 1959.

As if to make up for lost time, the company's accidental death benefit was considerably more liberal than the competition's. It was, in effect, "quintuple indemnity." Existing clients were allowed to purchase accident coverage of up to five times the amount of a new policy. If someone had $40,000 of insurance in force, for instance, he or she could add a $50,000 accidental death benefit to a new $10,000 policy. Premium rates for the new benefit were well below the industry average. The fine print in the company's contract was also less restrictive than the competition's. Even the most reputable firms issued policies with twenty or more exclusions (conditions of death under which they would not pay a claim). Northwestern limited itself to four. The new offering was enormously popular. Within six months of its introduction, the accidental death benefit was attached to nearly half of the company's new policies.

Two more new products indicated the interest of Northwestern, and the industry, in the growing young adult market. The graduated premium life policy, introduced in 1959, was basically a term product that gradually converted to whole life insurance. As the premiums rose, so, in theory, did the young person's ability to pay them. Lapse rates for the new product were high (12 percent in 1959), but graduated premium life became a popular alternative to term insurance.

The additional purchase benefit, first offered in 1963, was based on the same growing-income principle. Designed for younger buyers, it guaranteed a client's right to purchase additional $10,000 policies at six option dates (ages 25, 28, 31, 34, 37, and 40) and at marriage or the birth of a child. APB, as it is called, was designed to compete with the "guaranteed insurability option" offered by other companies. A major complaint about the typical option plan was that, in most cases, the additional policies were inferior to the original. They did not include the accidental death benefit or the waiver of premium for disability unless the client passed a medical exam, and the company's right to refuse a claim for fraud or suicide was renewed with each purchase. At Victor Henningsen's urging, Northwestern guaranteed that every policy purchased under APB would have the same benefits as the first, and that the suicide and incontestability clauses would date only from the original purchase. The company even provided ninety days of extra coverage automatically at marriage or birth, without an additional premium.

Northwestern did not move so boldly in a third area — nonmedical insurance. A growing number of companies sold insurance without requiring applicants to pass a physical exam. The only requirement was a normal medical history. Northwestern joined the trend in 1963, but its century-old insistence on careful risk selection made the company less than enthusiastic. A male between the ages of 31 and 40 could buy only $5000 of insurance without a medical exam — a limit that made many agents feel the new policy was only a token gesture.

There were other changes during the decade. The longevity of the American people continued to increase, and in 1963 Northwestern adopted a new mortality table (C.S.O. 1958) that better reflected the trends. The booming economy was also improving investment yields. The company raised its guaranteed rate of interest from 2 percent to 2.25 percent in 1963 and 3 percent in 1968 — still more conservative than the rates of most competitors. Improving mortality and investment returns caused a steady decrease in premium rates, a trend that affected the entire industry. The drop was especially noticeable in women's insurance rates. Northwestern did not even insure women between 1876 and 1933, but the company became one of the first large firms to recognize the female population's gains in physical health and economic status. Beginning in 1959, premium rates for women were significantly lower than those for men of the same age.

Many of the product and policy developments symbolized at least a modest retreat from the company's devotion to select-risk, level-premium whole life insurance. At heart, however, Northwestern remained a specialist. Speaking to the eastern agents in 1965, Donald Slichter sounded like the Edmund Fitzgerald of a decade earlier: "While other companies have multiplied, expanded, and diversified, we have increasingly emphasized that we are a specialty company, serving the individual as an individual and not as a mere number in a large group entity." At the same meeting a year later, Robert Dineen gave a speech entitled "Progress with Principles," a ringing endorsement of Northwestern's traditions.

The company's advertisements carried the same themes to a broader audience. In a series that ran in national magazines during the 1960s, Northwestern proudly proclaimed, "There *is* a difference!" Three qualities were highlighted: "High Investment Return! Favorable Mortality! Low Operating Cost!" With the exclamation points removed, the ads might easily have appeared in the 1870s.

Northwestern's insistence on principle proved extremely expensive in one area: the pension trust business. The company's agents had entered the field on their own initiative in 1938, and it was soon a major source of premium income. Federal authorities allowed tax deductions for any money spent by a corporate trust on employee pension benefits. During World War II, when salaries were frozen and corporate taxes were high, such benefits were often the only effective way to give an employee a raise. The pension market boomed.

The basic Northwestern pension product sold in the early years was the Special Retirement Endowment. Developed by actuary Elgin Fassel, it had an even lower premium and a higher rate of return than most products offered by group companies. A retirement income policy (insurance converting to an annuity at age 65) appeared later, and Northwestern became a national leader in the individual pension market.

Many Northwestern agents had long-standing contacts in the business world, and some derived nearly all of their income from pension cases. Relatively few in number, the specialists traveled across the country to develop cases for other agents, splitting the commissions and becoming wealthy in the process. Most of the client companies were small, but by no means all. In 1944 Dr. Charles Albright, who had left the home office medical staff to become the company's most successful agent, sold a group of 2500 policies to the Chrysler Corporation. By 1962 there were more than 21,000 policies in the Chrysler trust. Each was an individual contract issued after a medical examination.

Home office executives had strongly mixed feelings about the pension trust business. It brought in policies by the carload, but it also brought problems. The larger cases were costly to service, cumbersome to administer, and difficult to protect from competitors. Most importantly, Northwestern was flirting with group insurance, a fact that made many company officers uncomfortable. The Chrysler contracts, in particular, were viewed as a case of too many eggs in one basket. At the end of World War II, 20 percent of the company's pension business was concentrated in 1 percent of its 700 trusts. Northwestern provided sales aids and training programs for agents who were in the pension field but, at the same time, the company tried to slow down the flow of new business by imposing underwriting restrictions and by limiting the number of employees per trust. One veteran agent described the home office attitude as "driving with one foot on the gas pedal and the other on the brake."

Northwestern's fears were realized in the 1950s. Post-war changes in the tax laws and competition from group firms caused a gradual erosion of its pension trust preeminence. Agents continued to sell to new trusts, primarily in small companies, but the pension field's contribution to new premium dollars fell from 30 percent in 1951 to 15 percent in 1958. New sales were counterbalanced by surrenders of old policies, a trend that began soon after World War II and accelerated steadily. Nearly every former client purchased new coverage from group companies, which offered greater flexibility, lower costs, and dramatically lower agent commissions.

Northwestern modified its contracts to salvage some of the business, but it was a losing battle. The biggest blow came in 1962, when Chrysler decided to surrender every one of its policies. Between November, 1962, and October, 1963, Northwestern paid back Chrysler a total of $39,695,502. (The company's investment income for 1963 was slightly over $200 million; the impact of the Chrysler pay-out was clearly profound.) At least the payments were made in twelve installments. When Allis-Chalmers surrendered its policies in 1965, Northwestern had to write one check for $21,146,358.

Despite a staggering loss of business, Northwestern never seriously considered rewriting its pension trust cases on a group basis. The idea was mulled over but quickly rejected as risky, expensive, and an abandonment of principle. At the same time, the company was unwilling to abandon the pension field. A new employee plan series was introduced in 1965. It recognized, for the first time, that the needs of the corporate pension market were different from those of the individual market. New policies like employee life (with an invest-ment side fund) were offered. Within conservative limits, Northwest-ern guaranteed issue of policies to employees of very small firms, regardless of medical history. For somewhat larger companies, the underwriting rules were at least simplified. The employee plan series caused a brief spurt in Northwestern's pension business, contributing 9 percent of new premium income in 1966. But the inflation that began in the late Sixties convinced even the smallest firms to buy low-cost group products. The 1965 series was discontinued in 1971. Since that time, Northwestern has continued to look for a final solution to the pension problem.

Agents: Steady Growth

Northwestern's growth rate between 1958 and 1967 was as steady as a heartbeat. The annual ratio of new insurance to existing insurance averaged 8.5 percent during the period, never straying more than a percentage point from that figure. The sale of new products counterbalanced the decline of old ones so effectively that ten-year projections made in the late 1950s proved remarkably accurate.

Agents, of course, were responsible for every dollar of North-western's new business, and the company's steady growth reflected their high level of professionalism. Northwestern's field force continued to be perhaps the best trained and most productive in the nation. In 1962, 17.5 percent of the company's agents were Chartered Life Underwriters (against 2.8 percent for the industry), 37.7 percent held the National Quality Award (vs. 6.3 percent), and 10 percent belonged to the Million Dollar Round Table (vs. 1.2 percent). In every case the figures were significantly higher than they had been a decade earlier.

Even more impressive than the awards and educational attainments was the dramatic increase in productivity per agent. The rate of attrition for life insurance agents has always been extremely high. Although Northwestern kept twice as many of its new agents as the average firm, the company's general agents had to recruit at least 500 new people every year simply to keep pace with attrition. Even with a vigorous recruiting program, the number of full-time sales agents rose form 2384 in 1958 to 2481 in 1967, an increase of only 4 percent. At the same time, Northwestern's new business more than doubled, and its new premium income rose 70 percent.

Two agents virtually monopolized the production awards between 1958 and 1967: John Todd and Hugh Thompson. Todd led the company for four years with average sales of $6.4 million on 129 lives. He made his first appearance in the Top Twenty in 1937, six years after signing his full-time contract. Todd became a Chicago general agent during World War II, but he returned to the field with a vengeance in 1951. Working in the upper echelons of the Chicago area's business world, he remains one of the most successful agents in Northwestern history.

Thompson led the field for another four years, averaging sales of $5.9 million on 169 lives. He represented the younger generation. Thompson had joined the company in 1949 as a college student, and he grew rapidly under the tutelage of West Virginia's Deal Tompkins. In 1962 he became the first person ever to lead Northwestern in both sales volume ($4.4 million) and number of lives written (149). Thompson and Todd were both enthusiastic teachers; their presentations have helped to make thousands of agents more effective salespersons.

The person ultimately responsible for field performance was Robert Templin. A Marine in World War II and a Northwestern agent in Indiana after the war, he came to the home office in 1948. Templin began in the advertising and promotion section of the

Agency Department, but his role grew steadily. When Grant Hill retired in 1959, after twenty-six years as head of the department, Templin was named to succeed him. A gifted organizer and an astute politician, he became one of the most influential agency directors in the company's history. When the search for Robert Dineen's successor began, Templin was seriously considered for the presidency of the company.

Templin began to reorganize the Agency Department almost as soon as he was promoted. The management and merchandising functions were split, job descriptions became more specific, and the staff was expanded. The changes were part of a company-wide movement toward greater accountability and more efficient management.

Changes in the agency system itself soon followed. Northwestern reentered Mississippi in 1959 (after an absence of eighty-seven years), and obtained its first Louisiana license in 1965. The addition of Louisiana extended the company's reach to all forty-eight contiguous states. New general agencies were established in the fastest-growing sections of the country, including Long Island and southern California. In 1967 the number of general agencies totaled 101 — the first time the company had broken the 100 mark.

It was through his general agents that Templin's impact on the field was most visible. He culled the least productive managers and replaced them with generally younger, more progressive types. The same policy applied to the development of new territories. By 1968 nearly two-thirds of the company's general agents were Templin appointees.

The children of the baby boom were swelling enrollments at colleges throughout the country, and Northwestern moved to tap a growing market. College students had sold Northwestern products as early as the World War I era, but they were few in number and received no special attention. Recruitment efforts were stepped up in the mid-1960s. A formal college agent contract (specifying a minimum course load) was developed in 1966. Seventy-one contracts were awarded in 1966; the number doubled in the next year and tripled in 1968. Most college agents sold to their peers, and some were more productive than agents with decades of experience. At the same time, Northwestern continued its efforts to interest graduating seniors in full-time careers. By the mid-Sixties more than half of the company's new agents were college graduates.

Northwestern provided significant help to its young recruits, particularly through the Training Allowance Plan. Introduced in 1965, TAP is a program of dramatically increased commission rates for agents in their first three years — typically the least profitable in an agent's career. Although the 1958-1967 period was a time of slow growth in the field, TAP, the educational programs, and the district and general agency growth incentives helped to maintain the system's vitality.

Agents of all backgrounds had long been lobbying for improved benefits, and the home office heard their cries in the early years of Templin's administration. In 1961 Northwestern began to offer group health insurance coverage to its full-time agents. (The fact that it was a group plan caused some discomfort in the home office. When the benefit was announced, agents were reminded that Northwestern's specialty continued to be "individually tailored plans of permanent cash-value life insurance.") The retirement plan was upgraded five years later. Agents had been contributing to their pension funds with after-tax dollars since the plan's inception in 1942, a definite source of irritation. Beginning in 1966, the program was revised to allow pre-tax contributions. The new plan omitted an interesting feature of the old contract. It struck the clause stripping an agent of retirement benefits if he or she went to work for another insurance company.

Templin and his officers made significant changes within the system, but they also spent a great deal of time fighting competition from outside. Replacement of Northwestern policies became a growing problem, and agency superintendent Harold Baird became the leader of efforts to solve it. Some of the competition came from the proliferating number of small stock companies. The life insurance field grew from 1365 to 1724 companies during the period. Many of the fledgling firms offered "grand opening specials" in an effort to attract business. Donald Slichter cast Northwestern in the elder statesman's role, telling the eastern agents that "the flood of new companies are now trying to ride along on our coattails." Some agents responded to the threat too vigorously; a few were accused of libeling the youngsters. Robert Dineen was prompted to send the field a word of caution: "Agents sometimes forget that all of America's giant life companies were small once."

Another troublesome trend was the movement away from exclusive agents. In an effort to gain maximum volume, even established companies began to sell their policies through brokers and independent agents. Many field representatives found themselves in competition with their own products, and there was growing speculation that exclusive agents were a dying breed.

Perhaps the most serious threat arose, ironically, from the same economic prosperity that was boosting insurance sales. The continuing boom in the stock market attracted millions of speculators, and life insurance lost some of its attractiveness as a savings medium. The greatest number of people participated in the market through mutual funds, whose combined assets rose from $9.2 billion in 1958 to $53 billion in 1970. Mutual fund salespersons often worked in the same markets as life insurance agents, and many agents found it difficult to sell long-term contracts to prospects interested in short-term gains. By the late 1960s dozens of insurance firms had established mutual funds of their own.

The rise of other investment outlets had at least three effects on Northwestern and its competitors. It accelerated the trend to term insurance, which offered low-cost coverage for younger buyers. Term sales rose from 24.5 percent of Northwestern's new business (face value) in 1958 to 31.2 percent in 1967. Agents were disturbed because they considered term commissions equivalent to a vow of poverty.

Mutual funds also fueled an increase in policy loans. As early as 1959 Slichter was criticizing borrowers who used their insurance reserves "to pay for rainbows in other investment skies." Policy loans were only 4.7 percent of Northwestern's assets at the time, but Slichter's voice was as urgent as Francis Ferguson's would be twenty years later.

The stock market's third impact on life insurance was its encouragement of "borrow to buy" or "minimum deposit" selling. Minimum deposit is basically a means of minimizing premiums by maximizing loans. In the late 1950s, before interest rates skyrocketed, many people borrowed money from banks to pay their insurance premiums. When interest rates began to rise, clients turned directly to their insurance policies, borrowing against their cash values to finance payments. The practice gave policyowners a short-term source of investable capital as well as a tax deduction for interest payments. Agent commissions remained the same, but the company as a whole lost capital for its own investments and gained new business with high lapse rates and high acquisition costs.

Northwestern was one of the first insurance companies to take a stand against what has since been dubbed "mini-dipping." In his 1959 "rainbow" speech, Slichter condemned "borrow to buy" insurance as diametrically opposed to the true spirit of life insurance. In 1961 Robert Templin had harsh words for the "raiders" who sold their clients "an empty shell of debt." Northwestern released *Margin Insurance: The Other Side of the Story,* a pamphlet written by Robert Dineen, in the same year.

The Internal Revenue Service disliked the practice as much as Northwestern. Federal officials argued that it was an indirect use of tax dollars to fund insurance purchases. In 1964 the IRS required buyers to pay at least four of the first seven annual premiums or forfeit their tax deductions for interest payments — hence "minimum deposit" or, in the agents' jargon, "pay four and float."

Numerous Northwestern agents sold policies on a minimum-deposit basis, often as a defensive measure, but the Agency Department did all in its power to discourage the practice. Northwestern's pronouncements and the IRS decree did little, however, to halt what was becoming an epidemic.

Investments: Taking a Risk

Northwestern was pursuing some new rainbows in its own investment skies during the period. The company's assets increased from $3.9 billion to $5.5 billion between 1958 and 1967, and the money managers had little trouble finding outlets for the funds. They did, however, reshuffle the investment portfolio considerably. Old investments were retired. (United States bonds dwindled to 3 percent of assets, and the utility bonds purchased to replace them in the early post-war years shrank from 19 percent to 9 percent.) Areas of more recent growth remained important. (Mortgage loans held steady at roughly 36 percent of assets.) There was determined expansion in a new area of investment: equities.

Since the industry's beginning, life insurance companies had sought long-term, fixed-return investments to match the long-term, fixed-dollar policies they sold. They may have held anything from railroad cars to pasture land as security for a loan, but they were inherently reluctant to own, manage, or share the risk of loss in any of the investments they made. After World War II the booming economy created a lender's market that convinced many companies to move away from the safety of tradition. Bond managers turned to incentive financing, requiring a variety of "equity kickers" in loans

they made: stock rights, production payments, and partial owner-
ships. Mortgage lenders made their companies partners in large
projects and, in a growing number of cases, insurance firms bought
and developed real estate on their own. The risks were greater in the
equity field, but so were the potential returns.

Northwestern's emphasis on equities had actually begun in the
previous decade, and it expanded greatly in the next. Although the
company was not the first to participate in its investments, Northwestern was known for its aggressiveness during the period. This
stance was partly a response to market conditions, but it also reflected
the character of the people who managed the investment departments: Peter Langmuir in Securities, and Howard Tobin and Francis
Ferguson in Mortgage Loans.

Langmuir, a Yale graduate in economics, had come to Northwestern in 1947 as an industrial bond specialist, and within three
years he was manager of his division. In 1958 he was appointed to
succeed Slichter as head of the entire Securities Department. Langmuir had a solitary style and a single-minded devotion to money
management. When Slichter was named chief executive, Langmuir
was genuinely surprised that he would trade the pleasures of investment for the burdens of administration.

Under Langmuir's direction, Northwestern developed a reputation as "kicker-oriented." Virtually all loans were direct placements,
and premium dollars went out to everything from meat packing
plants to marble quarries, from greeting card factories to whiskey
distilleries. Every loan carried a fixed rate of interest, but Langmuir
often pushed for some extra incentive. This was especially true in
areas that involved some risk, like oil and gas extraction. (Slichter
once compared non-incentive loans on oil to "shooting dice with
some of the numbers rubbed off.") In 1960, for instance, the Finance
Committee approved Langmuir's request to loan $8.5 million to a
Texas firm with an option on an oilfield. Twenty-five percent of the
company's stock was transferred to Northwestern in the deal. It was
later worth $7.5 million, above and beyond the interest payments on
the loan. By 1967 industrial securities, many with equity kickers,
accounted for 23.5 percent of Northwestern's assets — an all-time
high.

Langmuir's department led the company into another area of
the equity field — the stock market. Northwestern was slower than
most companies to chase the bulls of Wall Street, but the market's

continuing upward trend made it difficult to resist. In the 1950s Northwestern had made some modest purchases of preferred stocks, which virtually guaranteed a fixed dividend. When Langmuir took over, the company shifted its emphasis to common stocks. In 1965 the combined stock portfolio held 7.8 percent of Northwestern's assets, up from 1.8 percent in 1958.

There was similar ferment in Howard Tobin's Mortgage Department. Residential loans tapered off from 18 to 13.5 percent of assets during the period, largely as a result of competition from other lenders. Northwestern found new opportunities in the commercial and agricultural fields. The "city loan" account grew from 12 to 13.3 percent of the portfolio during the 1958-1967 period. Northwestern invested hundreds of millions of dollars in office buildings, shopping centers, supermarkets, filling stations, and hospitals.

Most mortage loans were conventional, but Northwestern was among the first in the industry to participate in sale-lease arrangements. The company typically bought the land and buildings from a corporation developing a shopping center, for instance, and then leased it back on a basis that amortized the debt and paid interest. The developer had a source of extra capital, and Northwestern had an above-average rate of return. Sale-lease agreements were the counterparts of the equity kickers sought by the Securities Department.

Hospital loans were straightforward agreements, but they illustrate the Mortgage Department's characteristic thoroughness. Northwestern invested more than $100 million in hospitals, largely in institutions run by religious orders. The size of the account worried some board members, who feared that the company could never manage or sell the hospitals in the event of foreclosure. Tobin argued that the sacrificing labor of the nuns was a sort of endowment, and that their dedication was ample security for the loans. Nevertheless, his department researched the number of candidates, postulants, sisters, and retired nuns in every order that applied for a loan, making sure that the "labor force" was self-sustaining. When vocations declined in the mid-1960s, Northwestern gradually lost interest in hospital loans.

Of all the activities in the Mortgage Department, agricultural lending showed by far the most dramatic growth during the decade. Northwestern had been the industry's leading farm lender in the 1920s, and the massive foreclosures of the 1930s had made the company the leading farm owner. The arduous task of managing and selling the farms lasted through the war years. Northwestern was understandably reluctant to re-enter the agricultural market after the war; terms for new loans were restrictive. The company would not lend money to farmers outside the Midwest, and loans larger than $100 per acre were rare. The mortgage officers showed a strong preference for small family farms — 80 acres if they were one-man operations, perhaps 360 if the farmer had sons.

All of that changed completely. Tobin hired Francis Ferguson in 1951 and soon became his mentor. By 1956 Ferguson was the head of the farm mortgage division, and he succeeded in rewriting the rules that had governed the operation for thirty years. He took Northwestern from the family farm to agribusiness. He shifted the focus from the Midwest to the South and Southwest. Large irrigated operations became the investment of choice, and millions of dollars went out to finance the expensive dams, pumps, wells, and canals necessary to grow crops on arid land. The average farm loan climbed from $10,000 in 1951 to $63,000 in 1960, and some financed the development of farms as large as 100,000 acres. By 1965 irrigated farms accounted for more than 40 percent of Northwestern's agricultural loans.

Ferguson led his division in other directions as well. Northwestern money supported processing operations like feed mills and pre-packaged food plants. When the United States embargoed Cuban sugar following Castro's rise to power in 1959, the company loaned $13 million to develop the Florida sugar cane industry. Ferguson was always on the lookout for entrepreneurs. He once secured approval for a loan to a farmer who put heating elements in his asparagus beds, producing an early harvest that sold for extremely high prices. Under Ferguson, farm loans of all kinds rose from 3 percent of assets in 1958 to nearly 8 percent in 1967 — their highest point in the last fifty years.

Ferguson's performance made him the brightest star in the Mortgage Department, and Tobin took an active interest in his protegé's future. In 1962 he made Ferguson general manager of mortgage loans, a newly created position. In 1963 Tobin took an early retirement and moved literally across the street to a new job as president of the Wisconsin Gas Company. He had been on the utility's board for years, and he saw the move as both a new challenge and a way to make room for, as he put it, "a whale of a good man behind me." On February 13, 1963, only six weeks after Tobin's retirement, the board named Francis Ferguson vice-president for mortgage loans.

With responsibility for the entire mortgage operation, Ferguson found another new investment outlet: student housing. Northwestern had made dormitory loans in earlier years, but in 1964 the company began to take an equity interest in college projects. In some cases Northwestern built on university land and leased the dormitories back to the school. More often the company built off-campus and hired managers to rent and maintain the units. They were more spacious and more attractive than the typical college dorm; vacancies were rarely a problem. In 1965 student housing made up nearly 20 percent of Northwestern's new mortgage investments. By mid-1966 the company was financier and part-owner of housing for 13,403 students at 27 schools from coast to coast. New projects raised the capacity to 21,000 in 1967, and Northwestern buildings housed as many people as all the Hilton hotels in the country.

Peter Langmuir and Francis Ferguson were young, shrewd, and aggressive. They played key roles in raising Northwestern's net investment yield from 4.01 percent in 1958 to 5.04 percent in 1967 —well above the industry's 4.8 percent average. It was the first time the company's rate of return had been over 5 percent since 1929.

For all their skills, Northwestern's two investment executives were powerless to halt the growth in one area of the portfolio: policy loans. In 1966 the short-term prime rate (the rate charged by major banks on loans to their best customers) jumped from 4.5 percent to 6 percent. Most of Northwestern's policies carried a 5 percent borrowing privilege. Once other lenders passed the 5 percent mark, thousands of clients borrowed against their cash values. Loans on policies soared from 4.3 percent of assets in 1958 to 9.4 percent in 1967.

The demand was greatest in August of 1966. Northwestern paid out $113 million to its policyowners during the year, nearly three times the amount involved in the Chrysler surrender. By August nearly half of the company's cash flow was directed to policy loans. Langmuir and Ferguson found themselves with $23 million less to invest in 1966 than they had had the year before, despite a $48 million rise in company income.

Robert Dineen met more often with the Cash Committee in an effort to end the crisis. The company liquidated millions of dollars in stocks and bonds, and rolled much of the money over into investments with shorter terms and greater liquidity. Northwestern arranged standby bank credit, and the Securities Department began a concerted effort to rebuild the common stock and marketable bond portfolios. These measures enabled Northwestern to weather the storm with only minor damage, but the "credit crunch" of 1966 was a clear sign of harder times ahead.

The *Edmund Fitzgerald*

"Romance" is a word rarely associated with insurance companies, especially with their investment departments. To most laypersons, yield curves and portfolio rates are somewhat less than soul-stirring. With one investment, however — the lake ship *Edmund Fitzgerald* — Northwestern called up the romance of open water, blue skies, and summer winds. The ship was the best-publicized investment in the company's history, and the story of its career (and especially its demise) captured the imaginations of millions of people.

Lake shipping was a natural outlet for the company's funds. Northwestern was by far the largest insurance firm on the Great Lakes, and Edmund Fitzgerald had a lifelong interest in the freshwater seas. (He served as president of both the Wisconsin Marine Historical Society and the Milwaukee Harbor Commission after he "retired.") The post-war lake fleet was also, on the average, more than thirty years old. The demand for capital to build new ships became intense after 1954, when the United States finally agreed to join Canada in the St. Lawrence Seaway project. Fitzgerald had urged his investment officers to consider lake shipping years before, and they followed his advice. By 1956 the company's investment in Great Lakes carriers totaled $31 million, making Northwestern first in the field.

The company soon decided to build its own boat rather than finance construction for other firms. The decision was a byproduct of negotiations between Donald Slichter and the Oglebay-Norton company, a mining and shipping firm based in Cleveland. Oglebay-Norton was pursuing a loan for an ore project it was developing in Minnesota, but the discussions gradually turned to ships. In an agreement reached in late 1956, Northwestern announced plans to build the largest ship ever to sail the Great Lakes. The bulk carrier would be leased to Oglebay-Norton under a "bareboat charter" for twenty-five years, and the Cleveland firm would be entirely responsible for its operation and maintenance. This sale-lease agreement was identical to those Northwestern had already negotiated on several shopping center and office building projects.

Construction of Hull 301 began at the River Rouge shipyards

near Detroit in August, 1957. The Northwestern board gave the ship a proper name at its April, 1958, meeting, christening it the *Edmund Fitzgerald*. Fitzgerald himself abstained after suggesting several other names. Slichter (who became president at the same meeting) remembered the occasion as the only time the two men had disagreed in twenty-four years of working together. The ship became Fitzgerald's monument, a symbol of Northwestern's regard for his leadership. He professed to find his namesake "almost embarrassing," but Fitzgerald followed its career with intense interest. At his "4:10" birthday party in 1960, employees presented him with a painstakingly crafted model of the ship. It became one of his most prized possessions.

The *Edmund Fitzgerald* was launched with much fanfare on June 7, 1958. It was the largest object ever to hit fresh water, with a capacity of 25,891 tons and an overall length of 729 feet — one foot less than the maximum allowed to enter the Sault Ste. Marie locks. After a shakedown cruise and minor adjustments, the ship made its maiden voyage in September, carrying taconite pellets (low-grade iron ore) from the Minnesota shore of Lake Superior to the blast furnaces of Toledo. The *Fitzgerald* would make the same trip up to forty-five times annually for the next seventeen years.

When a steel strike idled the ship in 1959, its owners used the occasion to summon the *Fitzgerald* to Milwaukee, its port of registry. The visit was timed to coincide with the agents' annual meeting, and Northwestern held an "open boat" that attracted 26,000 visitors over three days. In 1960, its first full season, the ship broke a six-year-old record for weight in one trip and went on to set new records for season volume in both 1960 and 1961. The *Edward Ryerson* (two years younger and one foot longer than the *Fitzgerald*) took the volume lead in the next two years, but Northwestern's ship recaptured it from 1964 to 1966. The two carriers were the hardest-working ships on the lakes through most of the 1960s.

By 1970, 730-footers were a common sight in the shipping lanes. A new lock at the Sault enabled larger vessels to enter Lake Superior, and in 1971 the *Stewart Cort* broke the 1000-foot barrier. But the *Edmund Fitzgerald* was still known in maritime circles as a "glamour ship." It was a veteran carrier, a former champion, and a prize assignment for sailors. Its crew quarters were lavish in comparison with those on other lake ships; its guest quarters featured walnut furniture, deep pile carpeting, and a wet bar. Edmund Fitzgerald was a frequent passenger, and he knew many of the crew by name.

The *Fitzgerald* began its last trip from Lake Superior's western shore on November 9, 1975. The lake is notoriously rough in late autumn, and Captain Ernest McSorley soon found himself in a gale, with sixty-mile-an-hour winds and thirty-foot waves. As the journey continued, his ship began to take on water and developed a slight list. McSorley radioed the *Arthur Anderson* to stay close behind in case of trouble, but he had taken the *Fitzgerald* through severe storms in other autumns.

By nightfall of November 10 both ships were at the eastern end of the lake, where storm waves build to peak intensity. Seas were washing over their decks, and both vessels were lurching from wave to wave. The sheltered waters of Whitefish Bay were only fifteen miles ahead. In his last radio message to the *Anderson,* McSorley said, "I am holding my own." Then, at 7:10 P.M., the *Fitzgerald* disappeared from the *Anderson's* radar screen.

A night search began immediately, and it continued by land, lake, and air for weeks. All that the searchers ever found were an oil slick and scattered remnants of life boats and life jackets. The *Fitzgerald* and its crew of twenty-nine had gone down without even time to send a distress signal, much less lower the life boats. Coast Guard investigators later found the ship broken in half in 530 feet of water, its stern section upside-down and both halves 28 feet deep in mud.

Many employees remember a hushed feeling in the home office when the sinking was reported. They found it hard to believe that a large ship with such a long and distinguished career could fall victim to a Midwestern storm. Perhaps the person hardest hit by the news was Edmund Fitzgerald himself. At 80 he was already battling Alzheimer's disease (progressive senility), and part of his identity had slipped beneath the waves.

The *Fitzgerald* tragedy was the first fatal shipwreck on the Great Lakes since 1958. It was front-page news for a time, and a controversy about the cause of the sinking generated more publicity. The Coast Guard concluded that water had entered the cargo hold through "ineffective hatch closures." Others contended that the *Fitzgerald* had ripped a hole in its bottom while crossing a shoal. The lake carriers' trade association argued that the hatch covers were perfectly sound, and the group's leaders resisted calls for more stringent safety requirements. The seamen's union claimed that the ship was allowed to carry too much ore for storm conditions. There were allegations of navigational error, inaccurate charts, and poor maintenance of the

Whitefish Point light. The various parties could agree on only the basic facts: the *Fitzgerald* took on water, nosed into a huge wave, and never came up.

Although it aroused controversy, the incident might have retreated quietly to its place in the rich marine lore of the Great Lakes. In 1976, however, Canadian singer-songwriter Gordon Lightfoot released *The Wreck of the Edmund Fitzgerald.* It was an unusual combination of two venerable musical forms: an old-fashioned disaster song with the rhythm of a sea chantey. Lightfoot included it on an album, but the song became so popular that his company re-issued it as a single record. *The Wreck of the Edmund Fitzgerald* was on the Top 100 charts for five months, taking its place among offerings like *Disco Duck* and *You Sexy Thing.* It rose to the second position in November, 1976, and remained there for two weeks. Radios and jukeboxes all over the globe repeated the story of death in "the gales of November." The song also conferred an unusual status on Edmund Fitzgerald. He is the only life insurance executive in the history of the world whose name has become a household word.

Turning 110

Veteran Northwestern officers sometimes use words like "caretaker" and "interim" to describe the administrations of both Donald Slichter and Robert Dineen. Compared to the rebuilding problems of the previous period and the volatility of the next, the decade is remembered as one of calm and stability. There were no major crises between 1958 and 1967, no threats to the company's existence. Both presidents were vitally interested in continuing the deliberate progress of the Fitzgerald years. "Caretaker," however, understates the case. Slichter and Dineen were active presidents, and they presided over the company during a period of pervasive change.

On March 2, 1967, Northwestern took time out to celebrate its 110th birthday. A scene from *Shadow of a Giant,* the centennial musical, was resurrected in the home office auditorium, followed by a long round of speeches. Robert Templin said, "When the next history of the company is written, the last ten years will be given a lot of headlines." He looked back on the decade's highlights: new products, new premium rates, a new cafeteria, new tools like ISA, "and, of course, electronic data processing." Robert Dineen described the computer's rise as *the* event of the decade, and he placed it in a human context: "Far from being a 'giant brain,' the EDP system is more of a valued servant." Francis Ferguson retraced the company's steps into new areas of investment, areas that would not have been considered in 1950.

The last word, however, belonged to Laflin Jones. As the person most concerned with long-range planning, he looked ahead rather than behind, and he saw a new era coming: "No period will bear comparison with the forthcoming decade in terms of change, excitement, and opportunity," That, as it turned out, was an understatement.

Executives and Committees
1947-1982

Edmund Fitzgerald, the polished conservative who guided Northwestern from 1947 to 1958. Fitzgerald's central task was to rebuild the company after a prolonged period of stagnation caused by the Depression and World War II.

*Donald Slichter (top) and Robert Dineen, two presidents of sharply con-
trasting styles who continued the modest momentum of the Fitzgerald
years. Slichter was chief executive from 1958 to 1965, Dineen from 1965
to 1968.*

Top: *Leaders of the post-war decades (left to right): Laflin Jones, Donald Slichter, Robert Dineen, Edmund Fitzgerald, and William Cary (board secretary).*

Bottom: *The leaders of 1983. Northwestern executive officers gather after Francis Ferguson's last board meeting as chief executive. Left to right: Robert Carlson, James McKeon, Frank Kosednar, Russell Jensen, Edward Zore, Donald Mundt, Peter Bruce, Robert Ninneman, Ralph Harkness, Donald Schuenke, Dennis Tamcsin, James Murphy, Ferguson, Edward Flitz, Robert Carboni, James Ericson, Gordon Davidson, James Ehrenstrom, Harvey Wilmeth, Orlo Karsten, James Compere, and Richard Wright.*

Francis Ferguson, chief executive from 1968 to 1983 and current board chairman. Ferguson infused the company with a spirit of dynamism that proved essential in a volatile period. Bottom: *Ferguson at work with his executive assistant, Lucille Neff.*

Donald Schuenke, named president in 1980 and chief executive officer in 1983. A deliberate, workmanlike leader, Schuenke took charge at one of the most important turning points in the company's history.

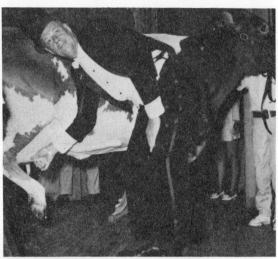

All in a day's work: Ferguson in tuxedo and tophat for a cow-milking contest at an annual meeting, and in bib overalls at dinner with Texas agent Bob Curl. Schuenke appears before the agents as a Star Wars knight prepared to do battle with the competition.

The Board of Trustees: from a schoolroom format in 1956 (top) to broader participation in 1980.

Top: *The Finance Committee at one of its twice-weekly meetings in 1960.*

Bottom: *Home office management and union teams meet at the bargaining table in 1978. Jake Jacobson, vice-president — personnel, is front and center.*

Since 1907 the Policyowners Examining Committee has conducted an annual review of Northwestern's performance and procedures. These photographs show the committees of 1965 and 1982.

(Top) Left to Right: *Lynford Lardner Jr., Dutton Brookfield, John Partridge, Lyman Ayres, and Dr. John Cowee.*

(Bottom) Left to Right: *Robert Scharar, Martin Stein, Quintus Anderson, Stephen Keller, and John Bissell.*

CHAPTER FOUR

The Sleeping
Giant Awakens

1967-1979

It is difficult to say precisely when the river pitched downward, the channel narrowed, and the first whitewater appeared. By 1967, however, it was clear that America had entered a rapids, and the nation was caught in a current of dizzying change. It bumped along from one rock to the next, scraping bottom on a few that appeared suddenly below the surface. It was the most tumultuous period in American history since World War II, perhaps since the Civil War, and it may not be over yet. The current slowed considerably by 1979, but the ride downstream has remained rough.

The Vietnam War was the major event during the first half of the 1967-1979 period. North and South Vietnam had been locked in a civil war since the mid-1950s, both sides struggling for control of a nation considerably smaller than North and South Dakota combined. The United States entered the fray in 1961, and its involvement accelerated through the Sixties. Men, money, and machines were poured into a seemingly unwinnable war. American troop strength peaked at 543,400 in spring of 1969, and American planes dropped more bombs than fell on all of Europe during World War II.

The Vietnam conflict became both the longest and the least popular war in American history. A wave of protest began to crest in the late Sixties, affecting everything from family relationships to political careers. The demonstrators and draft resisters, however numerous, were only one expression of a new mood in the country. The Depression, World War II, and the Cold War had encouraged a sense of solidarity, even uniformity, among the American people. By

1967 the lid was off. A new generation had attained its majority, with no memory of war, little experience of privation, and a powerful will to change. There was everywhere, it seemed, a rejection of the established order. Black militants — a minority of a minority — began to talk of separatism and revolution. Feminists — a minority of a majority — campaigned for rights more fundamental than suffrage. Consumerists took on corporations with a zeal reminiscent of the muckrakers of the early 1900s. Environmentalists assessed the price of progress and found it intolerably high.

There were activists in abundance, but others responded to the new mood by a massive turning inward. Young whites, in particular, experimented with a new lifestyle, one bolstered in part by new forms of music and a pharmacopoeia of non-prescription drugs. They first came to public attention with the "summer of love" in 1967, and their movement became a continuing media event, eventually choked with cliches. The young people were "hippies" and "flower children," forging the Woodstock Nation in the Age of Aquarius. Journalists chronicled in detail their communal lifestyles and outrageous hairstyles, their love beads and love-ins. Beneath the visual spectacle was an earnest belief that a new order was emerging.

The millions who made up the American matrix, the stable core whom Richard Nixon called "the silent majority," reacted to all of the movements with bewilderment, anger, and infrequent sympathy. They were drawn into an atmosphere of factionalism, often without consciously choosing sides. Like a rock cracking under intense pressure, American society was fractured into opposing camps: hawks and doves, hardhats and hippies, Uncle Toms and militants, consumers and corporations, over-30 and under-30. There were Okies from Muskogee, gays and straights, chauvinist pigs and pigs in blue uniforms.

The factionalism was mirrored by a strong undercurrent of violence. More than 47,000 Americans were killed in Vietnam, and the carnage was a regular feature on the evening news. Privileged whites on campuses and underprivileged blacks in ghettos took out different frustrations on their immediate surroundings. Ghetto violence reached a peak in 1967, when "civil disturbances" rocked a score of cities, including normally placid Milwaukee. The death toll was forty-three in Detroit, twenty-six in Newark. Robert F. Kennedy and Martin Luther King were slain in 1968, the same year that Chicago police clubbed dozens of protesters into submission outside the

Democratic national convention. In 1970 four students were killed during another war protest at Kent State University.

American troops were finally pulled out of Vietnam in 1973. A major irritant was removed, but the nation was soon hung up on another rock. The principals in a "third-rate burglary" at the Watergate complex in 1972 left a trail that led directly to the White House. By late 1973 there were new disclosures almost daily, and Richard Nixon's hold on the presidency grew increasingly weak. In 1974 he resigned, the first president to be forced out of office in the nation's history.

The social and political turmoil was matched by convulsions in the American economy. By the late 1960s it was apparent that the long post-war joyride was over. Lyndon Johnson had attempted to finance the Great Society and the Vietnam War simultaneously, contributing to a dramatic increase in the price of both guns and butter. The inflation rate crossed the 5 percent threshold in 1969, reaching its highest level since 1948. American productivity began to sag at the same time. The gross national product, measured in constant dollars, actually declined in 1970, bringing back memories of the 1957-1958 recession. Interest rates reached their highest point in a century in 1969, and two years later imports exceeded exports for the first time since 1893. A disturbingly large portion of the nation's imports consisted of petroleum.

"Volatile" had been a word reserved for temperamental actors, stormy weather systems, and South American politics. Now it was being applied to the American economy. Richard Nixon tried to end the growing chaos by imposing wage and price controls in 1971. The move led to a significant recovery, and some economists predicted a traditional post-war boom after withdrawal from Vietnam in 1973. In October of that year, however, the Arab nations imposed an embargo on oil exports to the United States. When the ban was lifted five months later, oil prices quadrupled. The nation soon found itself in the worst recession since the 1930s. The cost of living rose 11 percent in 1974, and unemployment soared to 9 percent in mid-1975.

The United States celebrated its two-hundredth birthday in 1976. The Vietnam War had been lost, but at least it was over. "Flower power" was a bittersweet memory. The ghettos were relatively quiet. Gerald Ford had returned a sense of decency to the White House. The economy was on the mend again. The American people had a chance to reflect on their remarkable history, and to realize that there had been some good news in the previous years: the first manned moon landing, a new relationship with mainland China, a society more open to different groups and different viewpoints.

Something resembling normalcy returned in 1976, but it was apparent that America had changed. There was a new mood of skepticism in the country, and a massive scaling-down of expectations. Economic uncertainty remained the abiding theme. Double-digit inflation returned in 1979, and another recession was imminent. Late in the year Iran captured the American embassy in Teheran. The United States, in the person of sixty-three of its citizens, was taken hostage. The years between 1967 and 1979 were one long rapids and, by the period's end, the nation as a whole had moved toward a bruised maturity.

It was against this background that Northwestern Mutual and its competitors tried to make progress during the period. The social, political, and especially the economic turmoil posed a challenge to every institution, including life insurance. There was more change in the industry than there had been at any time since the tontine fever of the late nineteenth century, and there was even an updated version of the 1905 Armstrong investigation that broke the fever.

Northwestern, in particular, changed more profoundly than it had since its first years in Milwaukee. Until 1967 the company was known in industry circles as a "sleeping giant" — the most stubbornly traditional of the top ten, a firm so quiet that few people outside the industry knew how good it was. The image was not entirely deserved but, compared with the tumbleweed behavior of some competitors, Northwestern had changed with all the speed of a glacier. By 1979 the giant was very much awake, and the company had displayed a dynamism and aggressiveness that some observers found totally out of character. Northwestern did not abandon tradition, but its method of pursuing traditional goals changed completely.

The major events of the 1967-1979 period are outlined in two distinct chapters, one dealing with internal developments and the other with external pressures. This chapter describes the events over which Northwestern had effective control: the selection of a new president, a new commitment to planning and growth, changes in the agency force and the product line, a new public image, reorganization of the company along functional lines, and the construction of a home office addition. Chapter 5 describes Northwestern's response to pressures from the environment: inflation, consumerism, social change, and the growing role of the federal government. The division is by no means crystal-clear. Internal changes were always made with an eye to the marketplace, and responses to the outside world always reflected the character of the organization. But the internal/external scheme may be a useful way to divide a period that contains enough material for a book of its own.

Francis Ferguson

Limited by his age to a three-year term, the most important thing Robert Dineen could do for Northwestern was to aid in the selection of his successor. Three strong candidates emerged: Laflin "Bob" Jones, Robert Templin, and Francis Ferguson. Jones had a depth and range of experience in the company that was absolutely unmatched, but he was only a few years away from retirement himself. Templin had become probably the strongest Northwestern agency leader in the twentieth century, but the board was not ready to break precedent by choosing someone from the agency side. Ferguson had proven himself as a gifted financier, an able administrator, and a man with what Dineen called "intestinal fortitude." In addition, Ferguson had the enthusiastic support of Howard Tobin, his old mentor. Tobin had already left Northwestern, but he and Dineen remained close friends. Dineen, through Tobin, became a Ferguson advocate, and the president's support was a key factor in the final election. On May 1, 1967, the board named Francis Ferguson the thirteenth president of Northwestern Mutual. He was, at 46, the youngest man to head the company in nearly a century.

Ferguson was born in 1921 on a dairy farm in upstate New York, not far from Rochester, and much of his boyhood was spent helping with the field work and chores. He stayed on the farm until graduation from high school, when he enrolled at Cornell University, across the state in Ithaca. World War II intervened, and Ferguson enrolled in a different institution — the Army Air Corps flight school. He was soon flying a B-17 on bombing raids over Germany.

Two experiences forced Ferguson to mature early. When he was thirteen his father died, leaving a debt-ridden farm for the family to manage in the midst of the Depression. An uncle took over the operation but, as the oldest son, Ferguson's responsibilities increased. Nine years later, on his fifth B-17 mission, his plane went down behind German lines, and he spent the next nineteen months in a prisoner-of-war camp. Ferguson was only twenty-four when Germany surrendered, but he emerged from the war with a rock-hard belief in self-reliance and an equally strong will to succeed.

In 1947 Ferguson completed his degree in agricultural economics at Michigan State University and went to work as a farm appraiser for the Federal Land Bank. He found the bureaucracy stifling, and had few second thoughts when Howard Tobin offered him a post at Northwestern in 1951.

The story of his job interview provides some insight into the characters of the two men. Despite their conservative image, good insurance company lenders often function like horse traders. Tobin asked Ferguson what he expected to be paid. The younger man mentioned $6500 as a fair salary. Tobin said he had planned to offer perhaps $500 less, and he proposed a deal: the lower figure for six months and then, depending on performance, the extra $500 plus interest. Ferguson declared that reasonable but made a counter-offer: "You take me at my figure and, if I'm not worth it, I'll give the difference back to you or you fire me." As Tobin recalled later, "When he said that, I knew I had my man. Here was a real trader." Ferguson got the job, at $6500 a year.

He began as a farm loan specialist and became an officer in less than a year. As described in Chapter 3, Tobin gave his new man unusual freedom. Ferguson rewrote many of the Mortgage Department rules, and compiled the impressive record that led ultimately to his election as president.

Ferguson served as understudy for sixteen months before Robert Dineen retired from the chief executive officer position. The new president visited scores of general agencies from coast to coast and immersed himself in the study of company operations. "As far as I was concerned," Dineen said later, "he was going to school." On September 1, 1968, finally, Ferguson took over the reins as head of the company.

The new executive's style was a real departure from that of his predecessors. Francis Ferguson is a man who inspires meekness in those with a capacity for it. Physically imposing, personally exacting, he took a visceral joy in the exercise of power as chief executive. He was plain-spoken, sometimes profane, and so candid that he often alarmed his public relations staff. But Ferguson is also a paradoxical figure. He has been variously described as a bull, a bear, and a fox. During nearly fifteen years at the helm, he was gruff and sentimental by turns, personally ambitious but dedicated to Northwestern principles, a careful listener but an autocratic decision-maker. He was flamboyant, a major figure in a major industry, and yet he was perhaps most at home behind the wheel of a tractor.

Informal to the bone, Ferguson brought a new mood to the company. His official duties included wearing bib overalls at a Southern agency meeting, T-shirts at Northwestern promotional events, and a tuxedo for a cow-milking contest with the Association of Agents president. (Ferguson lost on volume but won on accuracy.) To people on all levels of the company, he is known as "Fergie." It is not difficult to imagine Henry Palmer turning over in his grave. But Ferguson also operated on a scale different from that of earlier presidents. He hired a public relations consultant to represent the company in New York, a move some traditionalists considered immodest. In 1969 he announced plans for a company airplane. The move was controversial, but the plane saved time and money while it broadened Northwestern's scope. It was also a tangible symbol of Ferguson's intention to change things.

Even during his "apprenticeship" in 1967-1968, people formed definite impressions of the new leader, and those impressions crystallized in the following years. To some, Ferguson was a painful break with the genteel Northwestern tradition. To others, he was a breath of fresh air — or, more accurately, a whirlwind. To all, he was effective. He had a remarkably sure grasp of the issues. He knew what he wanted to do, and he got it done, without doubt, without delay. By the mid-1970s, he was being hailed as the right man at the right time, a dynamic leader in a volatile period.

Ferguson arrived at a time of maximum ripeness. Despite its "sleeping giant" image, Northwestern had changed significantly in the previous twenty years. There had been a steady evolution in its product line, its agency force, its investment strategies and, above all, in its computer systems. Fitzgerald, Slichter, and Dineen had brought Northwestern to a position of strength that Ferguson would use as the foundation for more pervasive change. Some of his administration's major accomplishments — planning, Extra Ordinary Life, agency growth incentives, reorganization — arose from seeds planted years before; they only came to fruit during Ferguson's tenure. The garden had been tended quietly and with care by an extremely competent group of senior officers.

There was also a subtle shift in the company's sociology. By the late 1960s employees who had come to Northwestern under the cloud of the Depression were slowly giving way to post-war recruits. The learned conservatism of the older generation was balanced, in the next wave, by a pent-up desire to grow, to innovate, to branch out.

Although other people and other conditions played supporting roles, Ferguson was at the center of the stage. It was he who focused the company's latent energy and translated its potential for growth into reality. Ferguson marshaled the forces of change behind him and brought Northwestern into the late twentieth century with a confidence that bordered on boldness.

Inventing the Future

Although he was born under the sign of Aquarius, Ferguson was emphatically not in sympathy with the counter-culture Aquarians of the late 1960s. He did, however, share one of the age's dominant traits: a determination to see things freshly, to ask basic questions and to search for answers without bias, without preconceptions. He had a native ability to spot sacred cows and a willingness to dispose of them. The result, as applied to Northwestern, was a corporate self-examination, and the elevation of strategic planning to a central place in the company's operations.

Northwestern had been involved in "planning" since the 1950s, but the process was something less than rigorous. Most research was retrospective: who bought what last year. There were sporadic attempts to identify issues and trends, but the efforts seldom played a major role in decision-making. When Northwestern changed — adding products, installing computers — it did so on the basis of current need, without a well-reasoned vision of the future. The company was not inclined to argue with its own success. In this it was not alone. As late as 1971, according to one study, only 10 of the nation's 1800 life insurance firms had substantial research and development departments.

The 1966 Policyowners Examining Committee sparked a change in attitude. Paul Knaplund and Edward Wells, vice-presidents of IBM and Boeing respectively, had seen the effectiveness of planning in their own companies. As members of the 1966 committee, they asked an eminently reasonable question: If life insurance is really a long-term business, why is so little attention being paid to long-range planning? Knaplund was chosen as the holdover member to chair the next year's committee, giving Northwestern's leaders a powerful incentive to answer the question.

In 1967 six top executives — Robert Dineen, Laflin Jones, Robert Templin, Victor Henningsen, Richard Mooney (general counsel), and Ferguson — left the home office to spend a few days at an Arkansas resort. There were no phone calls to return and no letters to dictate, freeing the six men to take a fresh look at the company's present and future. Out of this first planning rally — an annual event since that time — came a new interest in long-range planning.

Ferguson kept the momentum building. One of his first official acts as chief executive officer in 1968 was the establishment of a new department: Corporate Planning and Development. He described its mission as "the creation of an atmosphere of healthy inquiry about why and how at all levels of our company," and he called it "one of the most significant steps this company has ever taken." Laflin Jones, who was named the new department's head, became a board member at the same time — a sure sign of the planning function's importance.

The new assignment was a fitting capstone to Jones' long career at Northwestern. His father, Evan, had joined the company in 1889 and had served as its secretary from 1923 to 1935. Jones himself arrived in 1929, fresh out of Dartmouth College. He wanted to be a writer, and he viewed his job (Agency Department clerk) as only temporary. With Welsh tenacity, he stayed for forty-three years and became one of Northwestern's most influential leaders.

His rise was not meteoric. Jones stayed in the Agency Department for more than two decades, establishing the advanced underwriting division and heading the educational program. When Robert Dineen arrived in 1950, Jones was named his assistant, and he gradually became identified with Northwestern's research and planning efforts. He established the Markets Research Department in 1958 and became its vice-president five years later. When Dineen stepped up to the presidency in 1965, Jones replaced him as insurance vice-president.

Jones still found time to write. He authored a popular history of Northwestern in 1957 and prepared a variety of skits for company celebrations. He served brief terms as editor of both *Field Notes* and *Pillar*, the major field and home office publications. Jones is best remembered, however, for the plays he wrote, skillful presentations of the human dramas related to life insurance. *Stardust*, a sort of *Death of a Salesman* with a quietly happy ending, has been staged more than seventy-five times since 1953. A man of gracious reserve, broad views, and interests ranging from classical piano to philosophy,

Laflin Jones added a distinctive flavor to Northwestern Mutual. When he retired in 1972, Edmund Fitzgerald called him "the most practical intellectual I ever met."

In his new role as chief planner, Jones, characteristically, began at the beginning. He focused, first of all, on the consumer. How did his or her relationship with money change over the course of a lifetime? What were the dominant needs and desires? He then took a closer look at Northwestern, disregarding the entrenched patterns of the status quo. Who was the company? What were its principal qualities and resources? Jones then got to the heart of his assignment: devising a process that would insure the most appropriate fit between company and consumer, under changing conditions, year after year. His approach was ecological. Jones saw Northwestern, its market, and the entire society as organisms, living things that were interactive, mutually dependent, moving in a kind of dance. The purpose of planning was to decide the tune and the tempo that Northwestern would dance to in its particular role.

Jones had substantial help in his effort to, as he put it, "clarify the mental image of what we want the future to be." James McKeon was finishing his doctorate and teaching at the Wharton School of Finance in 1968. Impressed by his technical background and his capacity for hard work, Jones hired him to manage the new department. McKeon became head of Corporate Planning and Development when Jones retired in 1972.

There was also important input from a source outside Northwestern. McKinsey and Company, a management consulting firm with offices on three continents, had surveyed the life insurance industry on its own in 1964-1965, hoping to increase its knowledge and, not incidentally, to create a demand for its services. The effort paid off. In early 1969 Northwestern hired McKinsey to take an in-depth look at its operations, with special emphasis on possibilities for the future.

The results of the McKinsey survey were, to some officers, shocking. The researchers found much to praise — a top-quality field force, the industry's lowest net-cost standing, excellent penetration of the lucrative business and professional markets. But they also found reason for concern. Despite the innovations of the previous decade, Northwestern was losing ground in the industry. Its growth rates in new premium, insurance in force, and assets were all well below the industry average for the 1958-1968 period. The poor showing was not due to competition from the flood of newly organized companies. Among thirteen older firms offering similar products to similar clients, Northwestern ranked second-last in premium growth. Among all companies, ranked by insurance in force, it had fallen from eighth place in 1956 to twelfth in 1967.

Little was being done to reverse the trend. Recruitment of new agents had actually slipped backward. There were no agencies in one third of the nation's cities with populations larger than 50,000. After more than a century, the company was still a Midwestern institution. Nearly a third of its 1967 sales were in five states of the Old Northwest — Illinois, Wisconsin, Michigan, Iowa, and Minnesota.

Slow growth is by no means the same as slow death, but the trend concerned some members of management. The McKinsey staff also found internal problems. Mediocrity and complacency, they reported, were alive and well in the home office. Excessive reliance on the committee system had blurred the lines of authority. A tradition of conservatism had made people allergic to change. Board meetings were long on presentations and short on discussions. There was, at the same time, a clear awareness that change was coming, and both confusion and excitement about its potential effects. The McKinsey team found a company in transition, a giant stirring in its sleep but unable to stop dreaming of the past.

For the people at the very top, the final report held few surprises. Ferguson, in particular, might have been able to write it himself. But the McKinsey study had two major effects. First of all, the simple act of hiring a team of outside critics was a clear signal to everyone that self-examination and planning were top priorities. Secondly, the final report was a catalyst, a change agent. With the issues spelled out in black and white for everyone to see, Northwestern was virtually forced to respond.

The company had only two choices: to grow, relatively, or to shrink. Edmund Fitzgerald had faced a similar problem in the late 1940s. With costs rising and competition increasing, he could have adopted a growth strategy to keep pace with changing conditions. He chose instead to continue the emphasis on net-cost superiority, a decision that led to cost-cutting programs, modest product innovations, and a great deal of oratory about fiscal strength and philosophical stability.

Economic conditions had changed by the late 1960s. The issue was no longer growth itself but how much growth. No one had the slightest interest in being a high-quality also-ran, but some officials, fearing a strain on the company's resources, favored a modest expansion program. Their caution was counterbalanced by a widespread desire for more rapid change, especially among the younger agents and employees. The expansionists argued that faster growth would bring economies of scale into play, resulting in lower unit costs. And they felt an urgent need for a new climate in the company, one that would offer a new sense of challenge and opportunity.

With Ferguson at the helm, there was little question about the debate's outcome. In his first speech to the agents as president in 1967, he had declared himself in favor of growth, consistent with continued high quality. In his 1968 speech at the annual meeting, he put it more strongly: "Growth brings excitement and a heightened sense of destiny in home office and agency operations alike . . . . Planned growth will enhance a sense of accomplishment and purpose." Ferguson focused and enlarged the company's desire *not* to be an also-ran. Under his leadership, Northwestern crossed over to the fast track.

With its basic philosophy adopted, the company spent all of 1969 laying groundwork for the future. Even while the McKinsey survey was underway, nine task forces, split into twenty-two study groups, were taking an unprecedented look at the major issues facing Northwestern. The effort involved scores of people in management, grappling with questions that had been, to say the least, sensitive: group insurance, selling through brokers, mutual funds, and the pension market. The task force reports were submitted in July, setting the stage for the next step: formulation of the company's strategic plan. It was to be, in Ferguson's words, "the blueprint of where and why we want to move."

Laflin Jones wrote the strategic plan during a two-week "vacation" on Wisconsin's Door Peninsula. Its first sentence gave traditionalists little to criticize: "The purpose of NML is to continue to be the leading American company providing family and business security by specializing in life insurance and related services for the individual." The plan affirmed Northwestern's commitment to a relatively narrow product line and to a career agency force. Within its broad mission statement, however, there was room for innovation. The strategic plan called for new products like decreasing term and flexible policies, new approaches to the college and older adult markets, a new attitude toward agency management, and a new emphasis on policyowner services.

Above all, the plan called for growth. To maintain its position as "the leading American company" in individual life insurance, Northwestern had to expand its operations. Of all the goals set in the strategic plan, one was most important: $100 million in annual new premium by 1978. The 1968 figure was only $43 million; it was clear to all that Northwestern had a decade of hard work ahead.

As the strategic plan was being reviewed and revised during the last months of 1969, Jones and his staff turned to the next task: formulation of operating plans for each department and general agency. In the early stages of planning, the focus had been on the entire company and its context in society. Now, like an engine being disassembled, Northwestern was broken down into its constituent parts. Each executive officer and general agent was asked to submit a detailed plan for the next decade, complete with numbers: goals for new business, agent recruitment, investment yield, expenses, service time. The operating plans, coordinated by Jones and his staff, were the day-to-day applications of the strategic plan. Every work unit had a specific, quantifiable function in the company's plan, and accountability for performance was fixed.

By early 1970 the planning structure was in place. The strategic plan had few pretensions to literary merit or spiritual insight, but it became, in Ferguson's words, "a Bible to us." Its chapters and verses were the operating plans, based on ten-year projections, updated annually, reviewed at least quarterly.

The system was adapted to meet changing conditions. By the early 1970s a decade seemed like an impossibly long period, and five-year plans became the norm. Budget planning was added to the operational goals at the same time. In its basics, however, the planning process developed in 1969 has changed very little.

What lies ahead, the futurists are fond of saying, is not inevitable but inventable. The future Northwestern invented for itself in 1969 was a dramatic departure from its past. For decades net-cost superiority had been practically the sole determinant of Northwestern's course. There was enough new business to maintain a constant speed, but ranking first in sales was far less important than ranking first in value. Although Ferguson did not alter the basic course, he was determined to use some of the fuel stored by his predecessors. Northwestern decided that it could have it both ways, maintaining its quality while moving rapidly into new and larger waters. Slowly at first, the big ship gained a momentum it had not seen since the 1920s.

Ferment in the Field

Growth, of course, meant agents. Every dollar of new premium had to be brought in by people representing Northwestern in the field. The company's relatively slow growth in the 1960s was caused, in large part, by a relative lack of progress in recruiting. After a brief spurt in the mid-Sixties (614 new full-time agents in 1964), the effort tailed off (480 recruits in 1967). Northwestern products were sold through 2481 full-time agents in 1967, only 2 percent more than in 1960 and 11 percent more than in 1947. The number of general agents · stood at 101 — four more than in 1932. Despite high turnover and a dramatic increase in productivity, the company's field force was relatively stagnant.

Northwestern's central goal was $100 million in new premium by 1978, and it was obvious that rapid field expansion was the only way to reach it. The 1969 strategic plan called for the most ambitious agency-building program in the company's history: three new general agencies a year and, in existing agencies, an increase in the total number of full-time recruits from 500 to 600 a year by 1973. In addition, all agents were expected to increase their premiums by at least 6 percent per year.

Good will and impassioned speeches are no substitute for money when it comes to stimulating sales growth. In order to motivate existing agents and to attract high-quality recruits, Northwestern revamped its compensation system between 1968 and 1970. Renewal commissions were concentrated in the first three years after a sale instead of being spread out evenly over the first nine years, enhancing an agent's cash flow. Induction fees, a growth incentive first offered in 1953, were revised in 1968 to give general and district agents a larger reward for the production of their young recruits. Direct development fees, based on the production of older agents, were initiated in the same year.

Perhaps the most imaginative new "carrot" was the growth bonus, also introduced in 1968. It rewarded general agents for building potential in their operations. Every special agent under contract was assigned a quantitative value (based on age, length of service, and sales volume) that approximated his or her expected production to age 65. Just as an athletic team can be evaluated in dollar terms, a general agency staff was evaluated in points — more for its younger agents, fewer for those nearing retirement. If the point total rose from one year to the next, the general agent received a bonus — up to $12,000 annually. There was a powerful stimulus to recruit new agents who had decades of potential sales activity ahead of them. The veterans weren't forgotten, although some of them felt ignored at times. The company offered them desk clocks and watches to bring in new faces, and some general agents shared their bonuses with veterans who helped in the recruiting effort.

. The complexities of the new system were administered by a new department — Field Financial Services. Established in 1968, it combined tasks that had been scattered throughout the company. Its head was Richard Wright, who had come to the company two years earlier from the Hartford-based Life Insurance Agency Management Association (LIAMA). An expert in the financial relationships between home office and field, Wright brought a sense of rigor and professionalism to an area that was growing rapidly in importance.

The new incentives worked. It took a year or two, but the expansion effort gathered momentum. By 1975 Northwestern had the largest full-time field force in its history. An important part of the growth came from the development of new territories. The company opened fifteen general agencies between 1968 and 1975 — the greatest number since the 1900-1907 period. Five of the new agencies were in the Deep South, four were in California, and five more were scattered from Connecticut to Colorado. The remaining agency was based in Honolulu; its first head was Al Ostheimer, one of Northwestern's all-time sales leaders. In 1979 the company obtained a license to sell in Alaska, giving Northwestern a presence in all fifty states.

The combined growth of "scratch" and existing agencies boosted the number of full-time agents from 2570 in 1969 to 3532 in 1975, surpassing the Depression-era peak of 3479. The expansion was accomplished despite a high rate of attrition. Twenty-five percent of the full-time recruits in a typical year were still with the company five years later — a much better record than the industry average, but poor enough to make recruiting a never-ending job. Despite the turnover, Northwestern showed a net increase of 165 agents per year in the 1969-1979 period, nearly eight times the growth rate of the previous decade.

The McKinsey researchers had observed that the fastest-growing segment of Northwestern's future market was currently in college, and they warned that the company was overly dependent on an aging clientele. The first strategic plan, accordingly, called for a new emphasis on the "get them while they're young" approach. In 1969 the company set up experimental college units in twelve general agencies, with a staff person in each responsible for both agent recruiting and sales management. By 1972 there were fifty college units, and Northwestern was developing what it called "a field force within the field force." The number of college agents (all part-time) jumped from 71 in 1966 to 340 in 1971 and 459 in 1979. College sales were stimulated by the premium financing agreement adopted for the market in 1971. Northwestern, in effect, loaned students money to buy insurance, with payments accelerated after graduation. The emphasis on college marketing worked to Northwestern's advantage. By 1976, 10 percent of the company's full-time agents were former college agents, and many retained clients they had first met on campus.

When the goals for new premium and new agents were announced, Northwestern had insisted that growth would take place in a planned, orderly, manageable fashion. The company took several precautions to insure that its quality would not suffer as a result of expansion. The most important of these was the Quality Incentive, introduced in 1969. QI, as it was soon called, was a bonus paid to agents with superior earnings and superior persistency rates. An agent with 160 percent of the average agent's earnings and a first-year lapse rate of 2 percent or less was paid an extra 2.5 percent on renewal commissions. The increments may have been small, but QI payments amounted to thousands of dollars a year for many agents. In 1969 Ferguson estimated that the Quality Incentive program would cost Northwestern $3 million annually — a fair price, he felt, for a tool that would stimulate both production and persistency.

The company took other steps to assimilate its new agents and to maintain the quality and cooperation of the field force as a whole. The educational programs grew dramatically. Career Schools for newer agents were expanded from two to five a year. The Advanced Planning School, a weeklong clinic for career agents, began in 1968. Career Forum, a continuing education program for top producers with at least ten years of experience, was introduced in 1977. There was also an expanded effort to inform and support the agents. *Field-News* appeared in 1971 to keep agents up-to-date on company developments, and there was even a short-lived magazine (*Very Important People*) for agents' wives. Another 1971 development was the introduction of Operation Issue, a concerted home office effort to process new applications in time to qualify agents for year-end awards.

The dual emphasis on growth and support was reflected in changes within the Agency Department. Its staff was expanded and its functions were realigned. All general agencies were grouped into four regions in 1971, and four regional directors were appointed to provide better liaison and more efficient service. Marketing became a separate division at the same time. Its functions ranged from education to advertising, the common thread being the effort to help agents become more effective salespersons.

There was also change at the top. Robert Templin's title became "vice-president — sales" in 1968, reflecting Northwestern's new interest in volume. He was responsible for both the Agency and Field Financial Services Departments, and he moved closer to the administrative heart of the company. In 1971 Templin was elected to the Board of Trustees, the first agency executive to be so honored since Henry Norris in 1912.

As Templin's role grew larger, a new executive position opened up — director of agencies, reporting to Templin. Neal Creswell and James Pratt held the job for two years each, and in 1973 Dennis Tamcsin moved into the office. He was, at 35, the youngest executive officer in the company, and one year later he became a vice-president. Tamcsin, a Cleveland native of Hungarian descent, had worked as an agent and then as the general agent's assistant in Cleveland for five years before coming to Milwaukee in 1968. He was, like Templin and Grant Hill before him, both a Midwesterner and an ex-Marine, and he brought the same articulate enthusiasm to the office that his predecessors had.

As the "general agent for the general agents," the department head has always been required to monitor, motivate, and not infrequently prod the field personnel. Tamcsin, however, has managed the agency system during a period of unprecedented growth in both sales and recruitment. The company's vision of its future required a new emphasis on productivity, efficiency, setting goals and meeting them. The agency executive's job called for a delicate balance of toughness and tact that Tamcsin has been able to find successfully.

Despite the safeguards, the supports, and the stress on tight management, there was some concern about the price of growth. It cost thousands of dollars to finance the development of every new agent, and considerably more to establish new agencies. More than half of the first-year premium went to the agent, and it took time for new business to make a contribution to assets. An internal study done in 1969 showed that every $100 of new premium cost Northwestern $167 — $83 in expenses and claims, $75 in the reserve account required by law, and $9 in dividends. As policies remained in force, the ratio was reversed, and Northwestern's persistency continued to be the best in the industry. But there was intense interest in reducing the costs of acquisition. Commissions and claims could not be cut, and dividends were necessary to maintain a low net-cost ranking. Northwestern began to look at its legal reserve account.

The purpose of the reserve was to back up every policy's cash value and to pay potential claims, but there was more than one method of calculating its size. Northwestern had been using the net level-premium legal reserve method, which assumed that a firm's costs were spread evenly throughout the life of a policy. The commissioners reserve valuation method (CRVM) recognized that first-year costs were higher, and it allowed a corresponding reduction in the amount placed in reserve. Northwestern made the move to CRVM on its new policies in two stages, the first in 1974 and the second in 1978. Because the reserve per policy was smaller, cash values were smaller. That fact gave some agents second thoughts, but there was widespread support for the move. It reduced the $75 reserve cost of new business to $10 or $15. The "savings" were used to reduce premiums and to provide new capital for growth.

By the mid-1970s other factors had persuaded Northwestern to scale down its expansion program: soaring costs in both home office and field, the drag of policy loans on investment yield, economic uncertainty. Growth continued, but it took place vertically instead of horizontally. Only two new general agencies were opened after 1975, both in the South. The focus shifted to more intense development of existing agencies. The number of district agents jumped from 272 in 1975 to 304 in 1979 — the greatest increase since the mid-1950s. The roster of full-time agents in all categories grew from 3532 to 4220 during the same four years — the fastest rate of increase in the 1967-1979 period.

No company could increase its field force by 70 percent in twelve years without experiencing dizzying change, but there were some constants in the period. The most important was the continued preeminence of Northwestern agents in the industry. In 1974, when the growth program had been underway for five years, 25 percent of the company's eligible full-time agents were members of the Million Dollar Round Table and 40 percent were National Quality Award winners. Both figures were significant improvements over the previous period, and both placed Northwestern first among the twenty largest insurance firms. The number of Chartered Life Underwriters in the company passed the 1000 mark in 1973, and their proportion increased from 27 percent of full-time agents in 1967 to 33 percent in 1978.

There was similar constancy in Northwestern's market, as the agents continued to prospect among the highly educated segments of the middle and upper classes. A 1977 survey showed that two-thirds of the company's policyowners had college degrees (five times the national average) and half earned at least $25,000 annually (more than three times the average). In comparison with other buyers, Northwestern clients purchased larger policies that stayed on the books longer, and they were more inclined to come back for more. Throughout the 1967-1979 period, roughly half of all new sales were made to existing clients.

The necessity of hard work and long hours changed little for the agents during the period. Another 1977 survey showed that 80 percent of Northwestern's career agents were on the job more than forty hours a week, and two-thirds scheduled some evening and Saturday interviews. But averages conceal the diversity in the field force. The repeating sales leaders for the 1967-1979 period — John Todd for two years, David Hast for three, Lyle Blessman for three more — are a study in contrasts. An industry legend by this time, Todd ran a large and sophisticated operation in Chicago. Although he "retired" in 1967, he led the company in 1970 for the sixth time in his career. Hast, a Pittsburgh agent who joined Northwestern in 1949, called himself "a tortoise," plodding along methodically and making a multitude of contacts. He placed first in 1975 with sales of $12.2 million on 285 lives. Blessman, by contrast, had won the year before with a volume of $18.4 million on 29 lives. Working among the cattle ranchers and beet farmers of northeastern Colorado, Blessman typically closed his largest sales in the last month of the agents' year.

The performance of the field force as a whole was impressive. When the $100 million premium goal was announced in 1969, it seemed unrealistic to many inside the company. In five or six years, however, aided by expansion, greater productivity, and inflation, Northwestern's agents were closing in. In 1976 Francis Ferguson issued a "Bicentennial Challenge," urging them to reach the goal in the upcoming year. They made it with room to spare, bringing in $108 million of new premium in 1977, one year ahead of schedule.

Comparative figures for the industry gave Northwestern even more reason to celebrate. The face value of new life insurance policies sold by Northwestern rose from $1.4 billion in 1967 to $8.6 billion in 1979, a 514 percent increase. Ordinary insurance sales for all companies rose only 246 percent. Northwestern's new ordinary premium income grew 242 percent during the period, from $35.3 million to $120.8 million. The comparable figure for the entire industry was 112 percent, five points lower than the rise in the cost of living. Competing against companies with much broader product lines, Northwestern moved from twelfth place to tenth in insurance in force during the 1967-1979 period, and from twentieth to ninth in volume of new business. The sleeping giant was very much awake, and it was giving the other giants reason to worry.

New Offerings

With or without an agency expansion program, Northwestern's new business would have grown rapidly after 1967. The increase in the number of agents was paralleled by an increase in the number of products, and most were enthusiastically received in the marketplace. By far the most important new offering was Extra Ordinary Life (EOL). Introduced in 1968, EOL became, without question, the most popular Northwestern product since semi-tontine insurance was introduced in 1883.

Extra Ordinary Life is a hybrid contract, combining whole life and term insurance in a self-contained whole. Dividends are automatically used to convert a portion of the term insurance to paid-up whole life insurance each year, and in time all of the term element is converted. It is like dropping coins into a wishing well until money displaces all of the water. Unlike term insurance, EOL's premium is level throughout the life of the contract. Unlike whole life, dividends build up inside the policy. The result of this "marriage" is more continuous protection for less money.

The introduction of EOL was a major response to a major trend. As a result of lower mortality, higher investment earnings, and more spirited competition, premium rates throughout the industry had been dropping steadily since World War II. Northwestern followed the trend, but it remained a high-premium company, with correspondingly high dividends to maintain its net-cost ranking. There was pressure, especially from corporate clients, for products that would require a less formidable outlay of cash.

There was also internal pressure. Harvey Wilmeth, who became the company's controller in 1961, prepared a series of charts illustrating the ultimate use of Northwestern's revenue. Between 1900 and 1940, he showed, ten to fourteen cents of every dollar had been used to pay death claims. Most of the balance was applied to dividends and cash value increases. Between 1940 and 1960, as the nation's health improved, the share of the Northwestern dollar used to pay claims dropped to little more than a nickel. Wilmeth concluded that Northwestern had abandoned the insurance business for the savings business, and he argued for a substantial decrease in premium rates. As pressure from the marketplace increased, his view became more widely shared.

Extra Ordinary Life emerged as the solution to the problem in the mid-1960s. Its basic design was the brainchild of William Anderson, a Canadian actuary who had become head of the Toronto-based North American Life Insurance Company. William McCarter, a Northwestern actuary, met Anderson on a vacation trip to the Canadian Rockies. During a round of golf near Lake Louise, Anderson talked at length about the product he called "Special Enhancement." McCarter returned to Milwaukee aglow with enthusiasm. He tailored the basic approach to Northwestern's needs and rechristened it "Extra Ordinary Life." By November of 1965 he was ready to show it to the agents.

The new product was not welcomed with open arms. The agents feared that a lower-premium policy would mean lower commissions for them. McCarter and other officers cited studies showing that sales (and commissions) rose dramatically as premiums dropped, but they failed to convince the skeptics. The resistance softened when it was revealed that one of EOL's most vocal opponents in the field force was a leading salesman of North American's Special Enhancement policies. Legal obstacles remained. The New York insurance commissioner refused to authorize sale of the product in 1967, arguing that a virtual guarantee of dividends was a violation of state regulations.

Northwestern altered the contract's wording to satisfy the New York authorities and adopted a $20,000 policy minimum to appease the agents. On May 1, 1968, Extra Ordinary Life was offered to the public. Company officials had reason for optimism. Northwestern was the first major American firm to sell the product, and it had the dividends to make the policy work. Dividend payments had doubled since 1960, and the dividend scale had increased thirteen times in the previous sixteen years. The company's computer expertise was also more than sufficient to administer the complex new program.

Despite the built-in advantages, even the optimists were amazed by EOL's success. The new product replaced whole life as Northwestern's most popular policy in less than a year, bringing in 27 percent of all new premium during the first half of 1969. Some agents were surprised to find that first-year commissions of EOL sellers were rising at triple the rate of those who abstained. As more agents jumped on the bandwagon, EOL's lead widened. The new offering accounted for 34 percent of new premium in 1970, 44 percent in 1974, and nearly half in 1978. Extra Ordinary Life, teamed with the Insurance Service Account, was Northwestern's most powerful marketing innovation of the century.

EOL was the centerpiece, but it was by no means the only new product developed between 1967 and 1979. Change occurred so rapidly that the 1950s debate over double indemnity seemed, in retrospect, almost childish. The most radical departure from Northwestern tradition was disability income insurance, introduced in 1969. Designed to soften the blow of "economic death," it replaced at least a portion of a client's income lost as the result of injury or illness.

Disability income insurance, usually referred to as "DI," was introduced on this continent in 1907 and marketed widely for the first time in the boom years following World War I. As competition increased, underwriting standards fell. Some firms offered policies with standard premiums regardless of age. Northwestern, under William Van Dyke, showed absolutely no interest in following the trend, and the company's commitment to specialization hardened. The Depression soon killed the disability income market. As unemployment soared, thousands of policyowners found real or invented health conditions that kept them from working. They used their policies as a form of unemployment insurance. Claims mounted, and losses grew exponentially. Pacific Mutual, the largest and most liberal disability income writer, was declared insolvent and reorganized by California's state insurance authorities. Northwestern, with more than a hint of pietism, congratulated itself for decades thereafter on the wisdom it had shown in avoiding the fray.

Conditions changed in the late 1960s. The disability income market was growing again, and Northwestern began to see that the "living benefits" of DI might be an attractive complement to the death benefits of its other insurance contracts. The agents were already selling the product through other companies. When the home office surveyed the field force regarding new product development, disability income was the agents' highest priority. There was still some reluctance. Disability is, to put it mildly, somewhat harder to define than death, and Northwestern knew the hazards of entering a highly litigious and competitive segment of the industry.

When the top executives held their first planning rally in 1967, disability income was among the major topics of discussion. Ferguson and his colleagues knew that it represented a significant shift in direction, but there was surprisingly little debate. They returned to Milwaukee with the decision made to proceed. Two years of cautious development followed. Northwestern's actuaries designed a middle-of-the-road product, with relatively high premiums and few features that were not available elsewhere. It was offered for sale on August 1, 1969. The company had hired Kenneth Lafferty to manage its disability income effort at the beginning of the year. Lafferty came to the home office from a post as Midwest supervisor for Provident Life and Accident, a leading DI insurer.

Although they had been lobbying for it, Northwestern agents gave the new product a lukewarm reception. In 1970, disability income's first full year on the market, only 3000 policies were sold — barely one for every full-time agent. The product's contribution to new premium was only 1.5 percent of the total. Many agents had already established relationships with other disability income firms, and it was hard to convince them that Northwestern's version was superior.

As the company grew more comfortable with its new addition, the contract's applications were broadened and its terms liberalized. A substantially revised product appeared in 1974, featuring, most importantly, lower premiums. Sales increased accordingly. In 1979 23,000 disability income policies were sold, accounting for 6.6 percent of the company's new premium revenue.

Two additions to the term insurance line enjoyed faster starts. Northwestern had been selling term products for a century, but the company's attitude was steadfastly ambivalent. Time-limited coverage had an acknowledged place in the universe, but permanent insurance was the bright star the company followed. Northwestern sold term policies in the hope that they would be converted to whole life contracts, just as a dentist might install a temporary filling until the customer could afford a crown.

Following a national trend, Northwestern's term sales had

increased steadily since World War II, rising from 17 percent of face amount sold in 1947 to 31 percent in 1967. Consumers were indicating their desire to pay less for insurance. Extra Ordinary Life, designed to address the same desire, cut deeply into the term market. Term sales dropped to 12 percent of new business four years after EOL was introduced.

There remained, however, strong sales potential for low-cost, short-duration coverage. A 1968 survey showed that decreasing term products accounted for one third of the business Northwestern agents placed outside the company. Decreasing term policies were typically purchased by young people in their child-raising, home-buying years. The death benefit decreased every year, supposedly at the same rate as the client's financial obligations. The agent associations lobbied for a decreasing term contract separate from the riders the company had offered, and it appeared in 1971.

The battle for yearly renewable term (YRT) was not so easily won. Northwestern offered five- and ten-year term contracts, but they were sold as options to convert to permanent insurance. The contracts were not renewable without new evidence of insurability. In 1971 the agent associations argued for a one-year policy that would be automatically renewable and convertible. Some of the company's officers, notably Victor Henningsen, insurance vice-president, did not welcome the suggestion. Henningsen felt that a yearly renewable contract would be too easy to sell. He feared that clients would be less likely to convert their policies and more likely to let them lapse. The agents' rebuttal was simple: If you don't sell it, you can't convert it. A 1971 study showed that the agents had sold $53 million in YRT contracts through other companies, including more than $20 million to Northwestern policyowners. Despite spirited opposition, Northwestern began to issue yearly renewable term policies in 1972. Within a year they accounted for 17 percent of the face amount of insurance sold, second only to EOL.

There was comparable activity in the pension field, but it generated more smoke than fire. The old pension trust area was now variously known as "employee plans," "corporate products," and "tax-qualified business." All of the terms referred to insurance and annuity contracts used in the workplace as benefits. Contributions to employee plans qualified as tax deductions for employers, and the benefits were not taxable as current income for employees.

The tax-qualified area became by far the most complex segment of Northwestern's business. The company still sold employee life and retirement income contracts. In the mid-1960s it began to offer HR-10 (House of Representatives Bill 10) products for the self-employed and tax-deferred annuities for employees of public schools and non-profit groups. After 1967 Northwestern added variable annuities (qualified and non-qualified), flexible premium annuities, flexible investment variable annuities, and individual retirement annuities. Changes in market patterns, agent pressures, and federal regulations created a condition of nearly constant flux. Northwestern added, subtracted, and modified products virtually every year, each time causing actuarial headaches, each time forcing new encounters with the federal bureaucracy.

The variable annuity (VA) is a case in point. The stock market boom of the 1960s had spawned a wide variety of equity-based products, and Northwestern considered entering the field in 1967. After more than a century of guaranteeing fixed-dollar contracts, the company was reluctant to offer a product whose buyer bore the risk of loss. Robert Dineen declared that it "would represent a very important and fundamental move." After considerable debate, Northwestern decided in 1968 to introduce a variable annuity, with benefits based on the performance of a portfolio of common stocks. Before the product reached the marketplace, however, Northwestern had to organize a subsidiary (NML Equity Services) to advise the fund and train agents. The agents were required to register with the Securities and Exchange Commission. Separate accounts had to be established to isolate the VA assets from the rest of the company's funds. The groundwork proved useful later but, after jumping through all the regulatory hoops, Northwestern and its clients were caught in the stock market decline of the early 1970s. The assets of the separate accounts declined 16 percent in 1973 alone.

Within the maze of VAs, TDAs, IRAs, FPAs, and SPDAs, there was one simple constant — ambivalence. Northwestern shuffled and reshuffled the deck but, in the opinion of many, never really entered the game. As in the previous period, the company was unwilling to abandon the pension business but unable to commit itself to aggressive development of the market. A large part of the problem was Northwestern's reluctance to sell group products. The tax-qualified field was a no-man's-land between the group and individual markets, and the company could not decide what role to play in it. The relatively few agents who sold pension products had differing opinions about directions for the future. Home office staff who had the desire to expand the program had no authority to do so, and those in authority had no desire. The result was a stalemate, a continued drifting from year to year.

The problem was most obvious in the geography of the home office. Verne Arends, who had joined the company as a messenger in 1932, emerged as Northwestern's pension expert in the 1940s. He managed the employee plans division from the old Secretarial Department, far removed from the selling arm of the company. When the department was reorganized in 1968, employee plans became a division of Policy Benefits. In 1972, finally, Arends and his staff moved to the Agency Department. Its members, however, soon felt like the Israelites in Egypt. With an expansion program underway, Agency executives had little time or inclination to actively manage an area whose complexities were legendary. Products less specialized and more competitive received most of the attention. Agent training programs for the tax-qualified market were sporadic, and sales support was lukewarm at best.

Northwestern did not suffer from lack of knowledge. The company generated enough studies and reports to fill a small library. As one veteran actuary put it, "Northwestern knows everything about pension products except how to sell them." In a 1975 speech to the agents Ferguson said, "Ever since I have been in the home office, there has been a committee studying whether we ought to get into or get out of the pension business — except when another committee was about to be formed." He then announced the formation of another committee. This one, headed by James McKeon, made recommendations that would bear fruit in the 1980s. In the meantime, however, tax-qualified sales slipped from 18 percent of new premium in 1967 to less than 9 percent in 1979.

Throughout the period, Northwestern's actuaries tinkered with the product line, usually with better results in the non-pension areas. Responding to market forces and company policy, they constantly adjusted the mixture of price and benefits. The overall direction was toward liberalization. Dollar limits were raised, exclusions were pared, and recent offerings were continually upgraded. Outdated products were retired. The last endowment contracts — high-premium insured savings plans — were withdrawn from the market in 1978.

There were corresponding changes in price structure. The reserve rate was raised from 3 percent in 1968 to 4 percent in 1978, the highest it had been since 1869. Because the company guaranteed higher interest on investments over a contract's lifetime, it could charge less for insurance. This, coupled with lower mortality and new products like EOL and YRT, exerted a downward pressure on premium rates. For all Northwestern policies sold, the premium per $1000 of coverage fell from $22.15 in 1967 to $13.73 in 1979.

Change in products and policies was paralleled by change in the Actuarial Department's leadership. Victor Henningsen, a native Iowan whose first tongue was Danish, managed the operation from 1953 to 1968. He had joined the company in 1932 and earned a promotion to the officer ranks a year later, at the tender age of 25. A man of stubborn integrity, Henningsen was perhaps the staunchest defender of Northwestern traditions since Edmund Fitzgerald himself. He argued for innovations like the accidental death benefit and disability income insurance, but he is best remembered as a conservative — in his own words, "the 'no' man." Scrupulously honest, a lifelong perfectionist, Henningsen was not always easy to work for, but he was among the most widely respected figures in the company.

In 1968 Henningsen was promoted to insurance vice-president, succeeding Laflin Jones, and Russell Jensen was named the new head actuary. He was another product of the Iowa farm country and a Northwestern employee since 1954. Jensen managed the department for five years with quiet competence and sardonic wit. In 1973 Henningsen retired and Jensen took over most of his responsibilities. Northwestern went outside the company for a new chief actuary, hiring Dale Gustafson, vice-president of the American Life Insurance Association. Gustafson had long been impressed with Northwestern's quality, but the "stodginess" of the pre-Ferguson years had dissuaded him from seeking work there. In 1973, with a transformation underway, he willingly accepted a cut in pay to join the company. Gregarious, light-hearted, an enthusiastic teacher, Gustafson was far removed from the prevailing eyeshade-and-armband stereotype of the actuary.

Henningsen, Jensen, and Gustafson were markedly different in temperament and outlook, but they shared a common background. All were Scandinavians, all were Midwesterners, and all were products of the University of Iowa. The department they managed contributed a great deal of talent to other areas of the company, and it played a key role in the most pervasive product change in the company's history. The new offerings — EOL, DI, YRT, and others — represented a tangible shift away from the narrow specialist role of

earlier years. Their success was dramatic. In 1979 products introduced in the previous twelve years accounted for 60 percent of
Northwestern's sales.

The Quiet Company

Northwestern had long been one of the most conservative
advertisers in the insurance industry. The sleeping giant was also a
silent giant. Relying heavily on repeat business and the referrals of
satisfied customers, Northwestern had an exceedingly modest advertising budget. Its central campaign was the Karsh series — photographs of distinguished policyowners alongside their testimonials to
the value of life insurance. The series appeared in national news
weeklies from 1948 to 1968 with only the slightest variations, making
it perhaps the longest-running campaign in the industry's history.
With a new president, a rebuilt field force, and new products, it was
only a matter of time before Northwestern adopted a new image. The
process took a few years, but the company moved its light from under
the bushel and raised it high before the American public.

The Karsh campaign was extremely popular among the agents,
who used reprints as calling cards. In the late 1960s, however, it began
to fail. The testimonial approach had become commonplace, and
Northwestern found it difficult to recruit new executives and profes-
sionals for the series. The market was also growing away from the
campaign. As other firms were using psychedelic art and counter-
culture jargon to reach a new audience, Northwestern's advertisements
placed it squarely on the side of the "establishment." The company's
interest in the college market and the 21-35 age group was growing,
and photographs of graying executives were not appropriate to the
new emphasis. Yousuf Karsh received his last commission in 1968.

J. Walter Thompson of Chicago, Northwestern's advertising
agency, developed a new campaign based on an "individual " theme.
It featured photographs (and later paintings) of different types of
people, with a few well-chosen words stressing the unique qualities of
each and Northwestern's own emphasis on individual insurance. The
message was appropriate to the times, so appropriate that it became a
cliché. The pages of American magazines were filled with similar
tributes to individualism.

Richard Haggman, meanwhile, was growing restive. As Northwestern's advertising director since 1956, he had watched the effec-

tiveness of the company's campaigns diminish steadily. A 1970 Gallup poll showed that only 10 percent of the nation's adult males had ever heard of Northwestern. It was, by assets, the seventh largest insurance firm in the country, but it ranked only thirty-fourth in name recognition. Haggman was concerned that, despite dramatic change in other areas, the company was doing little to update its approach to advertising.

The 1970 Policyowners Examining Committee shared his concerns. Its members included Samuel C. Johnson, president of the Johnson Wax Company, and Marion Stephenson, an NBC vice-president. Advertising played a major role in both of their corporations, and they urged Northwestern to take a closer look at its own program. Johnson declared to Ferguson that the company's advertising budget was, to paraphrase slightly, "like spitting in Lake Michigan."

James Wilson, an Atlanta attorney who later became a Northwestern trustee, was named the returning member to chair the 1971 committee. There was significant pressure to address the advertising issue in the intervening year. With the active support of Ferguson, Haggman canceled the "individual" campaign and looked outside the industry for help. He found Stephen Greyser, a Harvard Business School professor with expertise in advertising. For several months in 1971, the two men worked on a systematic study of Northwestern's program. The result was a specialized counterpart of the company's strategic plan. It suggested, among other things, a first try at television advertising, provided that an "unusual media buy" could be found.

The unusual buy turned out to be the 1972 summer Olympics at Munich. An ABC team had traveled to Milwaukee in early 1972 to visit the Schlitz Brewing Company, already an Olympics sponsor. The network staff paid a courtesy call at Northwestern, informing Haggman that a one-sixteenth share of the sponsorship was still available. The cost was $1.4 million, nearly $600,000 more than the company's entire 1971 advertising budget. To the surprise of many, Northwestern agreed to participate.

Promotion began almost immediately. General agencies across the country became "Olympics information centers," giving away guidebooks and showing filmed highlights of the 1968 games. The theme of the 1972 agents' meeting was "In the Company of Champions," and the concluding speaker was Jesse Owens, a gold medalist in 1936.

One problem remained: how to use thirty minutes on the air. Northwestern and the Thompson agency conducted group interviews with people from the company's target markets, searching for themes that would strike the most responsive chords. The results showed that most people saw little difference among insurance companies. "Mutual" and "net cost" confused them, and they cared little about Northwestern's specialist role. Their basic requirements for an insurance company were simple. They wanted a firm that was big, that was old, and that offered value.

The survey results and a limited budget forced the company to keep its commercials simple. Filmed during June in the Chicago area, they featured one actor describing Northwestern's low-pressure agents, high dividends, imposing size, and century-old traditions. The one-on-one approach was intended to parallel the individual relationship of agent and client.

Haggman felt that the campaign needed a simple, memorable slogan that would unify and summarize the ten commercials. The Thompson agency had proposed "The Best-kept Secret," "The Great Unknown," and several others, but Haggman was less than satisified. On the train back from Chicago one evening, he and his assistant, Daryl Carter, began to make lists of alternatives. Haggman came up with "The Quiet Company," but he did not feel that lightning had struck. He kept the slogan as a tentative choice until his staff or the agency could find something better. The phrase wore well. Later research showed that it called up an image of stability, responsiveness, diligence, lack of pretense, thrift, and a host of other qualities. "The Quiet Company" was also, in 1972, a perfectly understated way to "introduce" a firm that had been in existence since 1857.

Few American businesses have had more successful debuts on national television. The Olympic games have always blended patriotism, wholesomeness, and drama. They were the most exciting event on the air during the late-summer rerun season, and viewer interest rose with the terrorist attack on the Israeli delegation — a stroke of "luck" that Northwestern would gladly have done without. The company's commercials were seen in 90 percent of the nation's television homes, well above projections. Their low-key approach was in marked contrast to the brass bands and fireworks of other advertisers. Subsequent surveys showed that viewers remembered them twice as readily as other insurance commercials. Northwestern soared from thirty-fourth place in public awareness to third. Clients began to write checks to "The Quiet Company." In 1971 only 15 percent of the company's agents felt that advertising was helping to sell insurance. After the Olympics 72 percent answered affirmatively. J. Walter Thompson concluded that Northwestern had gained more exposure for less money than any client in the agency's history.

The Olympics advertising coup was, for Haggman and his staff, the central event of the period, but there were other activities. With the Karsh reprints gone, agents felt a continuing need for print materials that would keep clients and prospects aware of their existence. In 1972 Northwestern began to publish *Creative Living*, a quarterly magazine featuring "lifestyle" articles. The editorial staff, based in New York, organized each issue around a theme, ranging from physical fitness to personal computers. Each participating agent provided a mailing list, and the cost of the publication was split between the field force and the home office. After a slow start, *Creative Living* became an extremely popular means of keeping in touch with customers.

Perhaps the most enduring result of the Haggman-Greyser study was the formation of a new department. Northwestern's communications activities — advertising, home office and field publications, public relations, consumer relations, and graphics services —were scattered throughout the home office. Advertising, for instance, was one of several units in the Agency Department's marketing division, and public relations was an arm of the Chairman's Department. Haggman and Greyser suggested greater coordination, and in 1973 Northwestern established the Communications Department. It became one of Robert Templin's responsibilities, and he hired a newcomer, Robert Carboni, to direct the operation. An energetic Easterner, Carboni came to Northwestern with twenty years of communications experience in the food and automotive fields.

The decision to make Communications a free-standing department was well-timed. Rapid growth, the rise of consumerism, and the impact of computer technology had combined to weaken the human links among the company's component parts. The new department's central role was to solve that problem, and it was among the first and most comprehensive efforts of its kind in the industry. Under Carboni's direction, Northwestern spoke with one voice to all of its various audiences: agents, employees, policyowners, prospects, and the general public. Agent publications were continually improved. Efforts to bring Northwestern to the attention of national periodicals were expanded. The Communications staff did much of the legwork for the annual Roots and Wings run, a contest between home office and field that began in 1978 with a challenge from a Louisiana agent. At Carboni's suggestion, the Association of Agents invited all home office employees to attend its annual show, which featured entertainers like Bob Hope and Glen Campbell. *Coverage* and *Management Bulletin*, employee publications introduced in 1972, were joined by Mutual Exchange (a confidential information network) in 1974 and Newsbreak (a home office television news show) in 1975. Northwestern enjoyed both a higher national profile and the continuing trust of its employees. A 1980 survey showed that 85 percent of the home office workers felt that the company kept them well-informed, and 97 percent had complete faith in the information they received.

Although Carboni and his staff were involved in a wide variety of activities, national advertising remained a central concern. The 1972 Olympics effort was, in the words of a later campaign, "a tough act to follow." Northwestern had neither the desire nor the budget to become as well-known as a General Motors or a Coca-Cola, but it maintained a modest presence on national television, sponsoring *60 Minutes* and occasional athletic events. The next major effort was the 1976 Summer Olympics in Montreal. Northwestern was absent from the airwaves for a year before the games, saving its money to meet the $2.5 million cost of sponsorship. The budget had nearly doubled since 1972, but the campaign was similar in other respects. Promotion was equally vigorous. The agents agreed to postpone their annual meeting to avoid conflict with the Olympics, and Northwestern made it known that two of its agents, Don Schollander and Billy Mills, had won gold medals in 1972. The 1976 commercials used the same low-key approach as the first Olympics campaign, although they appealed to a somewhat broader audience. (One featured a woman bank officer.) The results were, again, impressive. Northwestern's level of public awareness had fallen to 47 percent during a year without commercials. After the games it rose to 77 percent, and The Quiet Company was the sixth best-known of all American life insurance firms.

Television advertising was an established fact of life at Northwestern by 1976. Its budget was a fixed percentage of premium income, and media buys ranged from news specials to major-league baseball. Although the dramatic success of the first campaign would never be repeated, it was clear that Northwestern had entered the major leagues of insurance advertising. The giant spoke quietly, but its silence was forever broken.

The Rational Workplace

A corollary of growth was efficiency. The company's new public image was paralleled by a new internal structure, one based, above all, on functionalism. Northwestern made a concerted effort to eliminate the quirks and the anachronisms, the wasted steps and the overlaps, constantly adapting its structure to changing conditions. The transformation was not as vivid as the revolution going on in advertising, but it affected everyone in the company, from the night security guards to the Board of Trustees.

The structure of Northwestern in the pre-1967 years was based on common sense, habit, and personality. Each department had a well-defined territory, its borders outlined by subject area and clerical skill. The Treasurer's Department, largest in the company, kept Northwestern's books, whether the matter at hand was premium payments or general agency audits. The Secretarial Department, second largest, handled all transactions related to ownership and benefits, from beneficiary changes to death payments. The Actuarial Department also worked on policies, making all of the calculations affecting values. Personalities complicated the picture. One reason for the employee plans unit's presence in the Secretarial Department was the fact that Verne Arends was there.

Northwestern, in short, was organized vertically. The departments were as separate and parallel as a row of elevator shafts. The people at the top had access to every elevator and every floor, but other employees had to take the stairs. Horizontal integration was made possible only by a cumbrous tangle of committees and an intricate maze of mail routes.

The computer represented a fundamental change in the company's operating systems. When Northwestern committed itself to the daily cycle in 1955, information from a multitude of departments was centralized for the first time. Although the system was operational in 1962, it took several years for the company to respond to its new opportunities. The people preparing the input and using the output found some obvious shortcuts, but they still followed the old lines of authority. Policy loans, because they affected cash values, remained the province of Actuarial. Premium loans, because they involved premium payment, were Treasurer's concern. Death payments were in Secretarial, but surrender payments were in Actuarial. Various aspects of agency financing were handled by Treasurer's, Actuarial, and Agency. A piece of mail entering the home office was like the steel ball spinning into a pinball machine. It bounced from work station to work station, stopping here for an endorsement, there for an address change, another place for a value calculation. The resulting delays frustrated both agents and policyowners.

Donald Slichter recognized the problem as early as 1963, when he asked his executives for "a review of the organization of the company's work routines" relative to the new computer system. Little was done until 1965, when Laflin Jones became insurance vice-president. Jones took an interest in revising a structure that was growing less efficient daily, and he asked Frank Rice to suggest alternatives. Rice was an Iowa-born and Iowa-educated actuary who had joined Northwestern in 1951. He developed an interest in computers and became a data processing manager, later gravitating to systems work. A soft-spoken but tenacious man, Rice was an appropriate choice for a job that involved both organization and detail. With considerable help from all concerned, he began to unscramble the egg in 1966.

The process lasted more than two years. Rice learned the title, function, and often the personality of every member of Northwestern's management. He analyzed the responsibilities of each department and charted the workflows among them. With the company dismantled conceptually, Rice began to put it back together, seeking a structure that would maximize efficiency and minimize cost. The permutations and combinations were limitless, and Rice prepared literally hundreds of alternative charts. The work was no less painstaking than if he had been asked to engrave the company's bylaws on the head of a pin.

The final result, announced in 1968, was perhaps the broadest reorganization in Northwestern's history. The positions of secretary and treasurer were abandoned except for legal purposes. The Policyowner Services Department was organized to handle all work coming in *from* customers, whether they were paying premiums or changing an address. The new Policy Benefits Department was in charge of everything going out *to* customers, from policy loans to benefit payments. The Field Financial Services Department, headed by Richard Wright, was established to centralize financial transactions involving agents. The Administrative Services Department, under Charles Groeschell, was expanded to include all support functions within the home office, from the switchboard to the shipping dock.

Although the two Policy departments were new, their leaders were company veterans. Robert Walker, head of Policyowner Services, was yet another actuary who had shown a flair for administration. Born in Canada, he had joined Northwestern in 1946. William Minehan, in charge of Policy Benefits, was a Milwaukee native who had come to the home office in 1927, working summers while attending Dartmouth. Following graduation in 1931, he joined the Secretarial Department as a full-time employee. With the exception of military service and a brief stint as Edmund Fitzgerald's assistant, Minehan stayed in Secretarial for thirty-seven years, including sixteen as its executive officer. Although reorganization had a significant impact on his department, he welcomed the change. When Laflin Jones asked the executives for suggestions in 1965, Minehan wrote that "too many officers find themselves too directly involved in too many different activities too much of the time."

The reorganization was designed to solve that problem, among others. It shifted the company's axis from the vertical to the horizontal. It realigned the departments toward the groups of people who used their services, a genuine departure from the subject-area and clerical-skill basis of the old system. The transition was not painless. Some officers were reluctant to yield territory, and space allocation was a headache. Twenty-six work units moved during the reorganization, their members shuttling about the home office in an elaborate game of musical chairs.

There were no layoffs, and work routines changed relatively little, but Northwestern gained a great deal in efficiency. The ratio of policyowner letters answered within five days rose from 11 percent in 1969 to 80 percent in 1970. The number of days required to open an Insurance Service Account fell from six to one. And the twenty-seven committees meeting in 1968 were gradually pared to thirteen.

The 1968 realignment was only the most visible of several moves designed to bring more efficiency and precision to the company's operations. In 1969 Northwestern retained Edward N. Hay Associates, a Philadelphia-based consulting firm, to develop a salary evaluation system for management-level employees. The Hay system assigned points to each position, based on the knowledge, problem-solving skills, and degree of accountability it required. The points were then translated to salary ranges, formalizing a process in which there had been ample room for subjectivity.

The 1969 operating plans imposed similar rigor on the company's performance standards. Each department was expected to meet quantified objectives by the end of a year, whether its function was to approve insurance applications or to make mortgage loans. Progress was reviewed periodically during the year, spotlighting achievement (or lack of it) in a way that had never been so obvious before. In 1970 a cost-cutting program was grafted onto the operating plans. Executives were urged to watch for waste in their departments, and requests for budget increases were examined carefully. The process rankled many officers, who gave the cost-cutting team (Frank Rice, James McKeon, and Del Peterson) a distinctive nickname —"the troika."

Executives in some of the older departments developed their own approaches to more efficient management. In the Law Department, for instance, Richard Mooney, who became general counsel in 1965, took a fresh look at operating procedures that had changed little since the Depression. The results were an improved salary scale, a new emphasis on recent law graduates in recruiting efforts and, reflecting Mooney's own values, a shift to more democratic management. A Milwaukee native who had joined the company in 1945, Mooney was a first-rate investment lawyer, but he also developed a reputation as an unusually sensitive administrator.

Reorganization was practically constant after the first large step in 1968. Some of the changes were minor, like the employee infirmary moving from Personnel to Medical and back to Personnel. Others represented major shifts in direction, most notably in the area of underwriting. Northwestern had always taken pride in its careful risk selection, and the company's mortality statistics were enviable. After World War II, however, public health advancements and escalating competition caused Northwestern to review its policies. Without degrading its standards, the company took an increasingly liberal view of what constituted an acceptable risk.

The introduction of classified insurance in 1956 was a major step, but underwriting practices also reflected the change. In 1946 two licensed doctors had had to examine every application. By 1970 underwriting manuals were so complete that computers could begin approval of the most routine cases. There was a steady shift to lay underwriters for the more difficult applications. Doctors continued to set the standards and rule on the most complex cases, but their role became increasingly advisory.

Despite the changes, risk appraisal at Northwestern remained a two-headed operation. The Medical Department was administered by Dr. Jack End, a genial Milwaukee native who had joined the company in 1946. The Underwriting Department's executive was

Orlo Karsten, another in the line of Iowa actuaries who contributed so much to the company's leadership. Karsten had come to Northwestern in 1949 and left in 1956. After nearly seven years with two Dallas insurance firms, including a stint as vice-president of one, he returned to Northwestern in 1963 as Underwriting's assistant director.

The departments headed by Karsten and End were both involved in risk selection, but coordination was difficult at best. In 1977, finally, the medical staff was absorbed by the Underwriting Department. "Lay underwriters" became "underwriters," and the doctors acted as roving consultants and educators. At the same time, the Policy Issue Department was established to assemble and mail new policies and to create the necessary computer records.

An administrative change paralleled the change in organization. Karsten was named the head of Policyowner Services, and "Dr. Jack" was made responsible for health awareness programs and consultation on cases. The new director of Policy Issue was James Compere, yet another actuary. Since joining Northwestern in 1958, Compere had become the resident expert on the applications of computer technology to the company's insurance operations. The new Underwriting executive was Robert Ninneman, a lawyer who had arrived in the same year as Compere. Ninneman had joined the officer ranks as an assistant to Robert Dineen, and his pre-Underwriting experience included terms as the head of both Policy Benefits and Policyowner Services.

The four principals in the risk appraisal shake-up were not the only executives who saw their responsibilities adjusted during the 1967-1979 period. Ferguson tinkered with the organizational chart constantly, looking for the mixture of assignments that would challenge the younger men, reward the veterans, and establish the ideal flow of responsibility. Executives with a proven talent for administration often found themselves taking over departments somewhat remote from their own areas of expertise, but the results were generally positive.

Northwestern's executive staff grew as rapidly as it changed. The number of vice-presidents increased from six in 1967 to twenty in 1979. At the same time, the growing complexity of the business persuaded Ferguson to create more positions on the level between himself and the department heads. The number of people reporting directly to the president fell from eleven in 1968 to six in 1979. There had been executives with multiple responsibilities since 1950, when

Robert Dineen was hired to manage the insurance departments (Actuarial, Underwriting, Medical, and Secretarial). By 1974 nearly all of the departments were organized in clusters under four senior vice-presidents: Robert Templin (agency and communications), Robert Barrows (investments), Russell Jensen (insurance), and Donald Mundt (administration).

Mundt was a central figure in the executive shifts of the period. Born and educated in Nebraska, he joined the Law Department in 1952. He developed an interest in the human side of the operation and, working with Richard Mooney, began to play a large role in departmental recruiting. Peter Bruce and Fred Sweet, two of his recruits, have since become executive officers. Mundt stopped practicing law in 1970, when Ferguson made him William Minehan's successor as head of Policy Benefits. He prospered in the new assignment and became administrative vice-president two years later, with responsibility for the Data Processing, Administrative Services, and Personnel Departments. In 1977 he was promoted to executive vice-president and placed in charge of eleven of the company's eighteen departments. Easygoing, sensitive, and yet firmly grounded in Northwestern's objectives, Mundt has earned a reputation as one of the most astute managers of people in the company's post-war history.

The Board of Trustees, to which Mundt was elected in 1977, did not escape the wave of organizational change sweeping over Northwestern. Its size had been fixed at thirty-six members since incorporation in 1857, and by the 1970s Northwestern's board was among the largest in the industry. It was also, in effect, a two-tiered board. Since 1859 the Executive Committee, meeting monthly, had had the authority to approve everything from policy changes to general agent appointments. The Finance Committee, meeting twice *weekly,* ruled on every investment the company made, even the $10,000 home mortgages. It was only after the first "credit crunch" of 1966 that, for lack of business to conduct, the meetings were reduced to one a week. Both committees had real power, and other trustees arrived at the quarterly board sessions to find that major decisions had already been made. Both were also, because of the frequent meetings, dominated by Milwaukeeans, which seemed less and less appropriate as the issues faced by the board became increasingly national in scope.

Little change occurred until 1972, when revision of the Wisconsin Insurance Code was completed. The revised code required Northwestern to hold an annual meeting of policyowners, at which a majority of those present or voting by proxy would elect trustees. The form of the elections changed more than their substance, but two other provisions had a real impact on the board. The code removed both the thirty-six-member minimum requirement and the stipulation that a majority of members be Wisconsin residents. The board's size was gradually reduced to thirty, and a new effort was made to recruit out-of-state trustees.

A more fundamental shift took place in 1977, largely as a result of the changing make-up of the board. The Policyowners Examining Committee remained the most typical route to board membership; by 1977 nineteen of the thirty trustees had first come to the home office as invited examiners. Many of the newcomers were, like Ferguson himself, younger and more aggressive entrepreneurs. They were sensitive to the imbalance of authority among the trustees, especially so in light of court decisions defining the extensive legal liability of corporate board members. In 1977 Northwestern's board voted to sharply curtail the powers of the Executive and Finance Committees, to increase the number of its meetings from four to six a year, and to establish two new standing committees — Human Relations and Public Policy, and Insurance Products and Marketing. Some veteran trustees questioned the abrupt departure from tradition, but the 1977 decisions opened the door to deeper involvement and broader participation.

At every level — board, executive, management, clerical — Northwestern was gripped by a desire to "manage by objective" between 1967 and 1979. The phrase, coined by business expert Peter Drucker in 1954, described an attempt to bring the precision and the discipline of science to the marketplace. The approach stressed behavior over personality, results over effort. Northwestern went about its quantifying and codifying, functionalizing and organizing, all in an effort to set goals and to meet them, to know both the how and the why. Some traditionalists wondered if the company had lost something of its human dimension, like the botanist who forgets to smell the flowers. In the view from the top, however, the rational workplace was an absolute necessity in a world of persistent change.

From DALIS to LINK

The computer, of course, became the central tool of management science, the basic system of the systems approach. The data processing operation at Northwestern was a decade old by 1967, and it evolved even faster than the rest of the company in the years following. Technological developments sparked a quantum jump forward in the computer's powers and applications. The system's role in the company was enlarged, forcing change in some areas, facilitating change in others. "Eddie EDP" was, in effect, promoted from clerk-typist in the billing operation to administrative assistant in several areas, including the agency system.

The period began with a problem. In 1966 Northwestern purchased an IBM 360, a third-generation machine based on integrated circuits rather than transistors. All of the company's programs were written in Autocoder, a computer language that had seemed sophisticated in the late 1950s. IBM's engineers, in a move that rankled data processing managers across the country, gave the 360 a new native language — PL/1. Like a Norwegian speaking to a Swede, the 360 could follow the old programs, but only after some time-consuming internal translation. Committed to efficient use of its resources, Northwestern had no choice but to convert.

The timing was, to say the least, unfortunate. The Data Processing Department already had a substantial backlog of requests for service, and now a large portion of its staff was literally taken out of production. It may have seemed simple to outsiders, but the process of rewriting and modernizing all of the computer programs eventually required 200,000 hours of staff time.

The PL/1 logjam was one of several factors leading to an administrative change in the Data Processing Department. In 1970 Wil Kraegel returned to the Actuarial Department and Charles Groeschell took over the computer operation. Groeschell had been a central figure in data processing at Northwestern since his appointment to the original Electronics Committee in 1954. He was promoted from director of Data Processing to vice-president in 1972, but another level was added in the same year. Donald Mundt became a group vice-president with responsibilities that included Groeschell's department, and he brought his management expertise to a field where only the technically proficient had dared to tread.

The language barrier was broken in June of 1972. Groeschell, honoring a pledge he had made at the PL/1 project's beginning, had his mustache shaved off while the Data Processing staff looked on. The department now turned its attention to another conversion project, one that was substantially more productive.

The 360 was "upward-compatible." It could use magnetic tape, like the old 7080, but it could also operate with a new piece of hardware — the magnetic disk. The difference between disk and tape was significantly larger than the difference between a stick shift and an automatic transmission. It represented a fundamentally new way of driving the machine. In the old system, information was entered on punch cards. The cards were collected during the day, assembled in batches, and placed on the computer during the night shift. The machine passed through every inch of its policy record tapes, making the changes called for by the cards and, at the same time, generating premium notices and other scheduled materials automatically.

The tape-driven daily cycle had limitations. It offered overnight service, but it removed each department's access to its own files. Most of the significant data were on tape, and the only people who could retrieve information were the computer operators. The system was also relatively slow. To find one piece of information, the computer might have had to spin through an entire tape before arriving at the correct "address," just as you must spin through a tape cassette to find a particular song. And the system was redundant. The ISA tape file was organized by policyowner. The master insurance file included data on every Northwestern policy, including those owned by ISA customers.

Disks were faster than tapes. The computer could locate any address on any disk as easily as you can move a phonograph needle from one song to another on a record. Disks eliminated redundancy. They allowed data to be collected in a common pool, where it could be "massaged" — reorganized and recombined — in any pattern desired. Most importantly, the new system returned data access to the users. The computer was connected to visual display terminals, each with a keyboard and a screen. Anyone moderately skilled could press the appropriate keys to call up a specific piece of information, and not only see it but change it. The system became diffuse instead of centralized. Punch cards, printouts, and technicians gave way to the "on-line real-time" approach. Northwestern's operating employees could, to use a homely metaphor, do their own laundry instead of sending it to the cleaners in the computer center.

The tape-to-disk conversion project was named DALIS — Direct Access Life Insurance System. Although the Executive Committee approved DALIS in 1967, competing pressures delayed a full-scale effort. The project's staff started with something relatively small — new applications coming into the Underwriting Department. By 1970 a new business disk file had been created, and the underwriters were trained to use the company's first terminals.

The next step was daunting — conversion of the policy title data (names of owner, insured, and beneficiary) for two million policies. The material had been considered too bulky for the original conversion in 1962, but now it was assigned to a staff of forty-eight people. They typed information from the register cards onto computer forms and fed them through an optical scanner, which entered the data in the computer's memory. By 1972 the contents of 4000 file drawers had been transferred to approximately 50 platter-sized disks.

When the PL/1 project was completed in 1972, the DALIS effort gathered momentum. The original master file, with the financial history of each policy, was converted from tape to disk — a relatively easy step. Then file by file — policy loans, settlement options, investments — Northwestern's manual records were transformed from paper to billions of magnetic impressions on metal disks. As each step was completed, terminals were installed in the appropriate departments. The number of terminals in the home office rose from 19 in 1970 to 66 in 1974 and 230 in 1979. DALIS ceased to be a separate project and became an ongoing process.

The conversion effort is sometimes referred to as "going to data base." The various disk files were separate, but they were also integrated in a way that no tape system could duplicate. The library was in the machine. Anyone with proper authorization could locate any record on any disk at any time and, with some effort, combine and cross-reference the files in any number of formations. In 1975, for instance, Northwestern had three data bases — policy, agent, and new business. Two subsets of the policy base — the name file and the insurance file — were combined to yield, for the first time, a comprehensive master file of all policies arranged by owner. The number of data bases eventually topped a dozen, and the computer center's staff manipulated them in ways that would have seemed fantastic in 1967. The breadth and sophistication of the entire system would prove invaluable in the Update campaigns of the 1980s.

The leader of the conversion effort was Edward Flitz. A Milwaukee native and a graduate of the local state university, Flitz joined Northwestern in 1960 as a trainee. He became a programmer in the following year, but displayed a growing aptitude for administration. Flitz was named an officer in 1969 and assigned to key roles in both the PL/1 and DALIS projects. In 1972 he became Charles Groeschell's associate director and heir apparent. When Groeschell retired in 1978, Flitz took over the department. He saw the computer as a means to an end, and took pains to avoid the godlike posture that afflicted data processing managers in other firms. Unassuming, careful to keep the formidable jargon of EDP out of conversations with laypersons, Flitz offered a rare combination of technical proficiency and managerial skill.

Perhaps the most remarkable feature of the system being developed by Flitz and his staff was its mobility. Terminals extended the computer's reach from one closely guarded center to any location in the home office and, via telephone lines, to any location in the country. The most crucial locations outside the home office were, of course, the general agencies. In 1972, a few weeks after the PL/1 project was finished, Northwestern and IBM initiated a joint study on the use of computers in an agency setting. Completed in 1974, the study recommended a terminal system linking home office and field. A new project was born, named, appropriately, LINK — Life Information Network.

In a 1975 report to the agents, Ed Flitz declared that LINK would be "the greatest single breakthrough in company history in service to the field and your clients." Four pilot agencies were equipped with terminals and printers in mid-1976. The system was cleared for full application after several months of debugging, and the last general agency — Providence, Rhode Island — was connected in spring of 1977. To reduce strain on the home office computers, each local unit was powered by a mini-computer, linked to Milwaukee by leased telephone lines.

The system's abilities were impressive. LINK became a sales assistant, a secretary, a file clerk, and a bookkeeper. Agents could enter detailed financial data for their prospects and receive, overnight, customized proposals and ledger statements. When a sale was made, they could submit the basic underwriting information through the computer instead of the mail, and they could check on the status of pending applications without calling the home office. For their existing clients, agents could activate Insurance Service Accounts and provide up-to-date information on individual policies. LINK also helped with the housekeeping. It enabled agents to send and receive messages (LINKgrams), order supplies, and keep track of their sales activity. It even compensated for human error. The computer was programmed to reject incomplete applications, preventing a great deal of wasted time.

LINK was the most sophisticated agency computer system in the industry, and it quickly became an integral part of Northwestern's operations. Agent requests for ledgers (year-by-year accounts of a policy's monetary growth) nearly doubled after the system was installed. Orders for data reviews of individual policies topped 1000 per week. LINK reduced staff needs in both the home office and the general agencies, and it stemmed the rising tide of mail and phone calls between the two. The system also shortened the policy issue process by two to three days. Like all computer breakthroughs, LINK moved in two directions at once, extending the human reach while reducing the need for human effort.

The Data Processing Department must have seemed like a six-ring circus at times. Various phases of the LINK, DALIS, and PL/1 projects ran simultaneously, and there were constantly new jobs to do. Computer assistance was required in the design of new products, notably Extra Ordinary Life. Northwestern's planners began to use computer simulations in 1972, creating a variety of economic environments and analyzing possible responses to them. New sales tools were created, including conversion proposals sent automatically to term insurance owners and electronic estate surveys that were often twenty pages long. All of the special projects and long-term conversion efforts were ancillary to the daily tasks of keeping records, sending bills, and updating files during a period of rapid expansion.

The department periodically added employees and equipment to keep pace with the growing workload. Its staff precisely doubled between 1967 and 1979, increasing from 132 full-time workers to 264. A second IBM 360 was ordered soon after the first one arrived, and in 1969 the two were "married" in a simple ceremony, Francis Ferguson presiding. The union was equivalent to producing a V-8 from two four-cylinder engines. In 1971 Northwestern installed the first of its 370 series computers. The 370-155 was a lineal descendant of the 360, but it was four times more efficient. The price of new hardware fell even faster than the price of life insurance during the period. The original 705 had cost $1.6 million in 1957. It could store 280,000 bits (binary digits) of data and carry out 10,000 instructions per second. The LINK minicomputers installed in 1976-1977 had a capacity of 672,000 bits and a speed of 500,000 instructions per second. The cost of each local unit — including the minicomputer, two terminals, a printer, and even the cabinets — was less than $32,000.

Computers did more for less money, and they did it with fewer people. The growth of the Data Processing Department was counterbalanced by a relative decrease in the size of other departments. The total number of full-time home office employees grew from 1656 in 1967 to 1945 in 1979 — an increase of only 17 percent. Northwestern's insurance in force more than tripled during the same period.

There was a parallel shift in the make-up of the work force. The computer practically eliminated the lower-level clerical positions, and it promoted an increasingly dense concentration of skill in the home office. In 1958 — the effective beginning of the computer era — management staff (supervisors, specialists, and officers) made up 14 percent of the work force. Their ratio increased to 18 percent in 1967, and it reached 28 percent in 1979. There was similar growth on the upper clerical levels, creating a bulge in the middle of the company's hierarchy. The computer changed Northwestern's internal structure from a pyramid to a diamond.

In 1967 data processing was, to oversimplify, a centralized billing and filing system, with a limited range of other applications. By 1979 the computer was playing a central role in virtually every phase of the company's operations, from designing products to selling them, from approving applications to collecting premiums, from investing funds to paying death claims. The human networks at Northwestern remained strong but, on a functional level, the veins and arteries of the old system were reinforced (and in some cases replaced) by the cables and phone lines of the new. The company's dependence on technology reached a level that was probably never envisioned by the Electronics Committee of 1954. The commitment, however, remained the same: to use the best of modern tools, and to use them thoroughly, in support of an old tradition.

Northwestern Mutual Place

Since moving to Milwaukee in 1859, Northwestern had built new home offices in 1870, 1886, 1914, and 1932 — an average of one every eighteen years. The company, according to that timetable, was due for a new building in 1950, but slow growth during the Depression and war years made expansion unnecessary. (The face value of insurance in force increased only 15 percent between 1930 and 1945.)

It was only in the late 1950s that the home office began to feel cramped, and by that time the computer had arrived to alleviate the problem. Electronic data processing compressed and centralized the company's workflow, enabling Northwestern to grow dramatically without growing out of its headquarters.

For all its powers, the computer could only postpone expansion, not prevent it. Even moderate staff growth taxed the capacity of the home office and, beginning in the late 1950s, Northwestern mounted a nearly continuous effort to save space. The employee game rooms disappeared. The 1968 reorganization condensed work groups physically·as well as functionally, and Northwestern phased in precise space standards for each staff level. In 1970 the company leased part of a nearby warehouse to store everything from old records to surplus furniture. Despite these moves, shrinking space became a growing problem.

Northwestern's home office consisted of two buildings: the classic 1914 edifice and its functional 1932 addition. They were connected, but the structures were officially referred to as the south and north office buildings (resulting in two inelegant acronyms — SOB and NOB). Physical alterations in both units were the responsibility of the Building Advisory Committee (BAC), established in 1958. For years its concerns were limited to items like downspouts and floor tiles, but the committee's focus and composition shifted radically in the early 1970s. Hugh Macklin, serving a brief term as head of Administrative Services, was appointed in 1970. There were two more additions in 1971: James McKeon, manager of the planning effort, and Donald Schuenke, an investment lawyer who had come to Northwestern eight years earlier. In 1972 Donald Mundt joined the group and later became its chairman. The reconstituted committee began to discuss Northwestern's long-range space needs as well as the daily details. The shift in emphasis marked the beginning of an odyssey that would end only a decade later. Along the way, the BAC became perhaps the most overworked committee in company history.

The committee began its journey slowly, almost casually. During the last meeting of 1971, Macklin asked two simple questions: "Will we need to build? If so, when should we start planning?" The answers were slow in coming. A parking structure was proposed in 1972, and some thought was given to a new home for the computer center. But firm plans were dependent on hard facts. Early in 1973 the group asked Frank Rice to conduct a space study of the home office.

Rice concluded that the camel's back was nearly broken. Few

departments were intact by 1973. Data Processing, for instance, had spilled over from its original home on the second floor north to locations on five floors (including the basement) in both buildings. There was little room for new activities, and Northwestern was in danger of losing the efficiency it had so carefully fostered. The company could, in Rice's words, "survive to '75," but major adjustments would be necessary beyond that point. Short of putting desks in the washrooms or pitching tents on the roof, Northwestern's options were nearly exhausted.

The subsequent discussions were influenced by another factor. For years Northwestern had been quietly buying property in its neighborhood, an aging district of residential hotels and small apartment buildings, corner stores and small restaurants. The company demolished dozens of buildings and replaced them with parking lots. By 1973 Northwestern owned nearly all of the land between its home office and the lake bluff to the east. Expansion was now a demonstrated need, but the committee looked beyond the immediate problem. Its members pursued options that would accomplish three objectives: to provide space, to generate investment income, and to make full use of a spectacular building site.

One of the early prospects was a skyscraper. The BAC considered twin towers, one filled with offices, the other with apartments; a sixty-one-story high-rise with twenty floors of penthouse apartments; and an office building of fifty-five or forty-three stories. The First Wisconsin Center, Milwaukee's first and only skyscraper, was under construction across the street. The forty-three-story proposal was made in full knowledge that First Wisconsin's building was forty-two stories high.

Northwestern envisioned sharing its new building with other major tenants, but a consulting firm reported in 1973 that demand for office space in Milwaukee was slack. BAC members began to think of the skyscraper as a new home office, a shift in direction that put the future of 720 East Wisconsin in jeopardy. Demolition was never proposed, but selling the structure was. Representatives of the local electric and telephone companies toured the home office, but high maintenance costs and lack of expansion room dampened their interest. The BAC had decided, in the meantime, that Northwestern would be the sole long-term occupant of any new building. With no buyers for the existing home office and no need for a skyscraper, the committee began to scale down its plans.

There had been little enthusiasm for the idea of abandoning the home office. The proposal would probably have died if only because Ferguson opposed it. (He felt that the company's agents would never forgive the move.) The Building Advisory Committee was simply looking at every conceivable option, slowly, methodically, in detail. A high-rise home office was not the most radical proposal made during more than three years of discussions. A move to Arizona was suggested, presumably during a winter meeting. Other ideas included building offices across the country to decentralize the company, buying an insurance building in Appleton (Wisconsin) to house specialized functions like data processing, and renting new quarters in Milwaukee for the Investment and Law Departments.

Another option involved adding floors to the north building. The 1932 addition was eight stories high, but it was designed to bear another sixteen. The original architects had either expected rapid expansion or felt that their plans were timeless. Forty years later, it was obvious that they were not. One drawing of the proposed addition showed a glass-and-steel tower perched directly atop the dull granite of the north building, much like tail fins mounted on a Model T.

Aesthetic considerations aside, the proposal received serious attention. Speaking at the 1974 meeting of policyowners, Donald Mundt stated that an addition to the addition was the most promising of several options his committee was studying. This first open statement laid some rumors to rest, but it was also a real estate stratagem. Northwestern hoped that an announcement of plans to build in place would discourage adjoining property-owners from raising their prices. The company, in fact, was drifting steadily toward a decision to erect a new building.

The drifting finally stopped in the last months of 1975. The company had decided by that time to retain the south building, to keep all of its operations intact, and to drop proposals that would involve other companies as major tenants. The BAC came very close to settling on a modest addition as the answer to Northwestern's space problems. It was discussed as a six- or seven-story building to the east or north of the home office, linked to the 1932 structure by a simple upper-level bridge.

The board approved the plan in principle at its October meeting, and Northwestern assembled a project team in January, 1976. The overseer was Cushman and Wakefield, a New York-based real estate firm involved in everything from site planning to building management. The architects were Sasaki Associates of Boston and Poor, Swanke, Hayden and Connell of New York, participating in an unusual joint venture. The first firm was known for its skill in harmonizing a building with its landscape, the second for its expertise in designing financial office buildings. The general contractor was Allen and O'Hara of Memphis, a firm acquired by Northwestern after years of joint work in college housing developments.

There was one more consultant to be heard from — Building Programs International, a space planning company based in New York. Douglas Nicholson, the firm's president, made a forceful presentation to the Building Advisory Committee in February of 1976, saying, in essence, that Northwestern was on the wrong track. His staff had concluded that the existing home office was extremely inefficient. The north building, in particular, with its high ceilings and its maze of interior columns, defied efforts to organize workflow and traffic patterns rationally. Nicholson argued that a small annex would only compound Northwestern's problems, spreading inefficiency over three buildings instead of two.

His alternative was simple and sweeping: renovate the south building, tear down the 1932 addition, and erect a large general office building to the east. The original home office, its 1914 elegance renewed, would become a front door, a flagship, a symbol of Northwestern's heritage. It would house the top executives, public-contact departments like Communications and Personnel, and specialized groups like lawyers and actuaries. The new east building, set back to preserve the lake view, would be the operations center, housing the bulk of the clerical force. The two structures would be joined by a "connecting module" that might include common-use facilities like a cafeteria and a learning center. After streets were closed, the remaining open space would become a green plaza, setting Northwestern off from its surroundings. (The BAC had seriously considered a condominium project for part of the grounds.) Nicholson called the entire scheme "a campus arrangement," as attractive as it was functional.

After the BAC members "picked ourselves up off the floor," in Mundt's words, they had to agree that Nicholson made sense. By far his most controversial proposal was razing the north building instead of raising it. Demolishing a perfectly sound structure seemed inconsistent with Northwestern's traditional emphasis on thrift, and criticism poured in when the plans were announced. The top executives, however, became convinced that the new scheme represented thrift in the long run, that even a modest gain in efficiency over the years would more than justify the decision.

The details were worked out later. The new building took shape on the drawing boards as a sixteen-story glass-and-granite box. The first thirteen floors were reserved for Northwestern; the top three became growth space providing lease income until the century's end. The "connecting module" became an atrium, a gigantic window box with hanging lights, fig trees, flowers, and an oval pool. Engineers drew plans for a computerized system to heat and cool the entire complex. In its essentials, however, the scheme devised by Building Programs International became the blueprint for all the blueprints that followed. It was endorsed by Northwestern in July, 1976.

The Building Advisory Committee breathed a collective sigh of relief. Its members had spent more than three years reviewing a parade of consultants, studying a small library of reports, and debating the merits of dozens of plans. Now, apparently, the most difficult decision was made and, after so much dreaming, the project was nearing reality.

The development team established a timetable for construction. A parking structure was the only element of the project that had never been in doubt, and the final plans called for a 732-car garage just north of the 1932 addition. It was first on the schedule, to be followed by erection of the east building, renovation of the south building, demolition of the north building, and construction of the atrium. The contractors estimated that the entire project would be completed by autumn of 1979.

The projected schedule (and the projected costs) were, in retrospect, optimistic. Deadlines and budgets were revised frequently as the result of both design changes (particularly in the south building) and a series of complications that no one could have foreseen. Northwestern Mutual Place, as the development was named, was not the World Trade Center, but it was an extremely complex project. It involved construction, renovation, and demolition of major buildings, with each activity dependent on the others. The project team included four major firms, dozens of consultants, and scores of subcontractors. Coordination was extremely difficult at times. Most importantly, Northwestern put the project on a "fast track" to take advantage of a lull in the building industry. Design was often only one step ahead of construction, and cost estimates were extremely tenuous.

The members of the Building Advisory Committee — all laypersons with other jobs to do — were expected to make decisions on everything from the selection of sculpture to the direction of the carpet nap. They found themselves acting as referees, expediters, accountants, and apologists. Delays and overruns were announced with embarrassing regularity. In 1976 the committee instructed the contractors to trim more than 10 percent from the original budget estimate — an exercise that would later seem ironic.

On a bitterly cold day in the week before Christmas, 1976, Ferguson and Mayor Henry Maier detonated small charges of dynamite to break ground for the project. The blasts marked the official beginning of Northwestern Mutual Place. They also inaugurated a six-year siege. The first troops in a small army of laborers, tradesmen, and artisans marched to the site, bringing with them a sizable fleet of pile drivers, cranes, front-end loaders, and bulldozers.

For the construction crews, the project meant steady work in a time of recession, with opportunities for substantial overtime. For the home office employees, it meant noise, dust, and inconvenience, but the project also generated excitement, at least in its early stages. Scores of people who had never used a welding torch or sat in a crane cab watched in fascination as the work progressed.

The first steps were the easiest. The parking structure was completed by the end of 1977, under its authorized cost and only a few months behind schedule. Ironworkers finished the framing for the east building at the same time. Further progress was delayed by an unusually cold winter and a series of summer strikes, but the first floors were ready for occupancy in December, 1978. The company organized a massive desk-cleaning project in preparation for the move. It yielded thirty-three tons of garbage, including a thirteen-year-old orange and an impressive collection of used staples. Moving crews, their loads considerably lightened, made hundreds of trips to and from the new building, and by summer of 1979 their work was nearly done.

The east building, or "home office addition," contained 500,000 square feet of floor space, nearly a third more than the north and south buildings combined. Each floor was a massive rectangle of open space, broken only by a central elevator core and rows of offices along the perimeter. The design, or lack of it, enabled Northwestern to arrange its space in modular fashion. Cloth-covered dividers were positioned to create a reception area here, a specialist's cubicle there, giving the company a flexibility it had never known. An entire department could move from one floor to another without having to call the carpenters and electricians.

As the east building employees adjusted to new quarters, renovation of the south building gathered speed. It became the most
expensive and the most time-consuming part of the entire project,
largely as the result of major additions to the preliminary plans.
Virtually every square inch of the building was altered in some way.
"Improvements" made over a sixty-year time period were ripped out.
Whole floors were gutted for new facilities like a cafeteria and a
learning center. A new heating-cooling system and new elevators
were installed. Floor plans were changed radically. There were
hundreds of smaller jobs, like refurbishing the board room woodwork and re-installing antique water fountains on every floor. Work
crews encountered problems with nearly every step, and the planners'
orderly sequence of events fell like a row of dominoes.

Northwestern's consultants had assured the company that business could go on as usual during the renovation. It was an assurance
the BAC lived to regret. As the project progressed, work units were
shuttled around the home office like figures on a chessboard, and
departments were often split up in the process. Phone conversations
were regularly interrupted by the sound of jackhammers and power
saws. The entire building was either too hot or too cold for a time
during the changeover to a new mechanical system. Employees in
some departments returned to work each morning to find a fresh
layer of dust on their desks, and Northwestern expanded its maintenance staff to keep up with the problem. A delay in one area had a
ripple effect, causing delays in every step to follow. In early 1978 the
Actuarial Department was moved to the company auditorium for
what the contractors promised would only be a few months. Nearly
two years later, the actuaries were still there.

Demolition of the north building, which began in fall of 1979,
compounded the problems. The dust level in the home office increased,
and the impact of the wrecking ball sent disturbing tremors through the
south building. The low-bid contractor proved unequal to the task of
bringing down a structure designed to support twenty-four stories. The
firm had estimated that the project would take five months. One year
later demolition was only partially complete. Razing the 1932 addition
was the most sensitive element of the entire plan, and Northwestern
officials found the delays particularly embarrassing. After nearly a year
of frustration, they hired a new contractor to finish the job.

The 1967-1979 period closed with development of Northwestern Mutual Place still underway. The project was more than two

years behind the original schedule, and cost overruns helped to force the cancellation of long-standing plans for a physical fitness center in the south building. But the east building was finished, and most departments in the south building had moved to their permanent quarters. The landscaping crews were making progress, and preliminary work on the atrium — the last step — was beginning. The light at the end of the tunnel was growing brighter.

Northwestern Mutual Place was the most ambitious building project in the company's history. It was also a convincing symbol of Northwestern's commitment to Milwaukee and to the city's downtown. After a prolonged lull, a burst of building activity had begun downtown in the 1960s, much of it stimulated by Edmund Fitzgerald's activities. As chairman of the Milwaukee Development Group, an offshoot of the influential Greater Milwaukee Committee, Fitzgerald was the chief arm-twister, fund-raiser, and cheerleader for revitalization activities. He headed the group from 1959 until 1971, when Francis Ferguson succeeded him.

Ferguson led the campaign in new directions. In 1973 the original group was replaced by the Milwaukee Redevelopment Corporation, a private organization that acted as a planner and financier as well as a catalyst. Ferguson became its president and, largely through his efforts, the MRC raised $3 million in private capital before it even opened an office. His civic leadership and his company's building program were both major factors in the ongoing renewal of the central business district. Northwestern Mutual Place took its place among the efforts to make downtown, as Fitzgerald said in 1963, "the energizer of the community."

The Transformation

It was apparent to even the most casual observer that Northwestern underwent a transformation between 1967 and 1979. At the period's beginning the company was, depending on your viewpoint, stodgy or simply stable, reactionary or cautious, stuffy or merely dignified. There were palpable stirrings, but Northwestern's image as a sleeping giant contained an element of truth.

By 1979 the company was moving in a different dimension. It was faster, larger, leaner, more daring. Its field force had nearly doubled. Its sales volume had increased fivefold. It offered one of the most innovative products on the market. Its planning capacity and computer systems were vastly superior to the industry norms. It had become a presence, however quiet, on national television. And its home office was an elaborate blend of old and new. Quality and mutuality remained the abiding goals, but Northwestern pursued them on a substantially different scale.

The transformation was accompanied by a dramatic change in tone at Northwestern, almost a change in character. The company moved from an unhurried formality to a brisk informality. It became less hidebound, less rigid, and less dogmatic as it became more rational, more systematic, more productive. Some of the change can be traced to the times, but much of it is directly attributable to Francis Ferguson. A man with little patience for ritual observances and nineteenth-century protocol, he cut through accumulated layers of tradition. Ferguson contributed, more than anything else, an entrepreneurial spirit — an aggressive, results-oriented style of management the company had never known. He ran the business like a business. He ran it, more specifically, as if it were his own business. Every dollar saved, earned, or wasted was as important to him as his personal bank balance.

This approach had its drawbacks — what some considered an overemphasis on the person of the president, and an overcentralization of power. But Ferguson made even the drawbacks an element in the company's progress. His sense of personal investment infused Northwestern with a drive and a dynamism that were entirely new. To the old insistence on high quality and trusteeship — fairly passive virtues — Ferguson added a sense of entrepreneurial purpose. He made an organism of many disparate parts function with one intelligence.

The transformation was not accomplished without a price. Northwestern showed symptoms of an ailment one veteran agent called "volumeitis." In field and home office alike, as the scale of the operation increased, as new faces gradually outnumbered the old, as precise performance standards replaced the "do your best" approach, there was the loss of a certain personalism. The computer, for all its powers, did little to enhance a sense of community. Speed sometimes became haste, and efficiency sometimes crossed over to regimentation. Poor communication became a serious problem. "In my day," said one retired executive, "productivity was something to shoot for, but it wasn't a passion. Some of those fellows now are so hard-nosed that I wonder if they're having fun any more." The company went to some lengths to humanize its operations, but volumeitis was an inevitable side-effect of growth.

Acronymitis, a related malady, reached epidemic proportions during the period. Northwestern's alphabet soup thickened to a stew. Agents could talk, without flinching, of the ROR on SPDAs and the impact of the CPI on PLs. Acronyms, in fact, provide a shorthand history of the period: CP and D (planning); QI and AGB (agents); EOL, DI, and YRT (products); POS, FFS, and PB (reorganization); PL/1, DALIS, and LINK (data processing); and the BAC's plans for the NOB and EOB (home office).

Despite the serious and not-so-serious ailments, few in either home office or field would have turned the calendar back to 1967. Northwestern was a livelier company, doing more things and doing them, on the whole, better than in previous years. Growth entailed human costs, but many found the spirit of enterprise congenial. "Planned growth will enhance a sense of accomplishment and purpose," Ferguson predicted in 1968, and few in 1979 would have disputed his statement. The company's gains in size, productivity, and public awareness did nothing to diminish the pride that had long been a Northwestern hallmark.

In calmer times, Ferguson's achievement would have seemed remarkable enough. He might have been (and might still be) enshrined as the leader who brought Northwestern from the shadows to the light. In calmer times, he might also have encountered more resistance. Inertia is a basic human condition, and it was an extraordinary challenge to move a company as old and as large as Northwestern in new directions. Ferguson, with substantial help, did it. In the years between 1967 and 1979, however, there were other challenges to face.

Investments
1947-1982

Edmund Fitzgerald poses in 1966 with the lake ship named for him, easily the best-publicized investment in Northwestern's history.

Top: *This offshore oil rig, one of many erected since 1972, represents the largest single investment ever made by the company.*

Bottom: *Office towers, like this one in San Francisco, have been an important part of the commerical mortgage portfolio since the late 1960s.*

Top: *One of the housing units at Wailea, a Hawaiian resort community in which Northwestern has invested $37 million.*

Bottom: *Greenway Plaza in Houston, a sprawling complex that includes a hotel, office buildings, a shopping center, and a sports arena. Northwestern loans and equity in the project total $77 million.*

Top: *The company's investment team in 1977* (left to right): *Gordon Davidson, Glenn Buzzard, Donald Schuenke, Donald Windfelder, and John Konrad.*

Bottom: *Shopping centers, including this one in Vancouver, B.C., have been an investment of choice for more than two decades.*

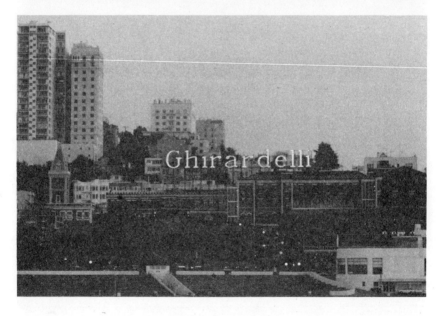

Northwestern's commercial investments range from modernistic office buildings to San Francisco's Ghirardelli Square, a converted chocolate factory in which the company owns a half-interest.

The Grand Avenue retail mall in Milwaukee, a dramatic blend of old and new that symbolizes Northwestern's commitment to downtown revitalization in its home city.

Top: *Northwestern's real estate investment trust (REIT) was listed on the New York Stock Exchange in 1971.* Left to right: *Robert Hack, president of the Exchange; Robert Barrows; Gordon Davidson; and Robert Silver, specialist on the REIT stock.*

Bottom: *Donald Schuenke signs the papers completing Northwestern's purchase of Standard of America Life Insurance from Sundstrand Corporation in 1982. Looking on are* (left to right) *Francis Ferguson; Walt Wojcik, Standard's president; and Ted Ross of Sundstrand.*

Advertising
1947-1982

"What if you had to be the executor of your own estate?"

NORTHWESTERN MUTUAL POLICYOWNER. *Life insurance with this company has played a vital part in the financial planning of Charles Stewart Mott. He purchased the first of 11 NML policies in 1899.*

Words of wisdom
about estate planning

By **CHARLES STEWART MOTT**
Engineer, Manufacturer, Philanthropist
and Director, General Motors Corp.

"OVER THE YEARS, I've known a lot of men who thought they had a good estate plan. Looking back, I see very few of them did.

"In light of this, I have a suggestion: put yourself in your executor's shoes.

Read your will, then read it again. List your assets and liabilities.

"If you're like most men, life insurance will be the major part of your estate. But is there enough life insurance? Is it the right kind and is it used most efficiently?

"Consider state and federal estate taxes, college for your children, living expenses for your wife, business obligations, personal loans, or a mortgage...all of these needs can be handled ideally

with policies of permanent life insurance.

"Besides, funds from such policies are available immediately, usually tax free. There's no waiting, no complicated probating procedures.

"One more bit of advice. A good estate plan is essential. Naturally, a good life insurance agent representing a good company can be of real assistance working together with your attorney and other financial advisers."

The Karsh campaign, featuring portraits of prominent Northwestern clients, ran without interruption from 1948 to 1968. It was perhaps the longest-running campaign in the industry's history.

Top: *Veteran Northwesterners admire the company's new logo in 1957.*

Bottom: *A series of print ads in 1981 emphasized the company's self-appointed role as a specialist.*

Top: *Richard Haggman (left), who coined the "Quiet Company" slogan as advertisng director, and Robert Carboni, head of the Communications Department since its establishment in 1973.*

Bottom: *Two "competitors" discuss Northwestern during taping of the television commercials introduced in 1982.*

CHAPTER FIVE

The Outside
World Intrudes
1967-1979

If archaeologists of the distant future recovered only insurance publications from our ruins, they would find little to guide them in a reconstruction of late twentieth-century America. *Best's Review* makes only passing references to Vietnam and Watergate in its 1967-1979 issues. *The National Underwriter* barely mentions ghetto violence and campus unrest. Northwestern's *FieldNews* has little to say about the baby boom and the flower children.

It is not, of course, the role of insurance periodicals to record or interpret the national news. Their editors have enough to do keeping up with events in the industry and its component companies. It is easy, however, in reading the trade journals and the company periodicals, to get the mistaken impression that life insurance is a self-contained world, a specialized backwater somehow removed from the rest of society. That has clearly never been the case; as the world changed, so did life insurance. After 1967 isolation was even less likely. Convulsive social and economic change rocked even the most stable institutions to their roots. In a sense, a new world was created, one in which the life insurance industry would never again be completely at ease.

In earlier years, passive management had been at least possible, if not desirable. A life insurance firm could coast along on the good work of actuaries twenty years gone, buying a computer for efficiency's sake, adding new products occasionally to appease the agents and preserve a market share. The major challenges were in the competitive environment, not in the social and economic spheres. As the scale of change enlarged in the late Sixties, coasting became virtually impossible. To take no action was to act, and often to lose ground. Northwestern Mutual and its competitors were marked by a progressive sense of embattlement during the 1967-1979 period. More and more effort was spent adjusting to conditions imposed from outside.

The pressures came from several directions at once. Inflation changed the nature of the basic insurance contract. Related economic ills inverted the investment picture. Changing mores demanded a new definition of social responsibility. Changing values demanded a new approach to employee and agent relationships. There were, for the first time in two generations, loud accusations that insurance firms were more interested in fleecing customers than in serving them. And the federal government's influence on corporate affairs reached proportions many considered uncomfortable. The industry found itself on the defensive, and self-determination became difficult, even dangerous.

Chapter 4 described the internal transformation of Northwestern Mutual. This chapter presents the other side of the coin — Northwestern's response to external conditions. The first half of the chapter describes economic pressures, particularly inflation and its impact on policy loans and other investments. The second half recounts changes in the social environment, from home office liberalizations and union unrest to consumerism and federal activities. The basic challenges were the same for all companies, but they provoked a multitude of reactions. Despite some wrong turns and false starts, Northwestern took the offensive more than once, solving common problems in ways that reflected a unique character.

The Inflationary Climate

Life insurance, as a financial industry, was most sensitive to changes in the economic weather. There were other clouds on the horizon after 1967, but the largest was inflation, moving across the country with unprecedented speed. After a brief rise following World War II, inflation had crept along at an annual rate of 1.7 percent between 1949 and 1967. It crossed the 5 percent threshold in 1969, and reached the double-digit level at 11 percent in 1974. After a modest decline, the rate galloped ahead to 11.3 percent in 1979.

The cumulative effect of continued inflation was devastating. It had taken from the 1850s to the 1920s for prices to double — more than two generations. After the deflation of the Depression era, the cost of living doubled again between 1942 and 1967 — a twenty-five-year time span. In the twelve short years between 1967 and 1979, prices more than doubled, rising 117 percent. Inflation was indeed a form of weather, a system of high economic pressure that sent a debilitating wind across the country. Once in motion, it was among the most self-sustaining of all economic forces. All the rhetorical rain dances, the cloud seeding of the Federal Reserve, and the windward shelters erected by some did little to dampen its impact.

Inflation is as much discussed as the weather, and as little understood. The hydrologic cycles and barometric pressures of meteorology have as their counterparts the business cycles and leading indicators of economics. In the conventional wisdom, inflation is too much money chasing too few goods. When demand grows faster than supply, as was the case following World War II, consumer prices are forced upward. Supply might catch up, but the result is not necessarily a stable economy. Higher prices generally fuel a demand for higher incomes, and high incomes, because they add to production costs, generally exert upward pressure on prices. The spiral can build indefinitely, like a poker game with no limit on the number of raises. The federal government, the agent of the people, complicates the process. A too-rapid increase in the money supply contributes to demand and devalues dollars currently in circulation. High levels of federal spending can also throw an economy out of balance. Inflation accelerated during the Vietnam War largely because the military program strained productive resources that were already struggling to meet a high level of demand.

Harvey Wilmeth has a different vision. Since joining Northwestern in 1947, Wilmeth has displayed a talent for statistics and a taste for ideas that have made him one of the most original thinkers in the company's history. In 1977 he advanced to the position of economist and free-lance intellectual. Wilmeth began a crusade to "rewrite economic theory" that has continued through his 1983 retirement. In his view, a key variable overlooked in all the economic equations is private debt. He shows that the much-publicized federal debt, as a percentage of the gross national product, has declined sharply since World War II, while the private debt ratio has nearly doubled. As businesses and individuals owe more and own less, so much is locked in debt that the money supply (relative to GNP) has actually declined. Inflation then is not too much money chasing too few goods. It is an expedient method of relieving the pressure of debt before it becomes intolerable. Wilmeth argues that new federal controls on the growth of debt are needed to supplement existing controls on the growth of money. The new restrictions, he maintains, would allow the government to increase the money supply (bringing interest rates down) without stimulating inflation.

Whatever its ultimate cause, the effects of inflation have been as real as rain. It dissolved the economic constants and brought a new sense of relativism to American life. It made financial decisions — from buying a house to building a factory — an elaborate game, one in which many of the cards were wild. It mocked gains that seemed impressive. Northwestern's assets increased 93 percent in current dollars between 1967 and 1979. In constant or "real" dollars, they declined 13 percent. Inflation caused a premature nostalgia. The prices of a loaf of bread, a pound of hamburger, and a gallon of gasoline had all crossed the one-dollar threshold by the late 1970s, making the prices of 1967 seem as distant as kerosene lamps and kitchen woodstoves. Inflation also added a touch of irony to the American scene. By 1979 an agent had to sell $1.5 million of insurance to qualify for the Million Dollar Round Table.

Few businesses are as allergic to inflation as life insurance. It has always been described as a long-term industry, one that operates in a fifteen- to twenty-year timeframe. Inflation radically foreshortened that timeframe, and the long horizon of the actuaries slipped into the fog. The fog analogy is appropriate. Like a ship captain at sea who finds the stars obscured, the instruments defective, and the destination uncertain, the life insurance industry suffered a massive dislocation. As the fog grew more dense, the captain could not guarantee his passengers a safe arrival. Life on deck continued as usual, but there was consternation on the bridge.

Inflation pushed operating costs to undreamed-of heights. It forced agents to sell more insurance simply to stay even. It mocked attempts to follow a stable investment policy. In ways that no one anticipated, it brought policy loan and federal income tax problems to crisis proportions. Perhaps inflation's most insidious effect was to change the nature of life insurance itself. It is a dollar business, and its financial mainstay has been a lifetime contract guaranteeing fixed benefits in return for fixed payments. As inflation galloped ahead, $10,000 of whole life coverage purchased in 1949 was worth less than $3,300 in 1979. The American economy created a new product — decreasing permanent insurance.

Most consumers expected to replace their cars and refrigerators periodically, but many were dismayed to find their life insurance wearing out. Some purchased new policies to keep their level of protection constant; other lost faith in "permanent" insurance. A 1976 study showed that whole life sales dropped nearly as fast as the Consumer Price Index rose. They stood at 31 percent of the nation's new business (face value) in 1979, down from 38 percent in 1970 and 42 percent in 1960. The trend to term accelerated, and there was growing interest in new products designed to change with the economy.

As a self-proclaimed specialist in whole life insurance, Northwestern was particularly vulnerable. If the company's product line had remained static, all of its recruiting, reorganizing, and computerizing after 1967 might have been largely wasted effort. In 1968, however, Northwestern began to sell Extra Ordinary Life policies, offering a high level of permanent coverage at a low level premium.

It is difficult to exaggerate the importance of EOL. The product appeared at the very beginning of the inflationary era, and it fueled a dramatic increase in whole life sales. Countering the national trends, permanent insurance rose from 69 percent of Northwestern's new business in 1967 to 88 percent in 1972 — the highest point in nearly fifty years. Due in part to EOL, the value of Northwestern insurance was enhanced despite inflation. In constant dollars, a customer's premium purchased twice the protection in 1979 that it did in 1949. The day of reckoning was postponed.

The Policy Loan Account

Timely product change enabled Northwestern to dodge one bullet, but another was on the way — the demand for policy loans. This one hit the company harder than virtually anyone in the industry. In 1893 Northwestern had asked the Wisconsin legislature for authority to loan money to its policyholders, in amounts based on each policy's cash value. The lawmakers obliged, establishing a variable interest rate with a ceiling of 6 percent. Customers had a ready source of cash in times of need, and the company had a rather attractive investment outlet. Its yield on invested funds was only 5.16 percent in 1893. Six percent, in fact, was well above the average rate earned for the next eighty years, and it seemed positively usurious during the depressed 1930s. By 1939 the prime rate charged by major banks had fallen to 1.5 percent, and in that year the New York insurance commissioner lowered the policy loan ceiling to 5 percent. Northwestern, like most of its competitors, applied the 5 percent rate to all of its new policies.

As the prices of hamburger and houses rose in the late 1960s, so did the price of money. In an effort to curb the growth of cash and credit, the Federal Reserve raised its discount rate (charged to member banks for new money) steadily after 1965. Fearing the loss of their money's value to inflation, lenders aggravated the trend by raising their interest rates sharply. The prime rate passed 5 percent in 1966, and three years later it reached 8 percent. It fluctuated wildly thereafter, peaking at 11.75 percent in 1974 and 15 percent in 1979.

During the Depression, policyowners borrowed to save their homes and to put food on the table. Life insurance cash values were a last resort. By the late Sixties, they offered the lowest interest rates available anywhere, and cash values became a first resort. Some people borrowed to meet personal or business emergencies, but a growing number used their loans as investment capital. The process was called "disintermediation," a pretentious word for a simple concept: eliminating the middleman. Instead of trusting their funds to insurance investment managers, policyowners made their own investments in certificates of deposit, Treasury bills and, by the late Seventies, money market funds.

Northwestern agents had long courted prospects in the upper income and educational segments of American society. They also sold large amounts of insurance to corporations, whose controllers watched the capital markets like hawks. The company took pride in the sophistication and economic stature of its owners, in part because their policies were much larger and more enduring than the industry average. Northwestern paid for that specialization. Of all the insureds in America, Northwestern policyowners were among the most likely to use the loan clause in their contracts. Their cash values were substantial, and many had both the knowledge and the will to explore investment alternatives.

Taken by surprise in the credit crunch of 1966, Northwestern had purchased more common stocks and marketable bonds to improve its liquidity. Despite these precautions, the company was shocked by the intensity of the next squeeze in 1969. The prime rate jumped from 6.75 to 8.5 percent in the first half of the year, and policy loan demand soared. By July the loan division's clerical staff was working sixty-five-hour weeks to keep up with the pressure, and there was still a two-week backlog of applications. Northwestern paid out more than $219 million in policy loans during the year. Nearly two-thirds of its new income went back out the door as loans — the highest ratio in the industry.

Borrowing activity rose and fell after 1969, generally in rhythm with the prime rate. After a short breathing spell, the rate surged ahead to 10 percent in 1973 and 11.75 percent in 1974. Loan demand reached a new high. Clerical workers processed 2000 applications for $4.9 million on one memorable Saturday, and Northwestern's net payout in 1973 and 1974 combined was nearly $400 million. After 1977 the peaks were nearly continuous. The prime reached 15 percent in late 1979 (on its way to 20 percent in the next year), and the company's loan disbursements averaged more than $2 million a day.

Although loan demand fluctuated, its effects were, like the inflation rate's, cumulative. The policy loan account was the fastest-growing segment of Northwestern's investment portfolio, increasing from $512 million in 1967 to $1.6 billion in 1975 and $2.5 billion in 1979. As a ratio of the company's assets, loans grew from 9.4 to 20.2 to 23.5 percent in the same years. The previous peak was 25 percent in 1933, and it took only a year to set a new record. (In 1980 the account absorbed 26.9 percent of assets; in 1981, 30.2 percent.) When the industry's loan activity was tallied at the end of each year, Northwestern was invariably among the national leaders — a distinction it would gladly have foregone.

The loan situation was aggravated by a growing trend to minimum-deposit selling. As described in earlier chapters, a minimum-deposit buyer systematically borrows against cash values in order to pay premiums. The loan principal increases annually, and clients claim their interest payments as tax deductions. "Mini-dipping" (or, more politely, "variable pay") is usually promoted as a tax-effective way to reduce premium outlays. As sales resistance to whole life products hardened with inflation, a growing number of agents overcame it by illustrating minimum-deposit plans.

Northwestern, already deluged with loan requests from existing policyowners, did not welcome new customers who bought with every intention of borrowing. Company officials had been railing against "borrow-to-buy" insurance since the 1950s, and now the campaign took on aspects of a moral crusade. Spokesmen attacked minimum-deposit as a perversion of the insurance contract, an unfair and perhaps unethical practice that hurt the company more than it helped individual agents. Ferguson came close to naming names at the 1973 annual meeting. He reported that the ratio of cash values withdrawn ranged from 15 percent in the lowest general agency to 37.6 percent in the highest, and he described one young agent whose customers had borrowed 82.3 percent of their cash reserves.

At one point Northwestern decided to bar highly "borrowed" agents from awards competition. The decision was reversed when the company found it could not distinguish minimum-deposit borrowing from the more general practice. All of the pronouncements may have slowed down the trend, but their fervor alienated some members of the field force. One agent noted that the home office willingly approved applications for very large policies, in full knowledge that they had probably been sold on a minimum-deposit basis. Another said that the company statements made him feel "like a Catholic selling birth-control pills."

Despite suggestions to the contrary, there is nothing intrinsically evil about policy loans themselves. Because the company, in effect, holds the policies as collateral, they are perhaps the safest investments available. But the unprecedented volume of loans gave Northwestern several reasons for concern. Policies stripped of their cash values are more likely to lapse than policies left intact. Northwestern's persistency remained the best in the business, but its overall lapse rate increased from 2 percent in 1967 to 3 percent in 1979.

Loan activity had an even more disturbing effect on the investment departments. During periods of peak loan demand, the investment managers found themselves without working capital. Because the peaks were impossible to predict, the investors diverted more and more funds to short-term, liquid instruments. Investment planning became a contradiction in terms, and long-term borrowers learned not to count on Northwestern for help in new ventures. Most serious was the drag on investment yield. With interest rates at record highs, new commitments were earning more than 10 percent by 1979. Lending funds to policyowners at 5 percent seemed, by contrast, like putting money in a sock.

The company also objected to heavy borrowing on philosophical grounds. Ferguson and other executives repeatedly described the situation as "unmutual" and "unfair." They described Northwestern's assets as an investment pool owned by everyone who paid premiums. The minority who withdrew funds from the pool hurt the majority by lowering the investment yield and therefore dividends. The non-borrowers never organized a protest movement but, in the company's stated view, the policy loan account represented a basic inequity.

For reasons more practical than philosophical, Northwestern moved aggressively to blunt the impact of policy loans on its operations. In 1969 the company raised its loan rate ceiling on new policies to 6 percent, reversing the action of 1939. The change was permissible in every state but New York. In 1970 Northwestern sent letters to the 341,000 policyowners who had borrowed, stressing the emergency nature of life insurance reserves and suggesting prompt repayment. Enough clients responded to at least cover the cost of the campaign. In 1974, when it was clear that the "emergency" argument had lost some relevance, the company sent another letter urging policyowners to at least pay the interest on their loans. It was, after all, tax-deductible.

A bolder step was taken in 1974. Working with a handful of competitors, Northwestern began a nationwide effort to seek legislative approval for an 8 percent loan rate. The campaign's field general was George Hardy, a company attorney since 1957 and its chief state lobbyist since 1962. Hardy spent much of his time between 1974 and 1979 on the road, talking with state legislators, insurance commissioners, agents, labor officials, and representatives of other companies. Roughly half of the states had no specific limits on policy loan rates, and they offered little opposition to the 8 percent proposal. The other twenty-five, however, had 6 percent ceilings (5 percent in New York), and few politicians were eager to raise the limits in a time of consumer unrest.

The 8 percent advocates argued that the old laws were out of touch with current realities, and they described a higher rate as a simple way to restore some balance to the situation. Hardy incurred the wrath of some competitors by suggesting that states require insurance firms to pass along the benefits of an 8 percent clause by either raising dividends or lowering premiums. Progress was steady but slow. It was not until 1980 that the new rate was legal in all fifty states.

In April of 1975, long before approval was complete, Northwestern became the first to announce an 8 percent policy in states that had passed the new bill. The most vocal opposition came from some of the company's agents. The new contract guaranteed higher dividends, but the agents feared the loss of a basic selling point, especially when no other company followed Northwestern's lead. (Northwestern stood virtually alone at 8 percent for two years.) Home office executives defended the move as absolutely vital, and they argued that it would soon become the industry norm. Agents, in the meantime, urged their clients to buy insurance before the loan rate went up. There was a flurry of term conversions and new sales just before the 8 percent contract went into effect on September 1, 1975.

Foreshadowing later events, Northwestern offered the 8 percent loan rate as an amendment to existing policies in the same year. The amendment campaign was a massive effort, one that would have been impossible in the pre-computer era. Every policyowner with cash-value insurance received a letter describing the advantages of the 8 percent clause: higher dividends for the individual and greater stability for the company. Nearly one-third of the company's policyowners accepted the amendment.

Speaking to the agents at their 1973 annual meeting, Ferguson had said, "Excessive policy loans are the greatest single threat to this company's position of cost leadership." The 8 percent campaign — the legislative maneuvering, the new contract, the amendment program — was the company's greatest single effort to meet that threat in the 1967-1979 period. Curtis Ford, the San Francisco general agent, quipped that, with the new 8 percent policy, "NML" would stand for "No More Loans."

That was not to be the case. Northwestern showed leadership and independence in the campaign, but it was soon clear that the new rate was only a stopgap measure. As the inflation escalator continued skyward, even 8 percent loans seemed like bargains. Policyowners continued to borrow heavily, and Northwestern resolved to find a more permanent solution to the problem.

Investments: A New Ballgame

Policy loans are technically investments. They require no strategizing, no negotiating, and very little paperwork, but they took their place alongside the utility bonds and apartment mortgages in Northwestern's investment portfolio. In 1979 policy loans absorbed nearly one-fourth of the company's assets, edging out corporate securities as the largest single item in the account. They dried up capital, hampered planning efforts, and held yields down. Like weak hitters on a baseball team, they forced the other players to work much harder just to keep Northwestern in the game.

The rest of the investment team was handicapped by the volatile economy as well as by policy loans. No aspect of insurance operations is as directly exposed to the environment as the investment function. A company can design products, recruit agents, install computers, and restructure departments largely as it sees fit, but it cannot change the economic weather. Investment managers can adapt to the climate, and adapt creatively, but they cannot grow money in a home office greenhouse. They were forced, after 1967, to operate in a context of inflation, recession, and sagging productivity.

Policy loans and economic turmoil combined to make investing an entirely new ballgame. Since the beginning of American life insurance, there had been a one-to-one correspondence between the insurance side and the investment side. Fixed-dollar, long-term policies were supported by fixed-dollar, long-term investments. That relationship broke down rapidly after 1967, and the investment departments were rocked by a series of dramatic inversions.

In earlier years a company could almost literally put thirty-year bonds or mortgages on the shelf and forget about them. After 1967 inflation eroded portfolio values as rapidly as it did insurance coverage, and continued inflation made long-term, fixed-rate investments seem impossibly risky. In earlier years there was pressure to get the money out into the field. After 1967, during periods of peak policy loan demand, there was no money to invest. In earlier years surplus cash and temporary investments were signs of inefficiency. After 1967 they became the highest-yielding investments available. In earlier years assets were managed to meet a predictable volume of death claims. After 1967 they were managed to meet an unpredictable volume of loans, lapses, and surrenders. In earlier years equity investments were viewed as extra risks with extra rewards. After 1967 they became virtually the only way to keep pace with inflation.

At Northwestern Mutual, the change in the game was accompanied by a change in the players. When Ferguson stepped up to the presidency in 1967, Robert Barrows succeeded him as vice-president — mortgages. Barrows was, like Ferguson, a native of upstate New York, a World War II pilot, and a former student at Cornell University. He had joined the home office mortgage staff in 1948 but spent most of his early career in the field. Barrows established the Dallas regional loan office in 1952 and served as its head until 1963, when he returned to Milwaukee as the manager of residential loans. A gregarious man with an active sense of humor, Barrows earned both the affection and respect of his colleagues.

Peter Langmuir, Ferguson's counterpart and sometime adversary in the Securities Department, had served the company with distinction since 1947. In 1967, at the age of 53, he suffered a fatal heart attack. Langmuir was the first executive to die in office since Michael Cleary, and his death was equally unexpected. His successor as vice-president — securities was John Konrad, a Wisconsin native who had joined the company in 1954. Trained as a lawyer, he had become Northwestern's expert in utility, energy, and municipal bonds, and he was the department's senior officer at the time of Langmuir's death. Konrad was, like Barrows, an affable, even-handed administrator. The Barrows-Konrad combination brought a sense of calm to the investment departments that was a distinct asset in a time of economic turmoil.

The Mortgage and Securities Departments had always functioned as autonomous units distinct from each other as well as the rest of the company. They competed for investable funds like college departments competing for the favor of their dean. The president had long been the ultimate arbiter, but after 1950, in typical Northwestern fashion, a committee took over that role. The Cash Committee, chaired by the president, met monthly to review the company's cash flow and to assign rough quotas to each department. Following the credit crunches of 1966 and 1969, it became obvious that more was needed. In a time of tight money and economic volatility, the company lacked a central focus in its investment efforts.

In 1973, accordingly, Robert Barrows was given a new title: senior vice-president in charge of investments. For the first time, Northwestern had a full-time executive whose sole job was to monitor, coordinate, and plan the activities of the investment departments. Conditions demanded it, but the move was also in harmony with the company's growing emphasis on the rational workplace.

Barrows' successor as the head of Mortgages was Glenn Buzzard, an Illinois native who had spent eight years in the Illinois regional loan offices before coming to the home office in 1955. By 1962 Buzzard was running the farm loan division, and seven years later he became the manager of all loan offices in the western United States.

There was structural as well as staff change. Reflecting a shift in strategy, two new departments were created in 1973. Real Estate split off from Mortgages under the leadership of Gordon Davidson. Born in Milwaukee and educated at Yale and Harvard, Davidson had become the company's commercial loan expert since joining Northwestern in 1953. Common Stocks split off from Securities at the same time. Its head was another Milwaukee native, Donald Windfelder. He was hired in 1954 as a superintendent of bonds, but his talent as a stock trader became increasingly apparent.

In terms of long-range planning, Barrows barely had time to warm the chair in his new office. In 1976 he was assigned to the President's Department as Ferguson's assistant and heir apparent. The new senior investment vice-president was Donald Schuenke. As the company's leading investment lawyer, Schuenke had shown an impressive ability to improve Northwestern's position in last-minute contract negotiations. As general counsel since 1974, he had also proven his ability to manage a complex department.

New faces, new departments, and a new structure enlarged the scope and increased the efficiency of the investment operation. The managers freely admit, however, that they were not quick to learn the new ballgame's rules. Years after inflation and interest rates had begun their upward climb, Northwestern was still buying long-term bonds and making long-term mortgage loans. No one expected inflation to continue, and high interest rates seemed to be a temporary aberration. Like impatient buyers at an auction, Northwestern's investors could not resist the temptations of an ascending market. In the early 1970s a 7 percent bond seemed like a gift from above. A few years later it was clear that Northwestern had been the giver.

Despite their slow start, the investment managers gradually developed a three-part strategy that carried the company through the period. It was based on a mix of long-term instruments, liquid assets, and equities. The lines between the categories grew blurry over the years, but Barrows and then Schuenke used all three as the foundation for investment planning.

The long-term investments formed the necessary base of the portfolio. They gave the company a steady, predictable flow of cash to meet death claims and ongoing expenses. Northwestern still bought the bonds of companies specializing in everything from aircraft to zinc, and it still loaned mortgage money to shopping center and office building developers. Bonds and mortgages made up 56 percent of the portfolio in 1979 — down from 77 percent in 1967, but still a majority of assets.

The investments seemed traditional, but their terms changed dramatically. Maturities were shortened. In a field once dominated by thirty-year terms, even fifteen-year commitments seemed dangerous. Dollar amounts increased. Northwestern had once loaned money to homeowners, small businesspeople, and family farmers by the thousands. In the early 1970s the mortgage loan minimum was raised to $250,000, and corporate loans of $30 million were no longer shocking.

Even more important was a steady shift to incentive financing. In the years just after World War II, most investments had been simple and straightforward — a specified sum for a specified period at a specified interest rate. Beginning in the late 1950s, Peter Langmuir had made incentive financing an art form. He negotiated for amendments to the basic contract that allowed Northwestern to share in the borrower's success. These kickers were viewed as gravy — a very rich gravy, in some cases, but never intended to replace the main course.

In the 1970s kickers became more the rule than the exception. Northwestern received a share of rental income from office buildings, production payments from energy suppliers, and stock warrants from a host of corporations, above and beyond fixed interest payments. Bonds and mortgages accounted for 56 percent of assets in 1979, but that figure is deceptive. The majority of new investments being made in both areas included some form of incentive.

The liquidity account, the second leg of the triangle, grew in response to the unscheduled demand for policy loans. By 1979 roughly 10 percent of the company's assets were invested in United States Treasury bills, commercial paper (corporate IOUs), and high-quality bonds — all easily negotiable in times of emergency. The liquidity reserve became, in effect, a fifth department. As short-term interest rates climbed progressively higher, its yields were the most impressive in the portfolio.

Northwestern's equity investments, the third leg, displayed a variety and a volatility that would have shocked earlier executives. As inflation continued, Ferguson and his executives saw the need for investments that would ride upward with the cost of living. Northwestern, in effect, tried to protect itself by taking risks. In three areas — common stocks, real estate, and energy exploration — the company abandoned its insistence on fixed returns and trusted its fortunes to the marketplace. Because of the risks involved, pure equities made up a relatively small percentage of the portfolio, but they included some of the most unusual investments in the company's history.

Common stocks had long been anathema at Northwestern. Although the market's post-war performance was spectacular,

Edmund Fitzgerald, Donald Slichter, and other executives repeatedly dismissed stock investments as gambling with the policyowners' money. They were also sensitive to the impact of mutual funds, which had diverted millions of dollars from life insurance. Temporary declines in the market were announced as good news.

The resistance had worn down considerably by the late 1960s. Northwestern introduced a stock-based variable annuity in 1968, and seriously considered developing a mutual fund of its own. Common stocks became an investment of choice, rising from less than 1 percent of the portfolio in 1958 to 4.6 percent in 1968, on their way to a peak of 7.4 percent four years later.

Northwestern, like many insurance companies, joined the parade just in time to see it end. After a 390 percent increase between 1949 and 1967, the Dow Jones Industrial Average flattened, rising a scant 1 percent in the next decade. Mutual fund redemptions in 1971 exceeded sales for the first time in history. In 1974, a particularly hard year for stockbrokers, Northwestern's common stocks suffered real and paper losses of $138 million, nearly a third of their value in the previous year. The company stayed in the market but, for safety's sake, limited its common stock investments to 5 percent of assets or less.

Northwestern's real estate ventures were somewhat less volatile and certainly more colorful. The most exotic were two resort communities, one on the island of Maui in Hawaii, the other near Hilton Head Island in South Carolina. Wailea, the Hawaiian community, featured 1500 acres of stunning oceanfront scenery well-removed from centers of population. Development began in 1971, the result of a joint venture in which Northwestern invested nearly $37 million. The original plans called for a luxury hotel, 2400 condominium units, and 661 single-family homes, served by golf courses, a tennis center, and a variety of shops. Moss Creek Plantation, the South Carolina property, was acquired through foreclosure in 1975. Plans for its development included 1200 single-family homes, 430 condominium units, and facilities for golf, yachting, tennis, and horseback riding. Moss Creek has been the site of the professional Women's International Golf Tournament since the mid-1970s.

Both Wailea and Moss Creek were designed in part to reach the affluent second-home market. Business was brisk at first (buyers were chosen by lottery for one Wailea project), but the real estate market entered a recession in the mid-1970s. Even the affluent lost interest in expensive second homes. Northwestern retained its interest in both projects, but the developers scaled down construction plans and timetables drastically.

The recession affected the company less directly in another way. In 1971 Northwestern launched NML Mortgage and Realty Investors, a real estate investment trust. REITs, mutual funds based on real estate rather than stocks, were a popular investment vehicle at the time. Policy loans were drying up the company's investment pool, and Mortgage Department employees in both Milwaukee and the field offices found themselves with time on their hands. The department's managers argued that an REIT would generate advisory fees and add to the staff's investable funds, allowing Northwestern to retain employees who might otherwise have been laid off. Ferguson, with some reluctance, approved the new venture.

Northwestern's REIT peaked early. Trading on the New York Stock Exchange was brisk, opening at twenty dollars per share in 1971 and rising to twenty-seven dollars in the next year. Like Northwestern itself, the new corporation invested the greatest share of its assets in long-term mortgages rather than equity ventures. After some initial success, the REIT was crippled by the recession. A disturbing number of projects was placed in "non-accrual status," a polite term for impending failure. The share price dropped to nine dollars in 1974 and never rose above thirteen dollars thereafter. The REIT fared better than most of its competitors, and it continued to pay dividends, but the outlook for its future growth was not promising. In 1982 Northwestern purchased all outstanding shares of stock and dissolved the trust. Only 12 percent of the original stockholders had remained.

Another real estate venture encountered problems of a different nature. In 1964, at Ferguson's urging, Northwestern had moved aggressively into the college housing market. Within three years the company had more rooms for rent than Conrad Hilton. The projects were immensely popular at first, but they quickly fell victim to a change in the market. Between 1967 and 1972 — the heyday of the counterculture — many students viewed any form of institutionalized housing as sterile and confining. Occupancy rates in all units plummeted to a low of 63 percent in 1971. The Kent State dormitory had been full in 1967. In 1971, a few months after four students were killed in a war protest, only 40 percent of the rooms were occupied.

Northwestern made the best of the situation. The most troubled units were sold, and several were converted to extended-care facilities by their new owners. The company kept fifteen of the properties and waited patiently for tastes to change. By 1979 occupancy levels in the remaining dormitories had returned to 97 percent.

Commercial real estate presented fewer problems during the period. Since the early 1950s Northwestern had invested millions of dollars in office buildings, retail stores, industrial plants, schools, and (later than most competitors) shopping centers. After 1967 the company's role shifted steadily from lender to owner. In its shopping center investments, for instance, the standard lease agreement gave Northwestern a share of each center's revenues, which rose rapidly as a result of both inflation and increased sales. The largest commercial investment was Houston's Greenway Plaza, a sprawling complex that included a shopping center, a luxury hotel, a sports arena, office buildings, and parking facilities for 5000 cars. Northwestern loans and equity in Greenway Plaza totaled $77 million.

Some of the agricultural investments were nearly as massive. The two largest — Gila River Ranch in Arizona and Atlantic Farms on the Virginia-North Carolina coast — showed how much Northwestern had changed since the days when most loans were made on one-tractor family farms. Gila River Ranch, acquired in 1968, covered 72,000 acres of arid but fertile land near the Mexican border. Northwestern spent millions on irrigation systems and developed the largest cotton farm in Arizona. Atlantic Farms, by contrast, covered 100,000 acres in the Great Dismal Swamp. Development there meant an elaborate and costly system of drainage. Glenn Buzzard, who actively managed both projects, said, "We went from watering the desert to draining the swamp. If we'd been able to combine their resources, we'd have had a hell of a property." Both were sold at a profit.

Of all the equity ventures, energy exploration was both the most radical and the most rewarding. Peter Langmuir had led Northwestern into the energy field in the 1950s. Based on his extensive contacts in the South and Southwest, the company had invested money in oilfields, natural gas wells, and pipelines. The investments were loans, but each included some form of equity kicker. There was a fixed-rate floor in each agreement, but there was no ceiling on potential earnings.

Ferguson shared Langmuir's interest, but he carried it one large step further. At his urging, Northwestern removed the floor as well as the ceiling. Years before the Arab oil embargo made the energy shortage a national obsession, Ferguson had concluded that petroleum was an undervalued resource, one whose importance could only grow. He also saw a logical fit between the massive capital requirements of oil drilling and the investable assets of his own company. To the surprise of both oil and insurance executives, he began to pursue deals in which Northwestern would share the possibilities of loss and reward equally with its partners. As inflation continued to erode the value of fixed-rate bonds and mortgages, Ferguson convinced his board that a tangible asset like oil was, in the new ballgame, a conservative investment.

In 1972 Northwestern joined a consortium of four energy companies bidding for offshore oil and natural gas leases in the Gulf of Mexico. The leases, off the coast of Louisiana, were awarded, and new tracts in Texas waters were soon added. Northwestern's stake in the original project was $44 million. By 1965 the company had invested $93 million in the Gulf; by 1979, $137 million. The offshore drilling platforms represented the largest single investment in Northwestern's history.

Business journalists were quick to see the ironies in a staid old life insurance company "wildcatting" in the coastal oilfields, and Ferguson received his share of ribbing at industry meetings. The last laugh was not long in coming. Although the initial Louisiana finds were disappointing, the Texas tract was far richer than anyone had expected. The payoff began in 1977 and has increased annually since that time. Northwestern's return on its offshore investment has been well in excess of 20 percent.

The company's growing interest in energy found other outlets. Northwestern invested nearly $30 million in natural gas wells in northwestern Texas, and more than $2 million in a Wyoming coalfield. Perhaps the most novel project was a rather short-lived solar energy experiment. In 1975 Battelle Memorial Institute, a non-profit research center, agreed to carry out a Northwestern-funded project to develop a solar-powered engine. Northwestern retained ownership of all patents. The $2.5 million investment was motivated in part by a desire to hold down irrigation costs on the Arizona ranch. The result was a fifty-horsepower irrigation pump dedicated at Gila River in 1977. It was the largest of its kind ever assembled, but it did not emerge as a cost-effective way to water the desert. The project proved two things: that the sun could be harnessed to drive machinery, and that it could not be done commercially.

In every area — energy, real estate, stocks, short-term accounts, bonds, and mortgages — the investment departments changed even more radically than the rest of the company between 1967 and 1979. At the beginning of the period, Northwestern's investors were still following rules that, in their essentials, were laid down in the nineteenth century. By 1979 incentive financing, liquidity reserves, and equity holdings had become a way of life.

The transition was not accomplished without some hesitation and a few missteps. Despite an ongoing program of portfolio improvement, Northwestern was still holding its share of old 2 percent sewer bonds and 3 percent railroad securities in 1979. But the policy-owners' dollars were going out to tidewater farms and deepwater oil wells, luxury resorts and industrial parks, singles apartments and cement plants. In some areas, notably energy, Northwestern showed the same aggressiveness that characterized its internal operations.

It was a difficult period for the investment managers. When the results were tallied, it was clear that Northwestern had lost ground in the industry. In 1967 Northwestern's pre-tax investment yield was 5.04 percent, well above the 4.82 percent industry average. In the 1970s yields rose to their highest point in a century, but policy loans hampered the company's performance. Northwestern's net rate of return in 1979 was 7.41 percent, compared to a 7.73 percent average for the industry.

Despite abundant problems, the investment staff found vitality in the challenges of the period. Their assignments were certainly varied: negotiating with cattle ranchers and winemakers, traveling to Hawaiian resorts and Alaskan oilfields, managing the Houston Rockets and financing the Milwaukee Brewers. Some developed a penchant for working out troubled investments, and others took pleasure in their new roles as venture capitalists. There were some major disappointments, but there were also some spectacular successes. The rules changed constantly, the lights went out more than once, and some of the players were forgettable, but Northwestern proved that it could compete in the new ballgame.

Social Change: Reaction and Action

The volatile economy was certainly the major external force affecting Northwestern between 1967 and 1979. Inflation, recession, policy loans, and investment turmoil all had a fundamental impact on the company's balance sheets. But no institution was immune to the social changes occurring at the same time. There was a new mood of skepticism and dissent in the nation, mingled with a distrust of those in power and an impatience with gradual change. In ways both trivial and profound, Northwestern found itself deep in the shifting social currents of the time.

As factionalism strained the seams of American society, the company's executives left no room for doubt about their own sympathies. In his 1968 farewell speech to the agents, Robert Dineen said, "We shall always remember this period in our national life as the era of dissent . . . . But the time will come when long-haired men, the hippies and the kooks will be just as much a part of the folklore as the bunny hop and the Charleston." In a 1971 speech, Donald Slichter blasted Ralph Nader and his cohorts as "an irresponsible disaster lobby." In 1975 a local citizens' group tried to give Francis Ferguson a tinfoil crown as "king of Milwaukee" for the power he supposedly exercised over freeway plans and urban redevelopment. Ferguson declined to comment on the honor, but his antipathy for the various social movements was well-known.

There was a minority view within the walls of the institution. Laflin Jones provided informal counsel to a group of activists at the University of Wisconsin — Milwaukee. William Minehan was a stalwart figure in the Christian social reform movement. Richard Mooney espoused a number of causes that set him apart from other company officials. A 1971 *FieldNews* article associated the firebombing of the Madison (Wisconsin) general agency with "the peace movement." Daniel Lourie, a Houston agent, wrote the editor to protest the inference and, to his surprise, received numerous letters of support from home office employees and other agents.

Reactions differed, but there was abundant evidence of changing styles at Northwestern. Terms like "cop out" and "turn on" began to appear in speeches. To the dismay of ardent traditionalists, pantsuits and miniskirts were seen more often in the home office halls. A 1972 Career School was pronounced "the hairiest ever," prompting an ex-barber in the class to bring his scissors to one of the sessions. The *Pillar* photographer posed bearded and mutton-chopped employees beneath the portraits of hirsute nineteenth-century presidents. A question about drug use was added to insurance applications in 1971. At least one agent used astrology to tailor his approach to prospects, and others adopted the techniques of "counselor selling."

They included, among other things, Perceiving Reality by overcoming the Egocentric Filter and making a Discovery Agreement with the client.

One reflection of the times was not so innocent. Northwestern received its first bomb threat in early 1970, and company officials found themselves unprepared to respond. The home office had always been an open building. (More than a few misdirected visitors wandered in hoping to buy stamps or pay their gas bills.) Although the first call was a hoax, it was suddenly clear that a well-placed bomb in the computer center, for instance, could cripple the company indefinitely. Within months identification cards were issued to every employee, video monitors were installed in the main lobby, and alarm systems were upgraded. Some employees muttered about "Big Brother" when tighter security measures were introduced. Ferguson replied, "Northwestern . . . is considered part of 'the Establishment,' which does make us vulnerable to attack."

As part of the Establishment, Northwestern could respond more positively to a different form of violence. In 1967, the peak of rioting in the nation's black ghettos, the life insurance industry launched its Billion Dollar Program. Members of the major trade associations were encouraged to invest money in projects that would create housing and jobs in the central cities. Although fewer than 10 percent of the nation's companies participated, it took barely a month to raise the first billion dollars in commitments. By 1969 the program had doubled its original goal.

Northwestern was a staunch supporter of the effort. Ferguson served on the industry's Urban Committee for two years and chaired it in 1969. By 1971 his company had invested $37 million — more than its proportionate share — in central city apartment complexes, nursing homes, and owner-occupied housing projects. The Northwestern Center for Industry, a large industrial park in Chicago's inner city, absorbed $16 million of the total. All of the investments were loans, made at market rates, and many were backed by federal guarantees. What distinguished them from other investments was their locations.

The results were mixed at best. The industrial park languished after its initial surge of development. Some of the housing projects became federal responsibilities. Despite good intentions and a few success stories, Northwestern and its counterparts encountered problems that money alone could not solve.

The Billion Dollar Program was only one expression of a new

emphasis on corporate social responsibility. As social and environmental problems received more public attention, the American people expected businesses to be part of the solution. Dollars once given to "charity" were funneled to "social concerns," and it became fashionable to advertise corporate good citizenship. Northwestern established its own Corporate Social Responsibility Committee in 1972, largely to monitor investment activity. The company pledged to make its investments work for the public interest, especially in the social and environmental areas. It is doubtful that the offshore oil wells or the Dismal Swamp drainage project would have won awards from the Sierra Club, but Northwestern's pledge was more than rhetoric. The company placed strict pollution controls on its industrial parks and, on one occasion, declined to invest in a housing project planned for a scenic section of the California coast.

At the home office, the light on the American flag outside was turned off and thermostats were turned down during the Arab oil embargo. Carpoolers received preferential treatment when spaces in the new parking structure were assigned, and the housekeeping staff learned to use phosphate-free cleaners.

In the view of some critics, corporations innovate in order to stay where they are. They become more liberal in order to conserve what they have — their reputations, for example, in a liberal time. Northwestern was no less socially responsible in 1979 than it had been in 1967, but fashions had changed and the emphasis was muted. The company no longer went looking for central-city investments. The Corporate Social Responsibility Committee found its mission increasingly indistinct. The annual reports no longer contained summaries of work in the area of "Public Concerns." The reports themselves, after being printed on recycled paper from 1971 to 1973, appeared on sheets fresh from the forest. In these respects Northwestern was no different from the overwhelming majority of American businesses.

A more abiding expression of corporate social responsibility was the company's attitude toward women and minorities. Since hiring its first female employee in 1880, Northwestern had not been a trailblazer in the field of women's rights. By 1908, 15 percent of the home office workers were women; by the mid-1920s, 75 percent. All, however, were single, and none were management employees. The first woman to enter the ranks of management was Louise Marie Newman. She became director of personnel in 1938, but had to wait until 1951 for promotion to the officer ranks. The post-World War II labor shortage forced a broader concession. Northwestern did not knowingly hire married women but, by 1956, the company allowed current employees to stay for up to five years after marriage. More than a few women left their wedding rings at home when they came to the home office for job interviews.

In 1951 Northwestern hired its first black employee, a young woman just out of high school. She was put to work in the Secretarial Department and told that, if she did well, other blacks might be hired. Despite enormous pressure, the young woman apparently convinced her supervisors that race was no handicap to performance, but progress in minority hiring was slow. In the mid-1960s Northwestern joined other Milwaukee employers in a campaign to promote equal opportunity in the workplace. The effort was informal and voluntary, but it did lead to a greater emphasis on the hiring of non-whites. By the end of 1970 there were eighty-six minority group members working in the home office.

It was in 1970 that the focus shifted from equal opportunity (leaving the door open) to affirmative action (inviting people in). Federal agencies were among the tenants in Northwestern's office buildings. Members of the Law Department discovered, to their surprise, that the company's role as landlord made Northwestern a federal contractor, subject to rather strict hiring guidelines. Instead of waiting for the compliance officers to visit, the company made a good-faith effort to develop its own affirmative action program. The demographics of every work unit were analyzed, and annual goals were set for the placement of women and minorities.

The federal authorities finally reviewed the program in 1975. As a result of their visit, the number of job categories was increased and long-range timetables were established for the "full utilization" of women and minorities. What had been a largely informal process was codified, and Northwestern learned to cope with a constantly changing series of federal guidelines.

The results were impressive. "Mother Mutual" was still a predominately female institution, but the distribution of women in the company was far more even. The ratio of women in official, manager, and professional jobs (federal categories) rose from 15 percent in 1970 to 43 percent in 1979. Their share of the technical jobs nearly doubled (to 68 percent) during the same period. Blacks, Hispanics, native Americans, and other minority workers became a more familiar sight in the halls of the home office. In the official/manager/professional areas, their ratio increased from 0 to 5 percent between 1970 and 1979; in the technician category, from 3 to 7 percent. Neither group was (or is) well represented in the highest levels of the company, but the days when women expected to type and minorities expected to work elsewhere had vanished forever.

The Human Environment

Affirmative action was the province of the Personnel Department, and few departments changed more radically during the period. Since 1937 the personnel function had consisted largely of screening, hiring, and keeping the records of clerical employees. Ferguson, first as head of a study group and then as president, broadened the department's scope to include all aspects of the human environment at the home office. In 1968 he hired Milford "Jake" Jacobson as the director of personnel. Polished, persuasive, and eager to initiate change, Jacobson came to Northwestern after seventeen years in a similar position at Montgomery Ward. Ferguson secured approval from the board to make him an executive officer. His position was the first new "cabinet level" post to be created since Robert Dineen arrived in 1950.

Under Jacobson, the Personnel Department grew rapidly and became a force for innovation within the company. Outmoded practices that had become part of Northwestern's folklore were abandoned and, uncharacteristically, new practices were adopted long before they became the industry norm. A compensation review led to higher management salaries and formal implementation of the Hay system in 1969. Two years later employees were allowed to smoke at their desks, ending decades of tar-stained washroom walls. Alcoholism and other drug abuse counseling programs were developed in the early Seventies. In every department there was a gradual shift to promotion by merit instead of by length of service, and the average age of the company's supervisors dropped sharply.

The most widely publicized step was taken in 1973, when Northwestern began to experiment with flexible hours. During World War II the Office of Defense Transportation had assigned different work schedules to urban employers in order to reduce the demands on public transit. The Milwaukee office gave Northwestern hours from 8:10 A.M. to 4:40 P.M. In 1946 the union won its demand for a 37.5-hour week, and quitting time was moved back to 4:10 p.m.

Before long the 8:10 — 4:10 schedule seemed as much a part of Northwestern as the free lunch. Beginning in 1973, however, the company allowed most of its employees to choose any starting time between 7:00 and 9:00 A.M. Some supervisors feared that their workers would lie in bed as long as they could. To their surprise, half of Northwestern's work force chose to arrive before 7:30.

A smaller wall was breached in 1979. Northwestern was perhaps the industry's last employer to prohibit not only coffee breaks but coffee as well. President after president pointed to the short workweek and the free lunch as exceptional benefits. The chief executives seemed to feel that any time spent drinking coffee, either at a desk or on a break, was a veiled form of theft. One fastidious officer feared that coffee stations would lead to an explosion in the building's "vermin" population.

Like an earlier form of prohibition, the rule was practically unenforceable. At any given time a substantial portion of Northwestern's management could be found at the Bilshure, the Pfister, Heinemann's, and various other coffeeshops in the area. In 1979, after years of determined opposition, Ferguson lifted the ban. Employees pooled their resources to buy percolators, and discreetly placed soda vending machines appeared in the home office for the first time.

Throughout its history, Northwestern had been like a Victorian parent, supportive but stern, wielding authority without a trace of self-consciousness. Rules that seemed arbitrary and old-fashioned survived at the home office long after they had vanished elsewhere. The post-1968 liberalizations were a retreat from that posture. They symbolized a cautious willingness to share power, to let workers control more aspects of their own environments. Jacobson saw the process as "doing good by doing good" — promoting productivity by encouraging morale. There is little doubt that the approach was successful. The number of days lost per employee fell steadily every year, and turnover in non-management positions dropped to its lowest point since World War II.

There was a paradox in the general movement. The growing flexibility in the company's personnel policies was matched by the growing rigor in its daily operations. The reforms initiated by Jacobson and his staff did not turn the home office staff into a dissolute pack of smokers and coffee-drinkers who worked only when they felt like it. On the contrary, Northwestern's post-1967 emphasis on the rational workplace required even greater intensity than before. Efficiency became a watchword, and performance was subject to regular review. The reforms were a subtle form of compensation for greater management expectations.

They were also a reflection of the times. However laudable the changes, they were influenced, if not caused, by developments in the outside world. The generation that came to work after 1967 was not inclined to respond to corporate parenting. Few people arrived expecting to stay until retirement, and even fewer considered Northwestern a religion. As Jacobson put it, "People wanted broader lives. They didn't put all of their eggs in the work basket." The liberalizations reflected the labor force's desire to be treated like responsible adults. There was little room for paternalism after 1967, and even less for the puritanism inherent in the coffee and tobacco bans.

As in so many other areas, Northwestern's personnel initiatives were timely. Ferguson's decision to broaden the department's role and Jacobson's enthusiastic response enabled the company to accommodate change before it had no alternative. Northwestern became an up-to-date, responsive employer, and in some areas, notably the flexible hours policy, the company was a highly visible innovator. The dynamism and the will to change that Northwestern displayed in the marketplace were apparent in the workplace was well.

Ironically, the various liberalizations were accompanied by labor unrest. The company's non-management employees had organized one of the nation's first white-collar unions in 1937. It was a home-grown, independent organization until shortly after World War II, when its members voted to become a local of the Associated Unions of America. The AUA was a Milwaukee-based white-collar union with locals scattered throughout the Midwest.

Labor-management relations at Northwestern were cordial. The biennial contract negotiations were generally spirited but never hostile. It was not unusual for Charles Groeschell, the company's chief bargainer, to go out and raise a glass or two with the union team when a settlement was reached.

By the early 1970s Donald Cameron, the AUA's leader, was nearing retirement age with no one to succeed him. He recommended that all of his locals affiliate with the Office and Professional Employees International Union, a branch of the AFL-CIO. It was a controversial suggestion. Some members of the Northwestern local feared that their group would lose its identity and its independence in a large international. Others argued that the move would mean a quantum jump in staff, financial, and data resources.

If affiliation was controversial among the members, it was absolutely horrifying to Northwestern's management. In an ominous message, Ferguson stated that the constructive relationship of previous years "would unquestionably be jeopardized and might well be severely damaged. The methods and the militancy of the AFL-CIO unions are well-known to all . . . . It would be a mistake for [members] to place their future in the hands of the AFL-CIO in the expectation that they will do better."

Despite his warnings, Northwestern's union employees, by a 76 percent vote, joined the other AUA locals in the move to the international. Like so many other developments at Northwestern, the transition was rife with acronyms. On May 1, 1972, NML Local 35 of the AUA became a chapter of Local 500 of the OPEIU (AFL-CIO).

To the relief of many, the new bargainers were not the strike-happy anarchists management had feared they would be. The 1972 negotiations were as businesslike as in previous years, and the two sides settled without acrimony. (Management agreed, among other things, that employees with at least five years of seniority would no longer be required to punch time clocks.)

The atmosphere was considerably more heated in 1974. Without coaching from the international, Northwestern's union leaders placed "informational" pickets outside the home office during an impasse in negotiations. It was a bargaining tactic, not a strike line, but the company's management was appalled. The union also held general membership meetings to discuss negotiations, an unprecedented move that prompted management to issue bulletins telling its side of the story. Bargaining sessions became more productive, and both sides yielded ground. The union dropped its demands for dental and eye care insurance, arbitration of merit raises, and other concessions. The company agreed to allow floating holidays for perfect attendance, compensatory time off, and voluntary payroll deduction of union dues.

There was more serious dissension in 1978 over an old issue: union security. For years the union had sought to make membership in the local mandatory, both to protect its standing and to incorporate the 30 percent of non-management workers who received negotiated benefits without paying union dues. The company had steadfastly refused to consider the proposal, describing a union shop as undemocratic and unwarranted. It was a strike issue, but the union's officers decided to press it. There had been change in the leadership of both the union and the company bargaining teams, and it was a time of mutual testing.

In the summer of 1978, after nearly twenty fruitless sessions, negotiations were moved to a federal mediator's office. The stalemate continued, and the union's officers called a general meeting to decide on a course of action. By a vote of 606 to 120, the members authorized their bargaining team to call a strike. The atmosphere at the home office was extraordinarily tense for the next two weeks. Pickets walked, arguments erupted, rumors abounded, and executives made elaborate preparations for a long strike. (Someone suggested helicopter landings atop the home office to bring in people and supplies.) At the next bargaining session, however, the company showed just enough flexibility to defuse the issue. Union security was still nonnegotiable, but management granted a 10.8 percent pay raise, agreed to consider seniority in promotions, and allowed union representation in the grievance procedure. The union had shown its strength, the company had shown its adaptability, and a strike was averted. The new contract was approved by a 91 percent vote.

The presence of a union at Northwestern, a benevolent employer in many respects, had long been paradoxical, and labor unrest was even more so in a time of personnel reform. The tension in 1974 and 1978 demonstrated, if nothing else, that workers were no longer content to accept the status quo without comment. No union members denied that Northwestern was a good place to work, but they showed a willingness to risk their jobs to make it, in their view, better. The turmoil confirmed that Jacobson and his staff were moving in the right direction at the right time.

Despite vehement disagreements at times, there was a notable absence of ill will between the company and the union. Personalities rarely intruded during the bargaining process, and the honesty and the clarity of negotiations generally impressed outsiders. Management and union were in some ways like mature marriage partners, each respectful of the other's role, willing to discuss issues openly, and able to get on with the relationship when an argument was over.

Sacred Cows and Sacred Bull

As Northwestern faced demands from its own work force, a much broader challenge materialized outside: the consumerist movement. It was in some ways a throwback. At the turn of the century life insurance had joined the list of businesses subjected to intense public scrutiny. The Armstrong Committee of 1905-1906 uncovered lurid scandals and flagrant abuses in the industry, and its findings led to a series of reforms that make up a substantial portion of insurance law today. There were echoes of the Armstrong investigation in the 1920s and 1930s, but the atmosphere was calm after World War II. Life insurance was a part of America's good life, growing with the country, contributing to its progress, providing peace of mind to millions. In the late 1960s, however, the industry quite suddenly found itself an object of suspicion, a symbol of corporate power and greed. The "muckrakers" of 1900 became the "consumerists" of 1970. In a world distrustful of giants, life insurance experienced a steady onslaught of criticism.

The movement began quietly enough. In 1965 Congress passed a law enabling discharged servicemen to convert their federal group life insurance to individual policies, purchased from any company listed by the Veterans Administration. Servicemen returned home to a flood of solicitations from competing agents, and in 1968 Senator Philip Hart of Michigan asked the VA to give them some means of differentiating among policies. Industry experts told the VA that it simply couldn't be done — a major mistake.

Hart had stumbled onto a consumerist's motherlode. Already known for his attempts to make big business more accountable to the public, he trained his sights on the life insurance industry. In a 1968 speech to a trade group, Hart said, "If it makes sense to tell consumers how much of what is in a package on the supermarket shelf . . . , it makes sense to tell them how much they are paying for death protection and how much they are saving when they plunk down an insurance premium." He threatened to introduce a Truth in Life Insurance Bill to match the Truth in Packaging Act he had shepherded through Congress.

The industry's response was slow and disjointed. In 1970 the Joint Committee on Life Insurance Costs recommended the interest-adjusted method of cost comparison. It was a relatively simple yardstick that took into account the time value of money. Insurance firms had traditionally arrived at the cost of a policy by subtracting dividends and cash values from total premiums at the end of ten or twenty years. The assumed interest rate in the illustrations was 0%. Interest-adjusted comparisons used the same basic numbers, but altered them under the assumption that policyowners could earn 4 (later 5) percent interest on their money elsewhere. The traditional method showed a net gain at the end of ten or twenty years; the interest-adjusted method showed, in essence, the net opportunity cost of buying insurance.

Some skeptics, notably Harold Baird of Northwestern, argued that it was ludicrous for the life insurance industry to impose a time-value standard on itself, particularly when no other industry used a comparable yardstick. Others contended that it was inappropriate to apply any type of investment criterion to the purchase of risk protection. The purpose of life insurance was not financial gain but financial security; applying an interest-rate standard to the product was like expecting an umbrella to grow. Opposition to the joint committee's proposal was vigorous enough to effectively kill it.

When the industry failed to establish its own standards of comparison, Hart was true to his word. In early 1973 his Antitrust Subcommittee opened hearings preparatory to introduction of a life insurance bill. The first person to testify was Ralph Nader, who called the insurance industry "a smug sacred cow feeding the public a steady line of sacred bull." He and a procession of other witnesses described the average firm as a dictatorial enterprise with overpriced products, misleading advertising, and unscrupulous agents.

The battle was by no means a one-on-one contest between Philip Hart and the industry. It became a genuine movement, nourished by a climate of skepticism and social unrest. Herbert Denenberg, a professor at the Wharton School of Finance, generated a great deal of publicity with statements like "The only thing 'guaranteed' by cash-value life insurance is continual erosion of its investment component." The industry did not take him very seriously until he was appointed Pennsylvania's insurance comissioner in 1971. A year later Virginia Knauer, head of the federal Office of Consumer Affairs, began to explore the issues of product comparison and sales practices. In 1973 Joseph Belth, an Indiana professor, published *The Consumer's Handbook*, which rated individual companies on the basis of a complex statistical system. During the busiest years of insurance consumerism (1970 to 1975), issues that had once been the exclusive province of actuaries and academics were discussed extensively in the nation's newspapers and magazines.

Insults were traded, threats were made, and statistics were lobbed back and forth like mortar shells. The rhetorical smoke grew dangerously thick, but some genuine issues emerged. One concerned the cost of life insurance: How much was for death protection? How much was an investment? What was the rate of return? Another concerned selling practices. In seeking a balance between their clients' needs and their desire for commissions, agents faced a potential conflict of interest. Horror stories were uncovered, like the one involving an agent who convinced an elderly widow to spend 68 percent of her income on insurance. There were questions about the permanence of life insurance; studies showed that nearly half of all new policies lapsed within 10 years. And there was concern about the effectiveness of regulation in states with small and politically pliable insurance departments.

Perhaps the least refutable claim concerned the obscurity of life insurance. In study after study, insurance companies were forced to confront the rather startling fact that consumers did not understand their product. A 1973 survey showed that most people found Einstein's theory of relativity easier to read than a typical insurance policy. In 1974 only 17 percent of consumers surveyed could distinguish between a participating policy and non-par insurance. Even Northwestern, a company in which net-cost superiority had been *the* overriding goal for decades, was not immune. In 1977, 42 percent of the Northwestern policyowners surveyed did not believe that there were price differences among life insurance companies. (Ferguson put his reaction mildly: "surprised.") Most consumers found informed shopping practically impossible. They might have kicked tires and pinched tomatoes but, when it came to life insurance, they trusted their agents.

As in the Armstrong investigation, rhetoric was followed by reform. In 1972 "Horrible Herb" Denenberg's office required Pennsylvania agents to give all of their prospects a *Shopper's Guide* identifying the ten best and ten worst companies from the standpoint of value. In 1973 Wisconsin, Northwestern's home state, became the first to require provision of interest-adjusted index figures before the client accepted a policy. Pennsylvania took that concept one step further in 1974, requiring disclosure data before an application was signed. In 1975 several states required a ten-day inspection period before a sale was considered final.

Partly in response to the initiatives of some members, the National Association of Insurance Commissioners began to play a broader role. In 1973 the NAIC endorsed the interest-adjusted method as its model of cost disclosure. Three years later the group approved a model regulation that required agents to give their clients both a buyer's guide and a policy summary before closing a sale. Wording and enforcement varied from state to state, but cost disclosure eventually became the law of the land.

Industry response to both the criticism and the regulations varied. Half of the companies were, by definition, below average, and some had a vested interest in cost concealment. There were howls of protest during some of the less-balanced investigations, and there was a great deal of self-righteous posturing about "demagogues" who insisted on "meddling" in the actuarial mysteries. There were also companies, including Northwestern, that found the basic message of consumerism congenial: life insurance should offer value, service, and efficiency. Even they, however, sometimes felt like doctors being operated on by first-year medical students.

Northwestern's executives, at least in their public statements, took pains to avoid defensive rhetoric in responding to the consumerists. The company had long been a standard of quality in the industry, a position that, ironically, caused some discomfort in the 1970s. Like a bright student in a slow class, Northwestern resented being lumped with some of its competitors. In 1972 Ferguson complained that blanket criticisms "tar us all with the same brush." On the other hand, the company saw that the informed public envisioned by the consumerists might well choose Northwestern. In another 1972 speech Ferguson called consumerism "one of the most positive and exciting things ever," and he added, "It can only help NML."

Northwestern, in fact, had little to fear from the various cost comparison methods developed after 1970. The company ranked sixth in Denenberg's *Shopper's Guide* and third in Dr. Belth's *Consumer's Handbook*. In 1974 the Hart Committee used 31 methods to evaluate the performance of products from nearly 200 companies. Northwestern finished in the top ten regardless of the method used. Wisconsin, one of the nation's most consumer-oriented states, prepared its own buyer's guide. A competitor facetiously called it "Northwestern's seller's guide" because the company ranked so high in the standings.

Although Northwestern's performance was commendable, some officers and agents found the results at least mildly disappointing. They had long been accustomed to a first-place ranking in the net-cost comparisons. There is no question that the various indices were subject to manipulation. Some companies moved up in rank by offering terminal dividends, available only if a policy was surrendered after a certain number of years. Others submitted only select-risk policies for comparison. And a growing number of firms adopted liberal dividend formulas that applied only to new business. In Northwestern's view, the practice represented systematic discrimination against existing policyowners.

Uneasy with some competitors and uncertain about some consumerists, Northwestern nevertheless maintained a quiet, cooperative profile in the industry. The company established its own Consumers Committee in 1972, composed of six officers and six agents. Northwestern generally complied with new regulations long before they were adopted by all of the states. Most significantly, the company reversed its adamant opposition to specific cost index and disclosure proposals. In 1970 Northwestern had almost single-handedly stopped a joint industry committee's approval of the interest-adjusted method. In 1975, two years after the NAIC endorsed the method, Northwestern was one of the few insurance firms to publicly support the move.

Daniel Gardner, the company attorney most involved in the issue, explained, "Northwestern Mutual ranks at the top no matter what method is used, and we recognize the interest-adjusted method does a better job than the traditional method." Only five states had adopted the NAIC's approach at the time. In 1978, when several companies challenged Wisconsin's strict disclosure rules, Northwestern was almost alone in its support of the state commissioner. And in 1979 company spokespersons testified on behalf of the NAIC's model disclosure regulation. Northwestern's reasoning was the same in every case: Better to accept state rules you can live with than to invite federal intervention that might be intolerable.

Developments on the federal scene were relatively few after 1975. Senator Hart closed his committee hearings in 1974 and introduced the Consumer Insurance Information and Fairness Bill a year later. It would have required, among other things, disclosure of lapse and profit figures before the time of sale, and regular comparison of actual and projected dividends throughout the life of a policy. The bill failed. Hart himself, known by now as "the conscience of the Senate," retired in 1976 and died of cancer late in the year.

Before his retirement, Hart had forwarded his files to the Federal Trade Commission, perhaps the government's most aggressive guardian of consumer rights. In 1979, after nearly three years of work, the FTC released a final report. It was a widely publicized summary of the major criticisms developed over the previous decade.

The report's authors concluded that the average rate of return on life insurance policies was only 1.3 percent. They found that arcane cost comparisons and insufficient data made informed buying impossible. They characterized the prevailing system as noncompetitive, discriminatory, and cloaked in secrecy.

The industry was quick to respond. The American Council of Life Insurance pronounced the report "reckless" and produced figures showing that the yield on insurance policies was 5.9 percent. Some executives questioned the motives of the FTC staff, and a few indulged in personal attacks. Others, like Northwestern's Dale Gustafson, stated simply that the report was not a good piece of work. Undaunted, the Commission actively sought disclosure rules more stringent than those adopted by the states, and Congress began to hear testimony on a new insurance bill.

The political climate changed before the debate could generate much heat. In 1980 Ronald Reagan and a substantially new Congress were elected in a landslide. Within months the Senate had drastically limited the FTC's authority to investigate American business, including the life insurance industry. The FTC report quite suddenly appeared to be the last large blast in a long salvo of consumer criticism.

Although the national mood changed, the consumer movement did not die in 1980. New organizations and new leaders appeared, less vitriolic, perhaps, and more constructive than some of their predecessors. The movement did not die, but it became sufficiently quiet to permit an assessment of its impact. In the critics' view, the major questions had not been answered and the essential reforms had not been passed. In the corporate view, life insurance had sustained considerable damage. Already battered by a volatile economy, the industry had lost its aura of sacredness. Agents encountered a public increasingly skeptical of their intentions.

Despite the shrill rhetoric and the sometimes capricious proposals, it is clear that the movement had a profound influence on the regulatory climate. As in the Armstrong investigation of seventy years before, the positive result of the outcry was an industry more responsive to the public it served.

The Growth of Uncle Sam

An ancient issue lurked just beneath the surface of the consumer debate: state vs. federal regulation. It had first come to light in

1866, when the Supreme Court ruled that insurance was not "a transaction of commerce" and was therefore subject only to state law. Five years later the National Association of Insurance Commissioners was organized to encourage at least general uniformity among the various state regulations. There was periodic agitation for federal regulation, both within and outside the industry, but there were no major developments until 1944. In that year the Supreme Court heard the famous South-Eastern Underwriters case. The Justice Department, arguing that antitrust laws applied to every industry, had indicted a multi-company insurance association for price-fixing. The Court ruled in favor of federal authority, and the issue was suddenly open again.

A year of frantic research and lobbying followed. The state-federal question went to the heart of constitutional law, and there were few precedents to rely on. In 1945 Congress answered the question by passing the McCarran-Ferguson Act. It left state regulation in place but required that every state pass statutes conforming to the federal antitrust laws. One of the major architects of the legal compromise was New York's insurance commissioner — Robert Dineen.

The issue lay dormant until the rise of consumerism in the 1970s. Insurance executives were struck by the fact that their most persistent critics seemed to be lodged in congressional committees and federal departments. Insurance was the last major financial industry that was relatively free of federal regulation, and the inadequacy of state controls became a recurrent theme in the testimony and reports. Senator Hart made his legislative intentions clear. Many regarded the FTC report as a stalking horse for federal control. A 1979 General Accounting Office study outlined in detail the weaknesses of state insurance departments. There was a growing movement to change the status quo.

In earlier years some industry leaders had openly advocated federal regulation. They had complained that dealing with every state in the union was time-consuming, costly, and often frustrating. The ranks of the pro-federal forces thinned in the 1970s. As one industry executive put it, "Would you rather be regulated by fifty monkeys, or King Kong?"

Some companies stubbornly resisted both state and federal attempts to reform the system. A few others, including Northwestern, became active allies of the state departments in their efforts to tighten local controls. In a 1975 speech Ferguson was the picture of pragmatism: "If the industry is unwilling to promote price competition and disclosure in the marketplace, we can expect a continuing battle to determine which governmental unit will fill the vacuum."

The campaign to federalize life insurance controls lost its momentum with the Republican ascendancy of 1980. It was, however, only one aspect of the government's growing role in industry affairs. The Employee Retirement Income Security Act (ERISA) of 1974 had added a dense layer of new regulations to the already complex pension field. The Securities and Exchange Commission had jurisdiction over equity-based products and, as more attention was focused on life insurance as an investment, the SEC's interest in the industry grew. The Privacy Act of 1974, applying to government documents, led to congressional proposals that insurance records (including investigative reports) be opened to clients. In areas ranging from energy investments to affirmative action programs, encounters with federal authority became more frequent and more intense.

As the acronymic maze of Washington grew in importance, Ferguson assigned one person to trace its course — Ralph Harkness. By 1970 Harkness was spending 25 percent of his time in the nation's capital, monitoring developments there and representing his company's interests. He had come to the home office in 1954 as Laflin Jones' assistant, and he had moved on to positions as an agency superintendent and a presidential aide. Harkness gradually became a roving executive, responsible for the Policyowners Examining Committee and corporate-community relations as well as federal affairs. His job description was as broad as his view of the company. With native dignity, good humor, and a sure sense of right and wrong, he became a gracious gadfly, a generalist who never hesitated to criticize what he felt to be deviations from course. Harkness was also the only executive, with the exception of Robert Templin and Dennis Tamcsin, who had joined Northwestern as an agent — a fact he allowed none of his peers to forget.

In 1978, with national concerns expanding rapidly, Ferguson appointed a full-time federal legislative counsel — Fred Sweet. An able lawyer with impressive political skills, Sweet coordinated Northwestern's response to both federal and industry developments. He had joined the company in 1968, just after graduation from law school. For the year preceding his 1978 promotion, Sweet worked in the U.S. Treasury Department as part of a federal-business exchange program. It was, he reported, a valuable orientation to life on the other side of the street.

Northwestern was not alone in its efforts to keep up with national developments. As the federal presence became more visible in the industry, so did the industry's presence in government. In 1973 the New York-based Life Insurance Association of America (dominated by the major eastern firms) and the Chicago-based American Life Convention (representing companies from the Midwest and West) agreed to a merger. A desire for more administrative efficiency prompted the move, but it also reflected the industry's desire to speak with one voice in the federal arena. Significantly, the new organization (the American Life Insurance Association) established its headquarters in Washington. The Institute of Life Insurance, the industry's public relations and research arm, joined the merger in 1976, and acronyms abounded. The LIAA and ALC had merged to form the ALIA; with the ILI aboard, it became the ACLI — American Council of Life Insurance.

Life insurance companies could soften the blow of death for their clients, but the industry could do nothing to escape the other American certainty — taxes. Of all the federal agencies, committees, and departments, none had a more tangible effect on life insurance than the Internal Revenue Service. In 1958 the government had let it be known that a new insurance tax law was necessary. When industry leaders met to plan their response, a major split developed. To oversimplify, it involved a preference for either investment income or total income as the basis of taxation. Most stock companies favored the first approach. They feared that mutual firms could avoid taxes by turning gains into tax-deductible dividends. Some mutual companies supported the total income method. They feared that stock firms would avoid taxes because their assets (and therefore investment potential) were relatively small — a result of their specialization in group, term, and other non-participating products. Northwestern, represented by Edmund Fitzgerald, was part of a group that favored the combined approach proposed by the Treasury Department.

Congress passed a tax law in 1959, retroactive to 1958. It used both methods in the calculation of taxable income, but it contained a novel series of compromises designed to preserve equity in the marketplace. The most significant, as it turned out, was a limit on the percentage of dividends that a mutual company could claim as tax deductions. Investment income, which became the major component of dividends, was divided into two accounts, one for the policyowners and one for the company. The IRS assessed taxes on the company

share. The formulas were without precedent in the annals of accounting, but the law worked for several years without major complaints
from anyone.

The lawmakers and insurance executives of 1959 could not
have foreseen the rampant inflation that began a decade later. When
the inflationary spiral rose, however, it pulled interest rates up behind
it. The investment income of insurance companies grew dramatically.
Under the 1959 formula, designed to solve a 1959 problem, most of
the income growth took place in the taxable company share; deductible dividends were reduced correspondingly. The cumulative effects
were staggering. In 1959 mutual companies (and stock firms that sold
participating policies) could deduct 90 percent of their dividend
payments from federal taxes; in 1979, the ratio was 50 percent.
Between 1959 and 1978, income taxes on all American corporations
rose 200 percent while after-tax income rose 350 percent. The life
insurance industry's position was reversed: a 500 percent increase in
taxes and a 300 percent gain in income.

Like their counterparts elsewhere, Northwestern's investors (and
policyowners) had the worst of two worlds. Already struggling, with
mixed results, to contain the damage caused by inflation and policy
loans, the investment managers faced the additional burden of geomet-
rically increasing taxes. As a ratio of net investment income, federal
income taxes rose from 7 percent in 1957 to more than 17 percent in
1979. The impact of taxes on the all-important investment yield was
equally dramatic. The difference between pre- and post-tax yields was
0.29 percent in 1957, 0.71 percent in 1967, and 1.33 percent in 1979,
when taxes reduced the net return from 7.41 percent to 6.08 percent.

Short of moving to Canada, Northwestern could do nothing to
avoid the law. The company could, however, take steps to blunt its
impact. The 1959 formula, in effect, taxed whole-life companies on
the difference between the interest they assumed they would earn (the
reserve rate) and the interest they actually earned. No one suggested
holding down investment yields, but it was clear that Northwestern
could make some adjustments on the other end of the scale. In 1968
the company raised its reserve rate from 2.25 percent to 3 percent on
new policies. The change reduced premium rates substantially, but it
also reflected a conscious effort to reduce taxes.

Although legal restraints and a desire for maximum fiscal
strength postponed larger steps, tax planning became a major home
office activity. In 1977 Northwestern, for the first time, divided its

policies into tax blocks and allocated higher dividends to those with higher reserve rates. In 1978, with both legal and psychological barriers removed, the company raised its interest assumption on new policies to 4 percent. It was the largest single move since Michael Cleary had reduced the rate a full point (to 2 percent) in 1947. Ferguson described it as "the course change that will bring the bow square into the winds that rock the boat most — taxes and inflation."

Not all Northwestern agents applauded the decision. A higher reserve rate meant lower premiums, and lower premiums meant lower commissions per $1000 of insurance. Many agents feared that, like the investment managers, they would have to generate even more income simply to stay in place. The Special Agents, Inc. (a name adopted by the Special Agents Association in 1976) was by far the largest of the field organizations. Its leaders carried the agents' concerns to Northwestern's management. In a series of rather stormy meetings at the home office, the group's representatives expressed their displeasure and requested a new compensation package. The company's executives refused, but they did agree to track the sales records of the 4 percent policies and to conduct a thorough study of agent income and expenses.

The results, released a year later, showed that the agents' earnings had more than kept pace with inflation during the 1970s. The study also supported the company's assertion that lower premiums led to larger policies and increased sales. In the first year of the new series, the average premium per policy increased 6 percent and total premiums 10.7 percent. A 4.7 percent gain in policies per agent accounted for the difference. They were meeting the challenge, but many agents wondered how long they would have to live on a diet of increased productivity.

The 4 percent decision created some tension between the company and its field force, but it quickly became a cloud with a silver lining. The increased reserve rate boosted sales and reduced taxes at the same time. More importantly, it stimulated home office efforts to apply the new formula to old policies. As described in the next chapter, it set the stage for Update '80 — the company's greatest marketing coup since Samuel Daggett borrowed money in his own name to pay the first death claim.

Change and Response

The life insurance business had survived periods of change before: the tontine excesses of the 1880s, the reform movements of the early 1900s, the boom and bust of the 1920s and '30s, the anemic investment climate of the World War II years, and the unprecedented growth that followed. The history of life insurance was, in fact, like the history of any other human institution: an endless cycle of change and response. It is doubtful, however, that change had ever occurred with the virulence and speed that were evident after 1967. The dollar value of traditional policies and the public trust in traditional companies eroded at the same time. Employees and agents demanded a new emphasis on personal freedom, and society demanded a new emphasis on corporate responsibility. Both the dense fog of economic turmoil and the glaring lights of congressional panels made it difficult for insurance executives to see ahead. Inflation was like a volatile element added capriciously to a chemistry experiment; its effects were both extreme and unpredictable. It turned the policy loan and tax formulas of an earlier time into monumental problems, and it made the investment strategies of a decade earlier seem as reliable as sixteenth-century maps of America. The insurance industry entered the heart of the rapids after 1967. In many respects change was the only force, response the only action.

At Northwestern Mutual, there was no panic in the employee cafeteria, and there were no reports of general agents going out in the desert to fast. The world did not end, but it certainly seemed to be spinning off its axis at times. Northwestern was forced to respond to bomb threats and congressional threats, union pressure and competitive pressure at the same time. The company recruited new agents and introduced new products while it was struggling to preserve old business. It emphasized strategic planning at a time when planning was both most crucial and most difficult. It spent enormous amounts of time erecting a new building just as it was erecting a defense against policy loans and taxes. An internal transformation was underway; developments in the outside world only added new pressures to an institution already coping with change of its own making.

There was a double irony in the company's position. Northwestern had always been an independent, even isolationist, firm. Like a small city, however, that suddenly finds its schools consolidated, its taxes raised, and a freeway through the heart of its business district, Northwestern found itself under the influence of forces beyond its effective control. As the outside world intruded, the company's independence was subtly compromised. Joint action with other firms became imperative, and environmental constraints played a larger role in decision-making.

Northwestern, under Ferguson, was aggressive as well as independent. The irony is that, after 1967, aggressiveness was really maintenance. Growth was necessary to preserve real economic size. Dynamic leadership was necessary simply to keep up with the pace of change. Like a canoeist in whitewater, Northwestern learned that the most effective way to maintain control was to move considerably faster than the current.

It was an accident that Francis Ferguson became president at the beginning of a convulsive period, but his response was no accident. The ironies notwithstanding, there was room to move after 1967. Ferguson set the tone. If Northwestern was no longer the epitome of independence, it could play a leadership role in the industry. If moving ahead meant keeping up, the company's response could be fresh and individual. The 8 percent program, the energy investments, the personnel initiatives, and the groundwork for Update '80 were all innovative approaches to common problems. Despite occasional wrong turns, Northwestern met the challenge of the outside world with the same informed vigor that characterized its internal operations. The company's competitive standing and corporate identity were both at stake. It goes without saying that anything less would have been insufficient.

The Workplace
1947-1982

Northwestern's neighborhood in 1960. The Northwestern Railroad depot (now gone) is in the foreground, the home office above and to the right.

Changing styles: the employee music room in 1948 (top) and the current cafeteria.

Top: *The Secretarial Department in the north building just after World War II.*

Bottom: *The current Policyowner Services Department in the new east building.*

Birthday parties: Francis Ferguson and Edmund Fitzgerald cut the cake at the 1957 centennial (top), and Ferguson cuts a somewhat more imposing cake at the 125th anniversary celebration in 1982.

Top: *Northwestern's first computer arrives at the home office in late 1957.*
Bottom: *The "electronic brain" in operation.*

Top: *LINK trainees learn the new terminal technology in 1976.*
Bottom: *The computer center in 1982.*

Upper Left: *Louise Newman, director of personnel in 1938 and Northwestern's first woman officer in 1951.*

Upper Right: *The Term Opportunity Program staff celebrates the completion of its effort in 1982.*

Lower: *The company held a lavish "4:10 Party" in 1960 to mark Edmund Fitzgerald's sixty-fifth birthday and his retirement as board chairman.*

The "home office addition" under construction in 1977.

Northwestern Mutual Place nearing completion: the east building in 1978 (top) and the entire complex in 1981.

Top: *The atrium in the home office is unveiled in 1982.*

Bottom: *Ferguson, Schuenke, and Donald Mundt at the opening of the walkway connecting the east and south buildings in 1982.*

Top: *Some members of the Girls' Chorus at the group's first concert, 1949.*

Bottom: *Retired employees at their annual summer outing in 1981.*

Top: *Balloons go up at the home office "fountain turn on" in 1980.*

Bottom: *Northwesterners go out to explain a new policy series to the agents in 1981.*

CHAPTER SIX

Northwestern in the 1980s:

How Far Do You Go?

Current history is best left to journalists. The distant past divides itself neatly into periods; the landmark decisions and events stand out obligingly. But the details of the recent past are too dense, the patterns too obscure to allow more than a tentative summary, and looking ahead is like driving into a snowstorm. It is difficult to see the road, much less the landmarks. Russell Jensen, Northwestern's senior planner, put it succinctly:

> Bells and whistles don't go off when a major change occurs. You don't call all the troops out on the parade ground one day and say, "Here's the new flag. Let's salute it." You're in the middle of living your life and everything is going on at once. You look at the facts and you decide. Things happen.

It becomes clear that the easy landmarks and turning points of the past were reached in precisely the same manner.

There is ample room for caution, but it is difficult not to conclude that Northwestern has changed profoundly since the beginning of the 1980s. Specifically, it has moved from a product orientation to a market orientation. The company has begun the shift from narrow to broad, from specialization to diversification. The decision, made gradually, without bells and whistles to announce it, represents perhaps the most basic departure from tradition in Northwestern's history. The details are hazy, the implications even more so. "How far do you go?" is the question of the Eighties.

This chapter, completed during the worst economic times since the Depression, brings Northwestern Mutual to March, 1983 — the end of its 125th anniversary year. The first section describes some of the more distinct developments of the years since 1979, including the Update projects, new tax strategies and a new tax law, direct recognition, investment flux, and the selection of a new president. Some of the events marked the solution of old problems; others represented new directions. All, in the context of a 125-year history, are late-breaking news. The second section attempts a tentative analysis of the move to diversification: the pressures that influenced the decision, its connections with the past, its implications for the future.

Late Bulletins

- *The First Update*. The 1980s got off to a fast start at Northwestern Mutual. Stung by rapidly increasing federal taxes, the company had already moved to a 4 percent reserve rate on its new policies. As early as 1977, even before the new rate was official, Northwestern had begun to explore the possibility of making it retroactive. The success of the 8 percent loan rate amendment program in 1975 convinced the executives that a broader campaign was feasible, and the project received top priority in 1979. Update '80 was born.

The program offered pre-1978 policyowners a chance to raise their reserve rates to 4 percent and to share in the resulting tax savings, which translated to a 14 percent average increase in the face amount of each policy — absolutely free. Nearly 1.5 million policyowners were eligible for a total of $4.5 billion in additional coverage. The program was tested in three general agencies in 1979 and offered nationwide in spring of 1980. To stimulate new sales during the campaign, Northwestern allowed additional purchase benefit owners to use one of their purchase options during the Update year.

Update '80 was an industry first. No other company had both the desire and the computer power to make such a costly, time-consuming program work. It began as a basic application of a venerable Northwestern tradition: treating all policyowners alike. It quickly became the focal point of the most intense marketing effort in the company's history. "Just watch our smoke," Ferguson promised the western region's agents in late 1979. The 1980 advertising budget was $5.8 million, triple the previous year's figure. The amendment campaign was re-christened "Get More Out of Life," and Northwestern was identified as "The *Usually* Quiet Company." The Super Bowl and other television buys brought the message to over 80 percent of the national viewing audience. For the first time, Northwestern sponsored a cooperative advertising program for its general agents, paying half the cost of local media campaigns. By autumn the home office staff was mailing 8000 offers, processing 5000 acceptances, and answering 900 toll-free phone calls every working day.

Ferguson couldn't find enough to say about the program. He called it "a showcase happening in our company's history" and "the most innovative thing that's ever been done in the industry." In one speech he brought back memories of the airily alliterative Spiro T. Agnew, calling Update '80 a "most magnificent manifestation of mutuality." Many agents did not share his enthusiasm, at least initially. Convinced that the campaign would lead to increased service demands and depressed insurance sales, they requested additional compensation. The home office refused.

The agents' fears were soon quelled. The Update year closed with a 67 percent rate of acceptance, and Northwestern reaped an abundant harvest of good will. In the company's long history, no single effort accomplished so much in so many areas as Update '80. In a time of sagging sales industry-wide, it helped to make 1980 the best year on record, with Northwestern agents posting a 16 percent increase in premium over 1979. In a time of rampant inflation, it provided substantially increased protection at no additional cost. In a time of rising lapse and surrender rates, it gave existing policyowners a powerful incentive to stay with the company.

Most importantly, the campaign was a convincing demonstration of principle. Coming on the heels of the highly critical FTC report, Update '80 made Northwestern a highly visible champion of mutuality and fairness. Consumerists applauded. Dr. Joseph Belth called the program "historic," and former Vermont commissioner James Hunt urged the NAIC to require that all companies follow Northwestern's lead. Update '80 proved that, in Ferguson's words, "Big business and good business are not mutually exclusive."

• *ModCo.* The Update campaign was a singularly creative response to an adverse tax situation. It enabled Northwestern to transform a burden into an advantage. Taxation, however, remained an abiding concern, and the company found another way to lighten its load: modified coinsurance.

In a standard coinsurance agreement, two companies share a given block of business, splitting everything from the receipt of premiums to the payment of death claims. Modified coinsurance (or "ModCo," as it was soon called) was different only in that it dramatically simplified the shift of assets and liabilities from the initiating company. In 1980 and 1981 Northwestern entered into ModCo treaties with two major reinsurance firms. The agreements were strikingly simple. In 1980, according to the company's annual report, Northwestern paid the reinsurers a total of $625 million, representing the investment income earned and the premiums paid on the Update '80 block and tax-qualified policies. The reinsurers, in turn, paid Northwestern a total of $622 million, their share of insurance costs and future benefit payments.

The key to the transactions was that most of Northwestern's investment income (the principal basis of taxation) went out to reinsurers and came back immediately as reimbursement for costs and benefits. It was no longer taxable income. As reported in the annual statements, Northwestern's federal income taxes dropped from $123 million in 1979 to $102 million in 1980 and $77 million in 1981. ModCo and Update '80 caused a dramatic reversal of the prevailing trend.

Made possible by an overlooked clause in the 1959 tax law, ModCo was used by scores of companies in 1980 and 1981. Some critics charged that it was a thinly veiled money-laundering scheme. Mutual companies replied that it was a forced response to the glaring inequities of an outdated tax law. In Northwestern's case, ModCo restored deductible dividends to their 1959 level. It also solved a risk problem. Nearly all of the policies covered by the treaties were those amended during the Update '80 campaign. Northwestern had just assumed an additional $3 billion in risks with no evidence of insurability, and it made sense to share the potential burden of increased claims.

Industry committees had been developing a new tax proposal for some time before ModCo was discovered. Their members found it difficult to balance the widely divergent interests within the industry, but there was universal agreement that reform was needed. ModCo gave federal authorities a different reason to favor change: billions of dollars in lost revenue. In 1982, finally, a stopgap tax bill was introduced. It contained dozens of provisions, including the abolition of ModCo, but two were of special interest to Northwestern: a grandfather clause protecting the ModCo savings of 1980-1981, and a minimum tax deduction of 77.5 percent of policyowner dividends. (The deductible ratio had fallen to 50 percent in 1979.)

The stopgap bill was largely the work of industry committees, and Northwestern was highly visible in the proceedings. Ferguson spent nearly a third of his time in early 1982 ironing out details and mobilizing support for tax reform. The Board of Trustees held its March meeting in Washington to review progress. It was only the third meeting held outside Milwaukee in the company's history. Fred Sweet, Northwestern's federal counsel, became the chief representative of a mutual company consortium working for the bill's passage. In an ambitious campaign called "Operation Contact," Northwestern sought "power referrals" from its field force. The campaign revealed that agents knew half the members of Congress personally, a distinct advantage in lobbying efforts.

Due in part to Northwestern's efforts, the bill passed with few revisions. It restored some balance to the tax climate, but the new law was clearly a temporary measure, applying only to the 1982 and 1983 tax years. A campaign for more abiding reform gathered momentum. The American Council of Life Insurance made Ferguson a member of both its board and its Tax Steering Committee. Northwestern was again at the center of the storm.

• *Direct Recognition.* As ModCo and the stopgap law brought some relief from the pain of taxation, Northwestern worked to remove another old thorn from its side: the demand for policy loans. The problem reached crisis proportions after 1979. The prime rate passed 20 percent in late 1980 and, following the established pattern, loan demand soared. Northwestern's net pay-out was $529 million for the year, more than $2 million every working day and nearly five times the 1977 figure. Of the $800 million in 1980 premium received by the company, policy loans, surrender payments, and commissions absorbed all but $1.4 million. New investment funds came largely from old investment earnings. In 1981 the net policy loan disbursement reached $567 million, and loans rose to a record 30.2 percent of assets.

Northwestern had long believed that heavy borrowing represented a basic inequity. As early as 1969, when the loan account was only 14 percent of assets, the company had considered direct recognition of borrowing activity in the allocation of dividends. Borrowers, because they contributed less to the enterprise, would receive a proportionately smaller share of investment earnings than non-borrowers. The idea was mulled over and modified through the 1970s. In a 1974 paper Donald Schuenke, Northwestern's general counsel, explored the legal aspects of the issue, concluding that direct recognition would probably meet the test of law. In 1976 actuaries Wil Kraegel and James Reiskytl prepared another paper that traced the history of policy loans and provided a cogent rationale for direct recognition.

Both papers were landmark studies in the field, but they did not end a stalemate that had developed in the home office. Some executives, notably Ferguson, favored a unilateral move to direct recognition on every policy in force. They pointed out that dividend decisions were a company responsibility, not a matter of contract. The nature of mutual life insurance (and the policy contract itself) required an equitable distribution of surplus — an impossibility when borrowers and non-borrowers received the same dividends. Others argued that unilaterally lowering the dividends of borrowers might be viewed as an indirect means of charging higher interest rates — a violation of contract that would land Northwestern in court. Legalities aside, they said, it would be patently unfair to tell clients one thing at the time of sale and then change the rules in midstream without consulting them.

More fuel was added to the fire in 1980, when the NAIC gave its support to a market-rate loan bill. The state commissioners proposed a floating rate based on Moody's Index of Seasoned Corporate Bonds, a measure that had shown relative stability in previous years. Northwestern actively supported the lobbying effort for the bill, and gave every indication that it would adopt the new rate as soon as approval was complete.

The home office deadlock was broken in 1981. No one had ever objected to direct recognition as applied to new business, but the conservation of in-force policies was Northwestern's highest priority. The company wanted to avoid, at all costs, extreme disparity in the treatment of old and new policyowners. The success of Update '80 convinced the skeptics that an amendment program could answer the in-force question. Northwestern moved to direct recognition on its new policies at the beginning of 1982 and began its second major Update campaign one year later. The dual approach, all agreed, would blunt the impact of policy loans without alienating either policyowners or regulators.

For several reasons, however, the company decided to retain its 8 percent loan provision instead of adopting the market rate. Only twenty states approved the NAIC bill in 1981, and Northwestern had no desire to delay action indefinitely. The stopgap bill had not yet become law, and it was clear that a higher yield on policy loans would mean higher taxes. Perhaps most importantly, marketing tests showed that consumers found a floating rate much less appealing than direct recognition. The new rate functioned exactly like the escalator clause in a mortgage contract. A policyowner who borrowed at 10 percent in 1982 might have paid 20 percent a decade later. The fixed 8 percent rate, by contrast, was a known quantity, and it made policy illustrations much more reliable.

Update '83 was launched with appropriate fanfare. The company offered underwriting concessions and other incentives to stimulate interest and to boost sales during the campaign year. The most important motivator was the record dividend allocation of $701 million, an 18 percent increase over the 1982 figure. Under direct recognition, most non-borrowers were offered a 9.75 percent rate of return, against 6.9 percent for clients who had stripped their policies of cash values.

The campaign was well-timed. Short-term interest rates had fallen to their lowest point in recent memory, and many consumers found a tax-sheltered 9.75 percent return extremely attractive. Preliminary results showed a 55 percent rate of acceptance. Compared to the activity of one year earlier, new loan requests slowed substantially, and there was a dramatic rise in loan repayments. After more than a decade of discussion, Northwestern had found a solution to the policy loan problem that was both equitable and effective.

• *Investments.* Direct recognition promised some long-term stability to the investment departments but, in the meantime, the economic climate remained volatile. The 1980s, in fact, have so far been a period of greater extremes than the previous decade. The prime rate and the inflation rate both reached peaks in 1980, the first passing 20 percent and the second rising to 13.5 percent. The bottom began to fall out in 1981, and the next year was one of the most disastrous on record. Inflation slowed to 3.9 percent in 1982, but that was the extent of the good news. Unemployment reached 10.8 percent. The real GNP fell nearly 2 percent. Business failures, idle factories, and families without homes recalled, for older Americans, vivid memories of the 1930s. There were promising signs of recovery in early 1983, but no one predicted a return to the prosperity of twenty years before.

Northwestern's investment managers made their way through the peaks and valleys with the same blend of caution and boldness they had shown in the 1970s. Investment planning remained a three-legged stool (fixed-rate instruments, a liquidity account, and equities), but there was a significant shift in strategy after 1979. Although traditional bonds and mortgages continued to make up the core of the portfolio, virtually every new contract contained some kind of equity kicker. The liquidity reserve, reflecting high short-term rates and peak policy loan demand, rose to nearly 13 percent of assets at the end of 1982. The third leg — equities — grew most rapidly in the 1980s. In an effort to boost the overall rate of return, Northwestern raised the proportion of its equity investments from less than 20 percent of new funds to nearly a third.

There was a corresponding shift in the company's structure. In 1973 the Real Estate and Common Stock Departments had split off from Mortgages and Securities, largely because they were involved in risk-taking rather than lending. By 1980 loan and risk were so intertwined that the division no longer made sense. Glenn Buzzard assumed responsibility for both real estate and mortgage loans in that year, and Gordon Davidson took over Securities when John Konrad retired. The Treasurer's Department was established at the same time to manage Northwestern's liquidity account (money market funds, preferred stocks, and marketable bonds). The new treasurer was Edward Zore, who had joined the company in 1969 as a stock trader. When Don Windfelder retired in 1982, Common Stocks became one of Zore's responsibilities.

As in the 1970s, equity investments were by far the most diverse in the portfolio. Real estate remained an investment of choice, with an increasing emphasis on outright ownership rather than complicated joint ventures. In 1982 Northwestern acquired a half-interest in Ghirardelli Square, a San Francisco chocolate factory that had been converted to shops and restaurants. In 1983 the company completed development of its wholly-owned Pacific Trade Center, the largest office and commercial complex in Hawaii. Other acquisitions ranged from a vineyard in California to an irrigated corn farm in Kansas.

Common stocks dropped to 1.9 percent of assets in 1981, largely as a result of liquidation to meet policy loan demand. It was their lowest point in more than twenty years. When a bull market materialized in 1982, the stock managers began to rebuild the account.

The company's investors became adept at a new form of equity venture in the early 1980s — the leveraged buyout. Northwestern typically loaned a group of investors (often the managers of the bought-out company) enough money to acquire control of a firm, in return for an ownership share and stock options as well as payments on the loan. Northwestern joined a consortium of insurance firms that purchased a two-thirds interest in Congoleum, a diversified manufacturer producing everything from floor coverings to naval ships. The company acquired a $40 million share of American Forest Products, which made Northwestern part-owner of 171,000 acres of California woodland and a collection of sawmills and lumberyards. Other targets of Northwestern-backed buyouts included radio stations, an office furniture supplier, and the leading producer of fried pork rinds in the nation.

Energy investments remained the cornerstone of the equity account, and Northwestern led the way into new fields. In 1980 the company recruited partners to develop a coal tract it owned in eastern Wyoming. Hampshire Energy, as the consortium was named, soon announced plans to build a $1.8 billion gasification plant capable of converting 15,000 tons of coal into 20,000 barrels of gasoline daily.

Buoyed by the continuing success of its coastal oilfields, Northwestern saw the venture as an excellent investment and a pioneering step toward national energy independence. Although environmentalists balked at plans to strip a prairie of its topsoil and ground cover, Wyoming's authorities approved the project. The plant itself was designed to generate its own power and release a bare minimum of pollutants. Hampshire Energy received a $4 million federal grant in 1980 to fund a feasibility study, and in 1982 the partnership was the lone finalist in competition for federal price and loan guarantees.

The only major obstacle to the project's success was its timing, the same block Northwestern had stumbled over in its early stock purchases, the REIT, college housing, and the resort developments. As the 1981 recession deepened, the price of gasoline moved steadily downward. The project lost much of its investment potential, at least in the short term. In December, 1982, Northwestern announced that development of the synthetic fuel plant had been postponed indefinitely.

The disappointments in energy and other fields were softened by an undercurrent of macabre humor. Investors joked about the neutron mortgage, which wiped out the developers but left the property intact.

Donald Schuenke, who became head of the investment departments in 1976, repeated a new definition of a joint venture: an agreement in which insurance companies begin with no knowledge but plenty of capital and end with technical know-how but no money. Glenn Buzzard described "the Julia Child recipe of finance," which produced deals so complicated that no one could identify the ingredients.

Humor was one sign that the investors had not succumbed to the rigors of an adverse climate. Northwestern, in fact, had developed a taste for the risks and rewards inherent in new ventures. Three 1982 developments — direct recognition, the stopgap tax law, and a slackening rate of inflation — gave the investment team some breathing room, but there were no indications of a retreat to the strategies of the 1960s. The net investment return, which increased to 7.8 percent in 1982, grew even more important as consumers became more yield-conscious. Northwestern never lost sight of its long-term obligations to policyowners, but innovation and risk-taking emerged as the clear paths to superior returns.

- *New Leadership.* In 1980 Donald Schuenke left the investment departments to accept a new position: the presidency of the company. His appointment ended years of speculation. When Ferguson took over the reins in 1968, he had said that no president should stay in office until his age forced him to retire. A decade, perhaps, was sufficient. After that time, he insisted, the fresh trails of the early years became ruts, and the executive could do little more than remassage his old prejudices.

In 1976, close to the ten-year point in his administration, Ferguson moved Robert Barrows from the investment side to the President's Department. It was clear to all that Ferguson was grooming a successor, and there was widespread support for the move. Barrows was a broadly human executive, a man with a healthy touch of irreverence. He had also proven his ability to see the broad patterns as well as the minute details of the business. Only a few weeks after his promotion, Barrows discovered that he had cancer. Despite last-ditch attempts to stem the disease, he died on May 20, 1977, at the age of 54.

Barrows' death was a deeply felt personal loss for Ferguson and many others in the company. It also forced a fresh evaluation of top-level personnel. Matters of succession aside, it became increasingly apparent to Ferguson and his board that the top job was too big for one person. The business had become so complex, the demands so manifold that no individual could manage Northwestern's affairs efficiently. Schuenke (shenk'-ee) emerged from a field of three as the board's choice to provide help at the top. On August 1, 1980, at the age of 51, he became Northwestern's fourteenth president and a member of the board. Ferguson retained the chief executive officer position and moved up to the board chairmanship.

Schuenke's promotion was announced as a move to more efficient management rather than an answer to the question of succession. Ferguson declined to set a retirement date, and he assured his colleagues that he would remain at the helm "for quite some time." The promotion, however, clearly positioned Schuenke as the man most likely to succeed. Like Ferguson, he spent the first year in his new job with no one reporting to him. He traveled across the country with his wife, Joyce, meeting the media, getting to know the agents, and broadening his view of the company. On August 1, 1981, Schuenke was named chief operating officer, with overall responsibility for fifteen of Northwestern's nineteen departments.

Schuenke is an alumnus of three Jesuit schools in Milwaukee: Marquette High School, Marquette University, and Marquette Law School. As a struggling young lawyer just out of Marquette, he spent a year selling insurance for National Life of Vermont. Although he freely admits that he was no threat to National Life's volume leaders, the experience later made him the only president in Northwestern's history who had ever made a cold call or closed a sale.

In 1958 Schuenke joined Standard Oil of Indiana and spent nearly five years providing legal assistance to the company's real estate staff. In 1963 he came to Northwestern, in the twilight of Donald Slichter's administration. Schuenke quickly established himself as a leader on the Law Department's investment team, specializing in real estate transactions. He became an officer in 1965 and an executive officer in 1974, taking over the general counsel position when Richard Mooney retired. His rise thereafter was rapid. Schuenke succeeded Barrows as senior investment vice-president in 1976 and moved to the presidency four years later.

The new president brought a distinctive style to the office. Schuenke is neither flamboyant nor physically imposing. He is, given his position, a remarkably unassuming man, even-handed, approachable, the kind of person you might as easily find on a suburban parish finance committee as on a major symphony board. He is, on the surface, a quiet man well-suited to managing The Quiet Company. But there is a great deal more below the surface. What has impressed

Schuenke's co-workers most is his thorough lucidity. He is a penetrating questioner and a willing listener, able to see through complex issues quickly and clearly. He is patient with details but impatient with intrigue, and so slow to anger that he is nearly unflappable.

Schuenke has some lawyerly qualities: caution, rationality, an eye for detail, and more than a trace of perfectionism. (He has been known to rewrite minor press releases.) But his approach is by no means clinical. Schuenke is a firm believer in reasoned management. He prefers to explore an issue thoroughly with his staff and then move to a decision on the firmest ground available. When conflicts arise, he is more likely to try persuasion than to pound the table but, in the absence of consensus, he has no difficulty making the final decision himself.

Schuenke is the first native Milwaukeean to serve as president since Edmund Fitzgerald took office in 1947. Fitzgerald was born into a Scotch-Irish family on the East Side gold coast. He was a lifelong member of Milwaukee's modest aristocracy. Schuenke, by contrast, is the product of a German-Polish family and a German-Polish neighborhood: Layton Park, a remarkably stable blue-collar community on the city's South Side. It was, and is, a bastion of some stereotypical Milwaukee qualities: thrift, lack of pretense, parochialism, reflexive honesty, self-reliance, a belief in labor and reward. Schuenke's father, who still lives in Layton Park, spent his entire working life in the sprawling Allis-Chalmers plant west of Milwaukee, rising from apprentice machinist to foreman and finally to superintendent.

The distance between Layton Park and Northwestern's executive suite is not as great as it might seem. Schuenke has long since left the narrow confines of the neighborhood, but some of the qualities he absorbed there translated easily to a home office setting. Schuenke's approach to his job is, above all, workmanlike. He did not actively seek the presidency, and he is neither overly fazed by its duties nor overly impressed by its trappings. He got the job, quite simply, by doing his best, and by expecting the same of others. Like his father, Schuenke comes to the job with a knowledge of the problems and a command of the tools. Whether assembling a project or repairing a flaw, he works with speed and concentration, and he takes extreme pride in the finished product.

- *Administrative Change.* Schuenke's promotion triggered the most sweeping realignment of top management since the 1968 reorganization. There was a rash of promotions, transfers, and retirements. Some positions expanded, others contracted, and a sizable group of newcomers entered the top levels, some of them considerably younger than the typical executives of the past.

James Ericson became senior investment vice-president when Schuenke was named president. A native of bustling Hawarden, Iowa, and another home office Scandinavian, he had joined the company in 1965 as an investment lawyer. Ericson began as a specialist in direct placement bonds, but he quickly became a sort of utility infielder. He rewrote agency contracts, handled negotiations for the first company plane, took part in the first offshore oil leases, and acted as legal counsel for the group that brought the Milwaukee Brewers to town. Ericson became Ferguson's assistant in 1972, and other promotions followed. In 1975 he took over the Policy Benefits Department and one year later replaced Schuenke as head of the Law Department. In 1980, again following Schuenke, he became Northwestern's investment chief. Ericson made investment planning a central priority in his new position. The shift to equities had a disturbing effect on cash flow, and Ericson instituted a system of reporting and projection that gave Northwestern a clear picture of its position from one year to the next.

Donald Mundt remained the executive vice-president, reporting to Schuenke, but his was the only senior-level job that did not change significantly. Robert Ninneman moved up from Underwriting to head all insurance operations. Russell Jensen was put in charge of the actuarial, planning, and research functions. Richard Wright, the first head of Field Financial Services, kept his controller's post and received added responsibility for the Data Processing and Administrative Services Departments. Ninneman and Wright reported to Mundt.

There was comparable change on the level below the group vice-presidents. Frank Kosednar, director of Policy Benefits since 1976, and Frank Rice, head of Administrative Services since 1974, literally traded jobs in 1980. Kosednar, a Milwaukee native and a Marquette University graduate, had joined the company in 1955, and he had been an officer in Policy Benefits since 1968. Jake Jacobson retired in 1981, and James Ehrenstrom replaced him as head of the Personnel Department. Ehrenstrom had come to Northwestern as a management trainee in 1958, shortly after graduation from Waukesha's Carroll College. After eleven years in the Personnel Department, he had moved to officer positions in Underwriting and Policyowner Services before rejoining Personnel in 1973.

Jacobson was not the only executive who retired. Between 1979 and 1983 Jack End, Ralph Harkness, John Konrad, Robert Templin,

Harvey Wilmeth, and Donald Windfelder all left the company for more leisurely pastures. As stalwart members of the old guard moved on, there were clear signs of a youth movement at the top levels of the company. Peter Bruce, who had first seen Northwestern as a summer law intern in 1969, replaced Ericson as general counsel in 1980. James Murphy succeeded Robert Ninneman as head of Underwriting in the same year. He had started in 1966 as an actuarial trainee, and he came to Underwriting as the manager of Update '80. Edward Zore, who became Northwestern's treasurer, was the third young executive appointed in 1980. He assumed responsibility for the company's liquid investments, and he heads the investment planning unit that reports to Ericson. Fred Sweet, the company's voice in Washington, was promoted to vice-president in 1982. Gary Long, a CPA who had left Western Publishing for Northwestern Mutual in 1979, was named controller in 1983. Of the five new executives, all but Sweet were raised in the Milwaukee area, and all five were in their middle to late thirties at the time of their promotions.

• *Reorganization: A Second Try.* There was an important change in functions as well as in faces after 1979. For more than a decade Northwestern had been striving to make the rational workplace a home office reality. In an effort to cut costs and promote efficiency, the work force had been divided into functional units and the units had been combined in functional departments. The company's axis shifted steadily from the vertical to the horizontal, and its focus shifted, in theory, from the skills of clerical employees to the needs of those being served.

In the late 1970s it became apparent that functionalism had been overdone, particularly in the Underwriting, Policy Issue, and Policyowner Services Departments. The division of responsibility within the departments made perfect sense in theory. Each was a honeycomb of highly specialized work units whose members labored at specific tasks with a minimum of distractions. In practice, however, an insurance application or a service request that entered one of the departments might have passed through dozens of hands before the case was closed. Accountability for overall performance was so diffuse that quality suffered.

Few home office functions have as much impact on an agent's livelihood as risk appraisal and client service. The departments involved determine which prospects will be insured, and how satisfied they will be as policyowners. The agents had once been able to discuss specific cases in detail with the medical staff and other home office workers. As the volume of new business soared, as the number of agents and home office employees increased, and as the computer's role enlarged, personal contact became difficult, and the potential for confusion grew exponentially. The home office received a growing number of complaints from agents about long delays, lost applications, and lack of accountability.

In 1979 a task force headed by Richard Wright began to explore the issue. "It will bring our service back to a level we're proud of," Donald Mundt promised the agents. The result was another reorganization in 1981. The Underwriting and Policy Issue Departments disappeared, replaced by a cluster of work units known simply as New Business. The country was divided into four regions, parallel to those established by the Agency Department in 1971. In each region one home office team was given complete responsibility for all new business, from pre-underwriting to post-approval processing. James Compere moved from Policy Issue to supervise the central and eastern teams; James Murphy moved from Underwriting to manage the effort in the southern and western regions.

There was comparable change in Policyowner Services, headed by Orlo Karsten. The department was regionalized, and service teams were assigned to work with each general agency. Specialists became generalists, as sixty-three job descriptions were compressed into six. The department invested more than 35,000 hours in staff training before the transition was complete.

The new systems promoted greater efficiency as well as greater accountability. In Policyowner Services, for instance, the number of pending cases dropped from 46,555 in fall of 1979 to 7860 in spring of 1981. Just as importantly, agents had one-stop service for the first time in decades, and many developed a close rapport with their home office counterparts. Errors, delays, and complaints diminished steadily.

• *EDP.* The 1981 reorganizations provided one more example of the computer's central role at Northwestern. Without the terminal technology developed by the Data Processing Department, one-stop service would have been absolutely impossible. Data-base systems collected volumes of information in one common pool, and terminals gave the regional teams fingertip access to any information they desired.

For Data Processing's managers, the hectic pace of the Seventies grew even more hectic in the Eighties. The decentralization process continued in areas far beyond New Business and Policyowner

Services. The number of home office terminals increased from 230 in 1979 to 640 in 1982. The department's staff continued to expand, rising from 264 full-time employees to 297 in the same years. The Update campaigns of 1980 and 1983 absorbed a great deal of energy. And there was continued change in the department's equipment. In 1981 Northwestern replaced one of its IBM computers with an Amdahl machine, in part to save money and in part to foster a spirit of wholesome competition between the two vendors' service teams.

Individual developments, however, have been overshadowed by another technological revolution. The disk/terminal systems of the 1970s gave data processing a remarkable mobility, but they had limitations. The terminals were simply remote units of the central computer, as intimately connected to the mainframe as an octopus is to its tentacles. The advent of the personal computer was a large step forward. Small but powerful machines and user-friendly languages removed data processing from the realm of the experts. The new units were more independent offspring than tentacles; they were not so much decentralized as detached.

The office of the future became the office of the present in 1982, at least in one department. Faced with a two- to three-year backlog of requests, the Data Processing Department began to promote do-it-yourself computing among the company's managers and administrators. The first small machines were installed in the Law Department in 1982. They were connected to the main computer, but they were capable of independent functions as well, including word processing, electronic filing, and personal programming. After a brief adjustment period, the lawyers and their aides found that the new system allowed them to do much more work in much less time. It was soon expanded to other departments.

The trend was even more apparent in the field. LINK I, conceived in 1974, had enabled the agents to order customized proposals, submit new applications, change policy data, and send and receive messages. The LINK minicomputers, however, were literally slaves of the home office mainframe. Their functions were determined by the company's management.

Even before the project was completed, development of LINK II had started. The second phase, begun as a pilot project in 1981, featured more powerful machines and broader distribution. (LINK II was available to special agents as well as district and general agents.) Most importantly, it gave the agents independence as well as access.

LINK II had all the features of LINK I, but it enabled the agents to program their own proposals, create and maintain client files, and process any type of written material. The system was operating in every general agency by the end of 1982, and installation in other field offices continued.

When Northwestern's first computer arrived in 1957, there had been foreboding as well as excitement. Some feared that the machine would cause a loss of human control, that it would place too much power in the hands of technicians. With the rise of small computers in the 1980s, just the opposite happened. Data processing was no longer the exclusive domain of the Data Processing Department. The department willingly surrendered power to other home office workers, and the home office (somewhat less willingly) surrendered power to the field force. Individual agents and individual managers had a powerful tool that they could use at their own speeds, for their own purposes. The computer had come full circle.

Diversification: Background

The early 1980s have brought more change to Northwestern than entire decades had in earlier times. Some events have been evolutionary: the shifts in investment strategy, the ongoing reorganization of the insurance departments, continued progress in data processing. Others have brought a sense of closure to some old issues. ModCo, the 1982 stopgap law, and direct recognition were at least partial solutions to the tax and policy loan problems. Still other events — the Update programs, the selection of Donald Schuenke as president — marked new directions.

All of these developments, however important, have been overshadowed by the central theme of the decade: Northwestern's move from a product to a market emphasis, from a specialist role to diversification. The decision was made gradually, and its full impact will be felt gradually, the details unfolding over a period of years. Although Northwestern has by no means abandoned its traditional emphasis on quality, the company's traditional outlook is changing dramatically. Northwestern will offer more products to more specific markets in a more integrated way than ever before — a basic change in perspective.

Northwestern is changing because the world has changed. Diversification is a response to a number of fundamental shifts in the social, economic, and competitive environmenťs. The company has never been a follower; trends that swept the industry have, in the past, left Northwestern untouched. The fact that Northwestern is changing its course in the 1980s indicates the magnitude of recent shifts in the marketplace.

By 1980 continuing social change had made the insurance market a moving target. For decades the prime prospect had been a married man with school-aged children and a wife who worked at home. In 1980 only 15 percent of the nation's households matched that description, down from 70 percent in the 1950s. There had been a startling increase in the number of both two-income and single-parent families. The divorce rate had more than doubled since 1965. People married later and had fewer children. There had also been geographic and economic shifts. The Sunbelt was growing at the expense of the Snowbelt. Women and minorities made up a larger proportion of the professional and managerial group. More people than ever were engaged in small businesses.

As the market splintered, attitudes changed. Most consumers still considered life insurance an absolute necessity, but they showed growing discretion in what they purchased and how much they paid. With the passing of the large family, many consumers had less to protect. With more than half of the nation's wives working outside the home, the need for replacement income at a husband's death diminished. With broader Social Security benefits and the nearly universal presence of group insurance, there was less felt need for individual coverage. With greater longevity, there was less fear of dying too soon and more of living too long. As the first children of the baby boom looked ahead to their fortieth birthdays, their focus shifted from protecting against losses to maximizing gains.

Some of the trends were reflected in statistical reports. As a ratio of the nation's disposable family income, life insurance outlays fell from 2.6 percent in 1965 to 1.6 percent in 1980. In 1979, for the first time in history, ordinary policies (individual permanent and term) made up less than half of the nation's insurance in force. Group coverage accounted for nearly all of the difference. There was also a dramatic shift within the ordinary market. In 1981 term policies accounted for 59 percent of the nation's new ordinary coverage, compared with 41 percent a decade earlier.

Economic change compounded the effects of the social trends. Face values withered in the heat of inflation. The volatile economy made consumers both less willing and less able to pay for permanent insurance. High interest rates made Americans extraordinarily yield-conscious. They had once been content with the passbook rates at their local banks, but by 1981 even small savers could earn nearly 20 percent interest by investing in money market funds. Millions of consumers turned to their cash values as a source of investment capital, and others began to doubt the wisdom of their insurance purchases. In 1981, 8.9 percent of the nation's ordinary policies in force lapsed or were surrendered, up from 5.2 percent in 1966.

The most far-reaching result of the trends was a pronounced change in the public's perception of whole life insurance. As consumers became more yield-conscious, as consumerists brought more information to the public, as inflation eroded the permanence of permanent insurance, the policy was split into two components: protection and investment. In life insurance theory, level-premium cash-value policies are not investments. Premium dollars are pre-payments for death protection, and cash reserves build up to pay the inevitable claims. In practice, however, more and more consumers expected whole life insurance to offer a competitive rate of return. The long-distance runner was expected to sprint as well.

This "unbundling" was aggravated by a trend within the industry toward investment-based products, notably universal life insurance. Developed in 1975 and offered commercially in 1979, universal life is notable for its flexibility. Premiums can be paid in any amount and on any schedule desired. As a fund accumulates, the issuing company withdraws some of the money for its expenses and some for term insurance coverage. The rest is invested for the policyowner. In structural terms universal life resembles a flexible-premium annuity with a term rider. In practice, after favorable treatment in the 1982 stopgap law, it resembles a tax-free money fund. Dozens of companies, riding the wave of record-high interest rates, introduced the product after 1979, and it received an enthusiastic welcome. Financial columnists pronounced it the perfect alternative to traditional life insurance.

Some older companies who offered universal life faced a novel problem: competing with themselves. As their agents promoted the flexibility and high returns of the new offering, long-standing policy-owners dropped their existing insurance and climbed aboard. One firm solved the problem, known as "churning," by simply abandoning $3 billion in "obsolete" whole life coverage and offering a "universal policy shell" instead.

Universal life was only one sign of dramatic change in the competitive environment. As consumers watched their insurance dollars more closely, the battle for business grew more heated. In 1960, according to an industry study, roughly 10 percent of all sales involved head-to-head competition between companies. By 1980 the figure had risen to 25 percent. Insurance firms outdid themselves in an effort to illustrate the highest returns, the greatest flexibility, the lowest premiums. Price wars developed, especially in the term market. Terminations, replacements, and churning reached epidemic proportions. In-force business became increasingly vulnerable.

The number of insurance companies remained relatively stable, rising from 1780 in 1970 to 1958 a decade later, but unexpected competition arose from a new quarter. In 1980 Congress authorized the gradual deregulation of the financial services industry. It was ironic that, after years of fighting off federal regulation of their own business, life insurance companies were threatened by deregulation in another sector. The walls between banks, savings and loans, brokerage houses, commercial credit companies, and insurance firms began to crumble.

There had been visions of one-stop financial service centers since the 1960s, and now the reality approached. Insurance agents already offered mutual funds and annuities. Interest-bearing checking accounts appeared. Credit card companies and retail chains bought life insurance affiliates. Insurance companies purchased stock brokerage firms. Banks began to broaden their investment options. More financial institutions offered more products and services to more people than ever before. At stake was the American savings dollar, and the competition for it promised to be a free-for-all.

As the marketplace became more volatile, independent general agencies lost ground to other distribution systems. In 1973 a *Best's Review* contributor stated flatly, "Almost everyone agrees that the so-called American agency system has seen its zenith. It is just far too costly." His prediction may have been premature, but rising costs and falling premium rates forced many companies to take a hard look at their field forces. By 1980 Northwestern was one of the very few that retained the general agency system in anything resembling its original form. Some companies, in effect, laid off their agents and offered their products through brokers. Others experimented with mass merchandising, and still others moved to the salaried branch manager system. Nearly all, in an effort to increase accountability, removed at least some of the distance between home office and field.

Like their companies, many agents found it necessary to broaden their horizons in order to prosper. There was a steady shift in emphasis from insurance sales to broad-based financial planning. In 1982 the American College, reflecting the times, offered a Chartered Financial Consultant (ChFC) curriculum to supplement its Chartered Life Underwriter (CLU) program.

All of these developments, from the splintering of the market to the broadening of the field, were a prime example of synergism — a popular word in the 1980s. The total impact of the trends was greater than the sum of their parts. Disparate outside forces combined to form a juggernaut, and the insurance business changed dramatically. Consumers, in brief, expected life insurance to cost less and to yield more. The implications were profound, and the industry's response took many forms, from abandoning the agency system to offering products like universal life. In the view of many, permanent cash-value insurance sold through exclusive agents had become a sunset industry, one whose demise was just over the horizon. Traditional companies were warned to change or perish.

Northwestern had ignored trends before. In the decade following World War II, when life companies branched out rapidly into health, disability income, group life, accidental death, and substandard insurance, Northwestern had resolutely refused to follow. The company saw no reason to tamper with its own success, and Edmund Fitzgerald became an eloquent champion of the specialist's cause. The prophets of doom who emerged thirty years later left many in the home office unimpressed. As a traditional company offering traditional products through a traditional agency system, Northwestern, like Mark Twain, found the reports of its impending demise greatly exaggerated.

The trends of the 1970s, however, cut considerably deeper than those of the post-war decade. Northwestern ignored them at its peril. There were abundant signs that the rhetoric of a Fitzgerald no longer applied, that the gulf between past practice and present reality was growing wider every day. The statistics were disturbing. Extra Ordinary Life had enabled Northwestern to reverse the drift away from permanent insurance, but the trend to term began to reassert itself in the mid-1970s. Term coverage rose from 28 percent of the company's new business (face value) in 1975 to 38 percent in 1980 and 48 percent in 1982.

Permanent insurance remained the greatest source of premium dollars, but there was an important shift in the type of permanent products purchased. In 1981, for the first time since EOL's introduction, it was overtaken in sales by the traditional whole life policy. No one was naive enough to believe that the 1950s had returned. Minimum-deposit buyers were simply using the higher premiums and higher cash values of the whole life policy to support systematic borrowing.

Life insurance sales as a whole flattened. After a 17.7 percent increase in new premium receipts during the Update '80 year, life insurance revenues grew only 7 percent in 1981 and a scant 0.5 percent in 1982 — the most disappointing sales year since 1970. Some of the lagging premium growth was attributable to increased term sales, still more to the faltering economy. But annuity payments, bolstered by the universal availability of individual retirement accounts, rose 363 percent in 1982, and disability income premiums increased 30.4 percent. The two non-life lines accounted for 22.4 percent of the company's new revenue in 1982, up from 13.8 percent in 1977 and 11.3 percent in 1972.

The tumult in the marketplace grew louder after 1979. Northwestern agents found themselves increasingly on the defensive, forced to explain in detail why their products were superior to new offerings like universal life. An Iowa agent complained, "I wear a fireman's hat all day long." Dale Gustafson, Northwestern's leading spokesman on universal life, admired the product's flexibility but considered its sellers' marketing techniques disgraceful. Universal life companies illustrated 13 percent returns but guaranteed only 4 percent, which Gustafson called a "cynical exploitation of a temporary circumstance" — high interest rates. If rates remained high, he argued, Northwestern's portfolio yield would soon catch up to the new-money illustrations. If rates continued their 1982 decline, the "new whizbang" would perish in competition with permanent insurance, which offered both stability and flexibility.

Universal life aside, competition became much more intense in the 1970s. As the insurance market contracted, especially on the lower end of the income scale, more companies tried to reach the upscale consumers who had long been Northwestern's prime prospects. Comparison shopping became widespread, and replacement ratios soared. Reported sales in which Northwestern replaced a competitor's policy rose from 2.8 percent of new business (face value) in

1969 to 7 percent in 1979. Replacement of Northwestern policies by others increased from 0.6 percent of new business to 2.2 percent in the same years. The company was winning more cases than it lost, but insurance competition was approaching a state of open warfare.

As competition increased, as new products appeared, and as attitudes changed, Northwestern's in-force business showed signs of erosion. The voluntary termination rate (lapses and surrenders) rose from 2 percent of all policies in 1967 to 2.5 percent in 1975 and 3.8 percent in 1981. The company's record was enviable, but it still caused alarm in the home office. In 1979, for only the third time in history, Northwestern paid out more money in surrender claims than in death benefits. (The first imbalance was caused by the Depression, the second by the huge Chrysler pension trust surrender in 1962-1963.) Surrenders outdistanced death claims by an even wider margin in the early 1980s.

Superior persistency had been called Northwestern's "secret of success" for decades. Renewal premiums were by far the greatest source of income, and maintenance of old policies was much less costly than acquisition of new ones. As lapses and surrenders rose, the company made conservation of the in-force business its top priority. The Update campaigns were convincing demonstrations of mutuality, but they were rooted in pragmatism. Northwestern was, in effect, "replacing" its own in-force policies with new ones. By offering existing customers the same features available to newcomers, the company hoped to discourage terminations. Equal treatment was viewed as both an ethical responsibility and a way to keep the "secret" of persistency.

The shift in product mix, the disappointing sales figures, the replacement activity, and the rising termination rates were all clear signs of some rather disturbing trends. It was the company's agents, however, who gave Northwestern the most compelling reasons to change direction. They, after all, were the ones out in the marketplace, making the calls and meeting the competition. As the environment changed, so did they. The company, after some hesitation, decided to follow.

Northwestern's agency system had undergone a paradoxical evolution since the 1930s. For decades the relationship between home office and field had been extraordinarily simple. The company manufactured a product, made it available to the agents, and left them alone to find their markets and make their sales. Northwestern

appointed general agents and monitored results, but that was virtually the limit of interference. There were no strings, no subsidies, and
there was very little in the way of sales support. The only requirement
was that agents sell Northwestern products and sell them well. No one
else was allowed to represent the company, and agents were expected
to honor the franchise.

This arm's-length relationship became considerably closer after
the Depression. The company developed a pension plan for its agents
in 1942. One of the industry's most sophisticated training programs
emerged in the late 1940s. Northwestern offered a variety of growth
incentives and subsidies in the 1950s, and expanded them dramatically
in the 1960s. LINK I, a standardized computer system, appeared in
1976, and LINK II followed five years later. All of these measures were
necessary to insure consistency and to promote sales, but they caused a
subtle erosion of the agents' independence. Although Northwestern's
field structure changed more slowly than any in the business, it was no
longer the pure entrepreneurial system of decades earlier.

The tide turned again in the 1970s. One indication of the change
was the rapid growth of minimum-deposit sales. Like the pension
trust business of thirty years before, it was strictly an agent phenom-
enon. The agents "mini-dipped" because buyers found the plan
attractive. The home office criticized it, with little effect, as a perversion of the permanent contract. Minimum-deposit was one sign that,
despite the closer ties, agents were becoming more independent.

LINK II, much to the surprise of the data processing managers,
became a focal point of the controversy and a symbol of the changing
relationship. The system made independent local programming possible. Many agents were already using computerized minimum-
deposit proposals (including some developed by a former agent who
had started an electronics service), and company officials feared that
the LINK II hardware would be used for the same purpose. They
decided, after prolonged discussion, that withholding technology was
no response to a broad policy question. LINK II was introduced
without restrictions. Northwestern did not encourage minimum-
deposit selling, but the company at least accommodated the trend.

A far more important sign of independence was the growth of
outside business. As more companies offered more products at lower
prices, the agents found it increasingly difficult to rely exclusively on
Northwestern policies. As premium rates continued to fall and term
sales continued to rise, they found it increasingly necessary to

broaden their offerings. A study of 1979 business showed that, of all the premium dollars generated by Northwestern agents, 39 percent went to other companies. Some of the outside sales involved group insurance and other products that Northwestern did not offer. The company's strict underwriting standards forced other prospects outside. In still other cases, particularly those involving term insurance, Northwestern's rates were not considered competitive. The agents, as always, were simply doing what they considered necessary to prosper in a challenging environment. Despite these qualifications, many officials found the 1979 study disturbing. Of all the statistics that compelled Northwestern to diversify, the 39 percent outside business figure was without doubt the most important.

The problem was compounded, ironically, by the agency expansion program that had made Northwestern a sales leader. The number of full-time agents continued to grow rapidly, rising from 3685 in 1977 to 4571 in 1981. Assimilation of new agents had been a concern since the expansion program began in the late 1960s. Northwestern's training program was excellent, but the constant appearance of new faces and the accelerating sales pace caused a slow drift away from the intense loyalty, almost the devotion, of earlier agents. An increasing number came from other companies and other insurance operations, and some found it difficult to automatically "think Northwestern." When a young Texas agent was asked about his previous experience, he said, "I brokered." When asked about his markets as a Northwestern agent, he replied, "I broker." His attitude was hardly typical, but the old patterns of loyalty had changed enough to cause real concern.

The general agents were most immediately affected. Their incomes were absolutely dependent on the Northwestern sales of the agents they managed. They recruited the agents, housed them, paid the utility bills, hired the secretaries, and shared in training expenses. Many were disheartened to find their field workers spending a substantial portion of each day in sales activity that contributed absolutely nothing to the agency. Some took direct action. By 1982 roughly 20 percent of Northwestern's general agents had signed agreements with other firms, typically for overriding compensation on cases placed by their sales representatives. They were functioning, in effect, as double agents.

The focus shifted to the home office. Many officials believed that Northwestern agents had the best of two worlds. They had exclusive access to Northwestern's products and universal access to nearly every other company's. As the volume of outside business grew, the exclusive franchise was in danger of being compromised.

The company had nurtured what many considered the finest field force in the nation, and the prospect of effectively losing it to "parasitic" competitors was chilling. In a 1982 speech, Schuenke reminded the agents that the home office-field relationship was "a two-way street." He continued, "Every time an agent sells a product outside of our system, it helps destroy that system." It was clear, however, that actions would have to accompany the words. Northwestern knew that, if the trends continued, there was an indeterminate point at which Northwestern's field force would no longer be Northwestern's.

Diversification: First Steps

As the pressures mounted, Northwestern had essentially three choices. The first was to do nothing, to maintain the status quo. Many feared that a non-decision would set a destructive chain of events in motion. Northwestern would watch other companies use its agents to grow at Northwestern's expense. As less business came to the company from its own field force, Northwestern would lose real economic size. As the company lost size, its agency system would become too costly to support, and it would either wither away or evolve into a sophisticated and independent brokerage force.

The second option was to abandon the exclusive franchise and contract with brokers to sell Northwestern policies. Brokerage would free the company to concentrate on product development and to define its specialist role even more narrowly. With a product line and a cost position widely considered one of the industry's very best, sales might reach undreamed-of heights. In time, however, because brokers have mixed loyalties and disparate levels of skill, there might be a gradual deterioration of underwriting quality, service, persistency, and therefore cost position. More importantly, a brokerage decision would sacrifice what was increasingly viewed as the company's most important asset — its field force.

The third alternative was to recapture outside business and recharge agent loyalty by giving the field force a wider range of products to sell, including, perhaps, group life coverage, health insurance, full-fledged pension plans, and more flexible individual policies. The company would attune itself to the marketplace more closely than ever before, identifying needs, designing products to meet those needs, and bolstering the ability of agents to solve a broad range of client problems. Northwestern would strive to gain the preeminence in several carefully chosen fields that it had already achieved in the ordinary life business, enhancing agent productivity and assuring company prosperity. Diversification would not only keep the agents from wandering, but would also insulate the company in the event that whole life sales really did become insufficient to support the enterprise.

Northwestern chose the third alternative. A basic reason for the decision was the perceived importance of client control. Company officials came to believe that, as the financial services industry became more competitive and more confusing, the key to success was the personal relationship between agent and client. Consumers were already deluged with direct-mail offers, advertisements, and blind phone calls from companies eager to manage their money. The informed counsel and the personal skills of its agents, the company reasoned, would give Northwestern a decided advantage in the competition for savings dollars.

It is important to note that, although Northwestern's focus shifted, the company never considered abandoning its commitment to cash-value life insurance. Diversification, ironically, was seen from the top as a way to preserve the company's preeminence in its traditional line. Ferguson described the new products to come as "extraneous" additions whose sole purpose is to bolster the agency system. Schuenke concurred, calling them "ancillary." Repeating a line used by every chief executive since Fitzgerald, he said, "We will never be all things to all people."

The decision to diversify was made haltingly, its elements unfolding over a period of three or four years. Perhaps the first large step was taken in 1979, when Northwestern commissioned two independent studies of the company's problems and prospects as it looked ahead to the 1990s. It was the first time since the 1969 McKinsey study that Northwestern had invited outsiders to make a top-to-bottom evaluation, and the impact was nearly as broad.

The two firms — Booz-Allen and Hamilton, and the Futures Group — submitted their reports in 1980. Both identified some impressive Northwestern assets: uncommon products, an upscale market, an excellent field force, an enviable cost position, and an insistence on quality. Both described the social, economic, and competitive challenges facing the company. They differed in specifics, but both firms recommended a significantly broader approach to the business. The 1990s study, as the two reports came to be called, urged Northwestern to move from a sales orientation to a marketing orientation.

Of all the terms in the ample lexicon of American business, few have inspired as much debate as "sales" and "marketing." On the surface, the distinction between the two is relatively clear. Sales begins with a product and works down to the customer. It focuses on creating the conditions (through advertising, sales support, selling techniques) that will stimulate demand for the product. Marketing begins with the customer and works up to the product. Its emphasis is on identifying conditions in the marketplace and designing products that will elicit the most enthusiastic response. Marketing can include, in addition, all the steps necessary to bring a product to market, from planning to design to manufacture to distribution to sales.

The distinctions are not so obvious in practice. Northwestern, for instance, established a markets research unit in 1958. Robert Templin became vice-president — sales in 1968. Marketing was added to the Agency Department's responsibilities in 1971. There was no clear consensus, but the marketing units were considered supplemental to the sales system, providing it with statistics and support. "Marketing" was a subset of "sales." This created a great deal of confusion in the early 1980s, when the terms were used almost as frequently as "life" and "insurance."

James McKeon emerged as Northwestern's most cogent and most vocal spokesman for the marketing concept, broadly defined. Laflin Jones had recruited him in 1968 to assist in the establishment of Corporate Planning and Development. When Jones retired in 1972, McKeon became the department's director, supervising an enlarged research effort and developing strategic and operational plans for the company. In 1975 he and Robert Walker, vice-president — Policyowner Services, visited Europe and Canada to examine the response of other insurance firms to prolonged inflationary periods. The Walker-McKeon report spurred the company, and McKeon, to look ahead with change in mind.

McKeon gradually developed a comprehensive vision of Northwestern's future, one in which marketing would become a central function. He foresaw the company reorganized along "lines of business" — the individual line, the group line, the pension line, the investment products line, and so on. Each would be managed by an executive whose staff had complete responsibility for everything from product planning to sales. Northwestern, in practice, would be unbundled into a number of smaller companies, each attuned to the needs and economies of its particular market.

The field force, in McKeon's view, would remain the key to success, but there would be a shift in emphasis from the individual agent to the agency as a whole. As the company diversified, so would the agencies. Each would continue to house generalists who made calls and brought in prospects, but they would split cases with other agents who had become experts in a particular line. The agencies would function like medical clinics, offering a variety of specialized services under one roof.

In 1980, largely in response to the 1990s study, Northwestern established a Marketing Department, and McKeon moved from the planning operation to become its vice-president. It appeared that the company was moving boldly toward a new definition of its strategy. In reality, however, the new department's responsibilities were a pastiche drawn from a variety of other departments. With the retirement of Robert Templin, McKeon assumed overall responsibility for the Communications Department. The employee plans division (the old pension trust unit) was transferred from the Agency Department, and the field financial services operation was moved from the controller's office. McKeon's research staff was much smaller than the one he had left in Corporate Planning. Supervision of the field force was still Dennis Tamcsin's responsibility, and his Agency Department retained a marketing division of its own. Tamcsin reported to Ferguson, McKeon to Schuenke. The new department represented an important first commitment to marketing, but many viewed the arrangement as a somewhat awkward transitional step.

The one area in which McKeon had an opportunity to develop a genuine marketing strategy was the pension field — a source of home office headaches for nearly forty years. McKeon had authored a comprehensive study of Northwestern's tax-qualified business in 1976, which led to his responsibility for the employee plans unit in 1980. (The unit's staff greeted the move with unbridled joy.) In McKeon's view, the pension field had caused so much discomfort because Northwestern insisted on treating it like the individual life field. He and his staff developed a nine-phase program tailored to the market's particular needs. Dividend rates on tax-qualified insurance products were raised, annuity rates and options were liberalized, plan administration and proposal services were computerized. Northwestern trained small groups of agents as experts in the pension field and returned them to their agencies to serve as in-house specialists. The company even organized, for tax purposes, a stock subsidiary through which its pension products will be sold.

One change was especially timely. Northwestern had been selling individual retirement annuities to self-employed persons since 1975, but an 8 percent front-end charge made them less than competitive. In 1981, as part of the nine-point program in the tax-qualified field, the company readjusted the contract and removed the loading. The SEC approved the changes in December, and two weeks later every working American was eligible for an IRA. Northwestern's IRA premiums increased 1146 percent in 1982.

None of the steps was a radical departure from company policy. Northwestern remained a provider of individual retirement insurance and annuity products, sold largely to companies with twenty-five or fewer employees. But the contracts were more competitive, service was more efficient, and the overall approach was more appropriate to the market. Sales results have been well ahead of the established goals. It appeared that Northwestern was finally finding its niche in a field it had entered reluctantly in the late 1930s.

Formation of the Marketing Department and adoption of a new pension strategy indicated Northwestern's desire to become a market-oriented company. An even clearer sign was the essentially new product line introduced in 1982. Northwestern had, over the previous few decades, moved a considerable distance from the "plain vanilla" whole life policy of the past. The 1982 offerings, however, were less the continuation of a trend than a new approach to the business. They met the competition, appealed to the markets, and accommodated the agents in ways more direct than ever before. "We're competing with dazzlers," Ferguson said. "It's time for us to move out the heavy artillery."

The most novel addition to Northwestern's arsenal in 1982 was Extra Ordinary Term. It is, like Extra Ordinary Life, a hybrid contract. It begins as a level-premium term-to-65 policy (60 percent of face amount) with a layer of extra term protection (40 percent). Dividends are used to replace the "extra" protection with paid-up additions to the original term policy. With that accomplished, they purchase paid-up whole life coverage, which becomes effective when the term policy expires at age 65. The owner ends up with cash-value insurance equal to roughly half of the original face amount.

EOT was hailed as "the best of both worlds" at its introduction. It combines the low premiums of term insurance and the permanence of whole life. EOT is a leaner version of EOL, designed for a leaner market. It has, however, no borrowing privilege, and its minimum face amount is $100,000. Northwestern hoped that, despite the high minimum, EOT would be used to upgrade term business rather than to replace whole life policies.

The new product was accompanied by other changes in the term line. Premium rates, which the agent associations had long criticized as excessively high, were reduced sharply. Northwestern launched a small-scale Update campaign to give existing term owners the benefit of the new rates. More riders, including the additional purchase benefit, were made available. And Northwestern developed a Term Opportunity Program that made it easier for term owners to increase their coverage or to convert their insurance to whole life policies.

There was comparable change on the other end of the scale. Permanent insurance rates dropped dramatically. Northwestern became one of the last firms in the industry to give non-smokers preferential price treatment. As other rates declined, the company offered an increasing whole life policy, whose premiums and cash values rose at a specified rate every year. The policy was a direct accommodation of the minimum-deposit trend; Northwestern was hoping to isolate the business rather than encourage it.

The company tried to accommodate substandard risks as well as minimum-deposit buyers. Instead of rejecting an application on medical grounds or charging a prohibitively high premium, Northwestern, beginning in 1978, sold many of its "rated" cases to reinsurance firms on a bid basis. The results were lower premiums for clients and more business for Northwestern. In 1982 the reinsurance program was responsible for 2000 policies with $8 million of annual premium.

A joint whole life contract was designed for clients who were either marriage or business partners. An indexed protection benefit (added in 1981) answered agents' requests for an inflation-sensitive product. The coverage (and the premiums) of IPB clients rose automatically at the inflation rate (Consumer Price Index) or at 8 percent, whichever was lower, every year. Although Northwestern hoped that its IPB rider would become as widely used as the accidental death benefit, it was attached to only 16 percent of eligible policies in the first year it was offered.

Although life insurance remained Northwestern's specialty, the non-life products received more and more attention after 1979. The annuity line was expanded and liberalized, particularly in the pension field. Disability income premium rates were lowered and the contract's coverage was broadened. In 1982 — to the surprise of some insiders — Northwestern was the nation's fourth largest disability income insurer, with more than $52 million of premiums in force.

All of the new contracts, riders, rates, and amendments gave Northwestern products an unprecedented flexibility. A client could, with the help of an agent, mix and match the products in any number of combinations, buying Northwestern term, for instance, and investing the difference in a Northwestern IRA. And all new cash-value sales were made on the basis of direct recognition. A record dividend increase and higher yields for non-borrowers made Northwestern insurance an extremely competitive investment. The company was going to market.

More radical ideas were at least discussed. One option was variable life insurance, a policy with fixed premiums and a death benefit indexed to investment performance. The company's actuaries also laid the groundwork for a universal life contract Northwestern could call its own. There was intense interest for a time in group health insurance, designed for the small business market. McKeon and his colleagues spent several months pursuing the idea in 1981, but the Board of Trustees expressed grave misgivings. Medical costs were rising out of control, health insurance firms were losing money, and huge premium bills were infuriating employers with group plans. The 1981 Policyowners Examining Committee concurred with the board, stating that group health insurance might be "dilutive of the company's excellence." In early 1982 the proposal was quietly dropped.

All of the products developed, discussed, and even dropped were tangible evidence of the shift in Northwestern's focus. The company was becoming less monolithic and more responsive, less genteel and more aggressive. The change was apparent in Northwestern's attitude toward rate of return. Investment yields and dividend returns had once been nearly as obscure, from the consumer's viewpoint, as mortality assumptions and expense loadings. Now, especially in the Update '83 campaign, returns were openly offered as evidence that cash-value insurance could compete with the "dazzlers" mentioned by Ferguson.

The change was apparent in the company's rhetoric. In Northwestern's reports and periodicals, terms like "financial services," "manufacturing capacity," and even "profit leader" began to appear where "insurance," "product design," and "operating gains" might have been used before.

The change was apparent in the company's television advertising. Northwestern had always been a generic advertiser, projecting its image quietly, gently, sometimes vaguely. The campaigns of the early 1980s were far different. They featured specific products and services. They mentioned costs. They used humor, not always subtly. They called Northwestern "a tough act to follow." In 1982 Santo Saliture, the company's advertising manager, said, "The gloves are off for good."

Despite the dramatic changes in both tone and content, Northwestern had not really made up its corporate mind in early 1982. The company had a Marketing Department, but the unit's marketing responsibilities were somewhat circumscribed. There was an abundance of new products, but none weakened Northwestern's reputation as a specialist in individual life insurance. Memos circulated and discussions went on endlessly, but there were no comprehensive plans to make diversification a reality. Northwestern had entered, perhaps in 1979, a transitional zone. There was confusion, anticipation, some tension. But there was also motion. Like a gigantic ship, one that takes miles to stop and miles to turn, Northwestern was gearing up for a definite change in course.

The Year of Decision

On March 2, 1982, Northwestern completed its 125th year of existence as a mutual life insurance company. That in itself was enough to make the year a milestone. For other reasons, however, 1982 may well be remembered as a turning point, a watershed, the end of before and the beginning of after. In 1982 Northwestern made up its mind.

Celebration preceded decision. The March anniversary was observed with appropriate fanfare. There were balloons, bands, gifts, and speeches, but the centerpiece of the home office party was an 850-pound cake, a high-calorie replica of the south building, complete with buttercream columns. The observance continued long after the cake was eaten. Northwestern's heritage was a recurrent theme in speeches, meetings, and reports. The company prepared commemorative calendars, assembled historical displays and, perhaps not incidentally, commissioned this book.

An even more lavish observance marked the completion of Northwestern Mutual Place. Demolition of the north building, renovation of the south, and construction of the atrium had continued since the end of 1979. By late 1981 only detail work remained: bricks for the plaza, fans for the second-story walkway, stones for the atrium pool. On July 16, 1982, home office employees paraded outside for the formal dedication. The executives made brief speeches. ("I have nothing against workmen," Ferguson said, "but thank God they're gone.") Champagne glasses were raised, and the project was officially completed.

The ceremony was followed in the next two weeks by a festive ice cream social for employees and their families, receptions for Milwaukee's business leaders and Northwestern's immediate neighbors, and special tours for agents attending the annual meeting. There had been nagging delays and costly overruns (and the plaza fountain still leaked), but Northwestern was confident that it had received value for its money. The Building Advisory Committee, its ten-year odyssey over, quietly disbanded.

Another Milwaukee project was dedicated a few weeks later and a few blocks west — the Grand Avenue shopping mall. It had begun several years before as a proposal of the Milwaukee Redevelopment Corporation, which was headed by Ferguson. Working with city officials and private developers, the MRC had developed plans for a multi-level retail center linking the downtown area's two major department stores — Gimbels and Boston Store. Its focal point was the Plankinton Arcade, an underutilized but elegant promenade with skylights, a fountain, and cast-iron railings. Milwaukee's main street had been known as Grand Avenue earlier in the century, and it emerged as the ideal name for a project blending new and old.

Skeptics came out of the woodwork, including the home office woodwork, when the plans were announced. Ferguson persisted. He lent his considerable weight to promotional efforts on the mall's behalf. More importantly, Northwestern provided $30 million of the $35 million in private capital required for the project, including an $18.7 million loan to the developers. When other investors did not step forward, Northwestern paid $5.5 million for all of the MRC's preferred stock, and the company purchased outright one of the old commercial buildings at the heart of the project.

The Grand Avenue was dedicated in August, 1982. Home office employees received an hour off to attend the festivities, and many heard Mayor Henry Maier call Ferguson "a civic fullback" and "the indispensable man." Northwestern's investment in the mall had been an act of civic faith, a tangible contribution to downtown revitalization efforts. As the project quickly developed a land-office business, it became clear that the investment was justified on financial grounds as well.

Northwestern Mutual Place and the Grand Avenue mall were important beginnings for the company and its home city, but 1982 marked an important conclusion as well. In September Francis Ferguson announced that, after more than fourteen years on the job, he was stepping down as Northwestern's chief executive officer. His decision was effective on March 1, 1983, when Donald Schuenke took over the reins. Ferguson remained chairman of the board and continued to represent Northwestern in the industry's campaign for permanent tax reform, but he planned, characteristically, to spend most of his time on the 1400-acre farm he had purchased in south-central Nebraska.

The decision was in some ways a throwback to the actions of an earlier executive — John C. Johnston himself. Like the company's founder, Ferguson was leaving a highly successful career in the city and moving west to open country. At 61, he wanted to return to his first love, and his son-in-law's decision to manage the farm gave Ferguson all the reason he needed to step down. In a farewell address to the management staff, he said that his first priorities included classes in welding and diesel mechanics. He announced no plans to start a mutual life insurance company in the wilds of Nebraska.

Ferguson's personal decision was made somewhat easier by a company decision. The 1990s study, like the McKinsey survey before it, had forced Northwestern to dredge up its preconceptions and examine them against current realities. The study, released in 1980, spurred endless discussions in the next two years. The Marketing Department was established and the product line was altered significantly, but no one felt that either move constituted an overall strategy. The company was flirting with the final decision like a nervous suitor.

The 1982 planning rally at Green Lake, Wisconsin, proved to be a turning point. In preparation for the rally, Ferguson asked his executives and a number of agents to describe their visions of Northwestern in 1992. The ensuing discussions were clarified to some extent by the concept of "driving force." The term, coined by management expert Benjamin Tregoe, referred to an organization's psychological core, the wellspring of its behavior, the motive underlying its strategies. Tregoe developed a list of nine alternative forces and warned, "Unless the driving force is recognized, attempts to change [the organization's] direction will be futile."

In a series of meetings before the rally and at the rally itself, the management team spent hours pondering what lay at the company's core. There was substantial agreement, finally, that Northwestern had always been a product-driven enterprise. It took its identity from the contract it offered: permanent, high-quality, low-net-cost, individual life insurance. There was also agreement that external forces made it necessary for the company to become an increasingly market-driven organization. No one suggested a retreat from high quality or low cost, but there was a new willingness to follow the lead of the marketplace.

Northwestern, at the same time, had no wish to abandon cash-value insurance or to surrender its initiative to blind market forces. The executives concluded that diversification was necessary, but they saw diversification as a way to broaden the time-honored circle of success, to strengthen the bonds between agents, policyowners, and the home office. If the home office made more products available, the agents would have less reason to write business with other companies, and policyowners would have less reason to seek the services of other agents. All concerned would receive more of what they needed. The company as a whole would be more efficient, more productive, and more interdependent. The result, looking ahead to 1992, was described as a "boutique." Northwestern's products would focus on living too long, dying too soon, and much of what occurred in between.

In a speech to the management staff shortly after the rally, Ferguson said, "Group insurance has been an issue around here for as long as I can remember. I am glad to tell you it is an issue no longer." One idol had fallen, and there were soon others. He announced that the company might broaden its focus to include other financial services, like personal investment assistance and cash flow management. At the same time, Ferguson pledged continued allegiance to whole life insurance. The future was taking shape.

The planning rally had crystallized an evolving sense of urgency. Action followed quickly. In June Robert Carlson was hired as a senior vice-president in charge of marketing. A Minneapolis native with a doctorate from the University of Minnesota, Carlson came to Northwestern after seventeen years with the Hartford-based

Life Insurance Marketing and Research Association. As the head of LIMRA's research unit, he had become one of the nation's leading experts on management and marketing strategy. He had also become a Northwestern policyowner.

The new emphasis on diversification and marketing required a new organizational structure. Since 1980 McKeon had headed the marketing effort and reported to Schuenke; Tamcsin ran the sales operation and reported to Ferguson. The appointment of Carlson enabled Northwestern to develop, for the first time, a truly comprehensive strategy. Both Tamcsin and McKeon reported to him. It was the first time in history (with the exception of Robert Templin's tenure) that the agency vice-president reported to someone other than the chief executive. It was also the first time since 1950, when Robert Dineen arrived, that Northwestern had hired a newcomer to fill a senior management post. The breaking of both precedents indicated the absolute importance of marketing in Northwestern's vision of the future.

Carlson moved from theory to practice, from research to application. After years spent as an observer and advisor, he was suddenly in charge of a major operation in a major company. Although the pace was considerably faster, Carlson had few adjustment problems. With the full support of Schuenke, he quickly developed plans to bring the company's structure and operating systems into line with its new emphasis on diversification.

September, 1982, was an extraordinary month at Northwestern. Carlson reported for work. Ferguson announced his decision to step down as chief executive. The real estate investment trust (REIT) was dissolved. And the company announced its acquisition of two smaller firms: Robert W. Baird and Company, and Standard of America Life Insurance Company. Baird, headquartered in Milwaukee, is Wisconsin's largest investment banking organization, with sixteen branch offices in the state and nine elsewhere in the Midwest. It offers a full range of stocks, bonds, mutual funds, and other investment products, all analyzed by one of the largest research departments west of New York. Standard of America, based in suburban Chicago, is a stock company specializing in group life and disability income insurance for the employer market. Its seventy-five agents also sell group health insurance in conjunction with a number of Blue Cross and Blue Shield organizations. The company is licensed to sell in forty states. Until the 1982 acquisition, Standard was a subsidiary of the Sundstrand Corporation, a high-technology aerospace firm.

The implications were not immediately clear. Baird's most important clients are individuals from the same income and educational strata served by Northwestern. Standard of America works in the same levels of the business market cultivated by many Northwestern agents. The acquisitions clearly gave the company opportunities to branch out into both financial services, broadly defined, and employer-sponsored insurance products. They were announced, however, as transitional measures that, in the meantime, made sense as investments.

The acquisitions were, if nothing else, an unmistakable public signal that Northwestern had changed. The company, after months of discussion, had done something. Smoke had erupted into flame. Whatever the specific implications, the Baird and Standard purchases may be remembered in years to come as early steps on the long road to diversification.

Northwestern looks at the world somewhat differently now. Some elements of its change in direction are definite. The company will sell a variety of group products. It will continue to concentrate on the individual market, but there will be new emphasis on small businesses, corporate executives, and other specific markets. As the company broadens its offerings, there will be a shift to agent specialization and an expanded commitment to the general agency system as a whole.

Other elements of the change are indefinite. Northwestern may manufacture and sell all of its own products, offer them through subsidiaries (formed or acquired), or diversify by negotiating "wholesale" agreements with other manufacturers. The company may offer fee services like cash management, and annuities may become only one part of its investment product line. Northwestern may acquire or form an agreement with a bank. The word for Northwestern in spring of 1983 is "poised," on the verge, on the edge, on the brink of a new strategy whose details are as yet indistinct.

Diversification: Impacts

It is more than a little foolhardy to evaluate a work in progress. Northwestern is dancing to music that is still being composed. But the dance has begun. The company is becoming, in the minds of its leaders, a market-driven enterprise. It will offer products markedly different from those of even the recent past. Its home office management and its general agencies will be structured differently. A constellation of forces — social, economic, competitive — has pushed Northwestern from narrow to broad, from product to market. The company is hoping to transform its problems into opportunities.

There are precedents for the change in direction. Northwestern had succumbed to market pressures and introduced semi-tontine insurance in 1883. But the tontine era ended with the Armstrong investigations of 1905-1906, and Northwestern entered a long period of retrenchment. In the 1920s, under William Van Dyke, the company refused to follow its competitors into the group, disability income, and health insurance fields. In the 1950s — the next round of diversification — Edmund Fitzgerald identified himself as an ardent keeper of the specialist's faith. But the company's response to the changing needs of its agents and its markets accelerated. Classified insurance was offered in 1956, an accidental death benefit in 1959, Extra Ordinary Life in 1968, disability income in 1969, and yearly renewable term in 1972. All marked significant (and often controversial) retreats from the narrowly defined specialist posture of earlier years.

All of the product innovations, however, were risk-based contracts written on the lives of individuals. Group insurance of any kind was a taboo of the first magnitude, and health insurance was particularly suspect. Non-annuity investment products and fee-based services were not even considered. As Northwestern moves farther afield in the 1980s, the gap between past and present will grow wider than ever before.

The company's decision to diversify has been made in full knowledge of the risks involved. There is the risk inherent in any new venture — the possibility of failure — but indecision may be an even greater risk. There is the danger that the costs of developing new products and new systems will jeopardize the economic welfare of old policyowners — the same risk faced, and faced successfully, in the expansion program of the late 1960s and 1970s. There is the danger that the demands of diversification will be more than the senior management can absorb. Northwestern has fewer executives than most firms of comparable size, and the company's bench is not particularly deep.

The insurance side is beginning to resemble the investment side. When the company's investors mounted their diversification campaign, branching out into the equity markets, start-up costs increased, cash returns were delayed, and there was a greater need for staff with expertise in particular fields.

Perhaps Northwestern's basic challenge is to find a niche for its new products. The company has no intention of peppering the marketplace with dozens of new offerings. It will concentrate its efforts in a few carefully chosen fields and move deliberately to gain preeminence in them. But the economy, the public's buying mood, and the tax climate are all volatile. Product design in the Eighties is like firing a bullet at a target barely visible and constantly in motion.

There is a more subtle hazard involved, one identified by Laflin Jones in a 1972 speech to the agents: the danger of economic elitism. Jones stated that insurance was "almost exclusively a family business" in his early years at Northwestern, and he voiced concern that it was becoming so entwined with tax leverage and fiscal gymnastics that it risked identification with "economic privilege." As the company's focus on the upscale consumer intensifies, will its clients be limited to those sophisticated enough to follow the arguments? As sales continue to shift from the kitchen table to the president's desk, will insurance lose some of its social utility? Economic pressures have pushed agents to where the premiums are, but is there any danger of losing touch with the basic nature of the business: indemnity? Similar questions were asked by Jones in 1972, and they are worth rephrasing in the 1980s.

Some individuals have wondered, at least privately, whether the risks are worth all the effort. One might ask if the air is so full of buzzwords — synergism, driving force, client control, market needs, boutique, scenario — that the light of reality has been obscured. Inflation, after all, has only been a major problem since the late 1960s, and rampant inflation (with correspondingly high interest rates) is the root cause of the major industry trends: policy loan demand, eroding face values, rising unit costs, the income tax burden, universal life, equity investments, and the mental splitting of the policy into protection and investment. What if long-term stability returns? What if inflation drops below 3 percent and unemployment falls to less than 5 percent? Will the time spent on diversification have been wasted? Probably not, in Northwestern's view. History is cumulative. The company is betting that, whatever happens in the future, the world has changed irrevocably.

There is, finally, some new pressure on the company's character. Throughout the first eight decades of this century, Northwestern honed an image of itself as the lone specialist, the sole keeper of the simple faith. The company was, to borrow the phrase of a potential competitor, "a breed apart." In time that image became an identity.

Northwestern was like a clothes shop specializing in tweeds, a purveyor of the classic and refined. Let the rest of the world, it said, jump from leisure suits to designer jeans. Quality will find a market. (Northwestern also resembled, in the view of some, a wind-up toy that kept going despite conditions or terrain.)

In the 1980s, as The Quiet Company becomes more aggressive, as the marketplace becomes a key factor in decision-making, as the specialist diversifies, the old image will have to be at least partially abandoned. Has the company's dollar been cut free of the gold standard? Has Tiffany's merged with K-Mart? Hardly, but there will be tension as Northwestern moves toward a new definition of itself.

It is noteworthy that, as the company has prepared itself to change, a passage from the annual statement of 1888 has become a credo: "The ambition of the Northwestern has been less to be large than to be safe; its aim is to rank first in benefits to policyholders rather than first in size. . . ." The passage is emblazoned in bronze on the wall facing the east building's entrance, and it is displayed prominently in scores of offices and conference rooms. Written a few years after the company entered the tontine fray, it dates from another period of massive uncertainty. As Northwestern changes in the 1980s, the credo could become a rich but hollow relic of the past, like the American frontier so widely venerated and so utterly gone. It may also serve as a touchstone, a totem, an ancestral voice reminding the caretakers of the present that some constants still apply.

All of the risks and all of the implications are worth pondering, but a sense of perspective is equally important. Northwestern's decision to diversify is not a turning point in human history. The walls of the temple will not collapse when the company introduces group insurance. The developments to come are the result of a business decision, made after a dispassionate assessment of the facts. The bottom line is the balance sheet.

Fitzgerald's insistence on specialization was no different, despite his sometimes impassioned rhetoric. (Fitzgerald, in fact, seriously considered buying a group life company in the early 1950s, and drew back only after deciding that Northwestern could not spare the executive talent needed to manage the firm.) In the 1980s, with pressures considerably more intense, no one had the slightest interest in dying on the barricades for a moribund ideal.

The plain truth is that Northwestern had no other choice. Given the tumult in the marketplace, the accelerating trend to term insurance, the growth of outside business, the desire to preserve a top-flight agency force, and a host of other factors, diversification emerged as the strategy most likely to insure Northwestern's future prosperity. The implications were profound, but the alternatives were forbidding.

A central question remains unanswered, and is perhaps unanswerable. How far must Northwestern go before it becomes a different sort of enterprise? When a bakery owner begins to sell cold cuts and cheese, at what point does the bakery become a delicatessen? How many products must Northwestern add, and how successful must they be, before the company loses its identity as a life insurance company? How far do you go? No one knows.

After 125 Years

Life insurance is a simple business — on paper. When the theories are applied, when the enterprise encounters the marketplace, the business is anything but simple. Looking back at 125 years in the history of one company, what stands out is the endless interplay of choice and circumstance, change and response, individual personalities and the corporate personality. There have been no simple decisions. There have been no predictable patterns. But the interplay produced a character, one that has been tested and tempered for more than a century.

Northwestern Mutual began as the obsessive dream of an impetuous patriarch. John Johnston left the scene early, but his dream came true for a small group of Milwaukeeans. Northwestern became a Midwestern upstart, growing with its region, developing in almost complete isolation from the industry's centers. In 1874 Henry Palmer became president, and it is he, more than anyone, who set the tone for all that has followed. In thirty-four years at the helm, he infused the company with a rigid insistence on quality, on trusteeship, on simplicity, on caution. Palmer's Northwestern was a stern, even stuffy, enterprise, but every president who followed has stayed the course he set. When the industry became more diverse, Northwestern, under William Van Dyke, remained simple. It became a de facto specialist in individual life insurance. When a major depression and a global war threatened the industry, Michael Cleary kept the old principles intact, and he tempered the old sternness with his human warmth. There were challenges in abundance, but the responses were unfailingly consistent.

Between 1947 and 1983 the challenges have been nearly continuous. The pace of change has become increasingly hectic, the issues more complex, the trends broader. Northwestern has been pushed by degrees from its insistence on specialization to the threshold of perhaps the most dramatic change in its history.

Five presidents have served the company since 1947. Their styles have run the gamut from the polished conservatism of Fitzgerald to the shrewd simplicity of Ferguson. Each has had a particular role to play: Fitzgerald to rebuild the company after fifteen years of forced atrophy, Slichter and Dineen to maintain momentum, Ferguson to commence a second rebuilding in a context of extreme volatility. Schuenke's first task is clear: to manage the diversification effort without endangering the company's surplus or jeopardizing the character passed down from Palmer.

After 125 years and 14 presidents, Northwestern remains a stronghold of tradition in a traditional industry. That has been both a burden and a blessing, an anchor and a keel. The felt presence of the ancestors has encouraged inertia at times. Things were done in certain ways because they had always been done in those ways. Change was painful. Initiative was frowned upon in some quarters. Like any self-contained society, Northwestern built up an impressive body of customs and rituals. At the same time, tradition gave the company a spirit of shared purpose, a sure sense of where it had been and where it was going.

In the recent past, especially since Ferguson became president, tradition has been placed in context. There has been a fresh willingness to experiment, to modernize, to depart from past practice. The results are apparent in everything from the product line to the personnel policies, from the computer center to the organizational chart. But the ancestors are still a voice in the inner ear of the company's management.

Nothing symbolizes Northwestern's dual personality better than the two buildings that comprise its home office. One is a Roman temple adapted to business use, a stern but graceful granite shrine whose interior is an orderly maze of marble and brass. The other is a glass-and-granite box, a shrine to efficiency whose interior can be rearranged at will. The buildings, like the company, are traditional and modern, antique and contemporary, looking backward to Rome and ahead to the twenty-first century. Significantly, the principal executive offices are in the old building.

Tradition notwithstanding, the company has changed a great deal, especially in the recent past. After 125 years, is Northwestern still a specialist? It is remarkable that the question can still be asked. Some companies are literally creatures of the marketplace, changing policies and practices from year to year in response to the perceived mood of the buying public. What has made Northwestern refreshingly different is its adherence to a philosophy. The company has changed to meet new demands, but it has not, at least until recently, strayed from its self-appointed role in the industry. From a narrow product standpoint, however, the answer to the question is, or soon will be, "No."

What remains? Is Northwestern still the same company it was on its 100th birthday? No more (or less) than you are the same person you were in 1957. Like most human institutions, the company has evolved in response to changes in its leadership and shifts in the environment, but it has evolved along lines established in the distant past. For all the changes that have occurred, and for all those soon to come, life at Northwestern is little different from the patterns of earlier decades. The employees troop into the cafeteria for a free lunch every day, just as they have since 1915. Agents pay their own way to the annual meeting, as they have since 1907. The Policyowners Examining Committee still holds court every year, another practice begun in 1907. The Sportsmen's Club's musky outing is still well-attended. A newly organized band offers noon-hour concerts in the atrium. Agents and executives still wrestle (politely) at the November meetings. Newly appointed members of management, including executives, are still expected to provide candy and cigars for their co-workers on the day of their promotions. Employees are more likely to mingle at the copy machine than the water cooler, but the home office is still a human workplace.

More importantly, Northwestern has shown remarkable constancy of character in the large things as well as the small. What are the elements of that character? An almost religious devotion to competitive excellence. Equal treatment for all policyowners. A belief in the personalism and professionalism of a highly skilled agency force. A blend of fiscal restraint and willingness to invest in quality. Consistency of thought. Independence of action. A lean management structure. An insistence on efficiency. These are nineteenth-century qualities that give the company a distinctive outlook in the late twentieth century. From the standpoint of character, Northwestern remains a specialist.

The company is certainly not without its human frailties and inconsistencies. It has been complacent, even smug, at times. Agents and employees have found its management paternalistic on occasion. Some have characterized its attitudes as both elitist and parochial. But Northwestern remains, to many, the standard by which the rest of the industry is judged.

In an important sense, Northwestern's character reflects the character of the city that has been its home since 1859. The people who make and administer the company's policies are, after all, Milwaukeeans. They have names like Wankowski, Gegenhuber, and Schuenke. Their hometown is an industrial city, a city built by immigrants. It is not an especially glamorous place, not a center of fashion or a setter of trends. It is, however, an extraordinarily livable city. Milwaukee has metropolitan attractions and metropolitan diversity, but it is a human-scale community. Its pace is leisurely. It has more neighborhood bars than nightclubs. The downtown area is modest, the streets are clean, the parks are spacious, and dozens of neighborhoods serve as focal points for their residents. These qualities have earned Milwaukee a reputation as a "big small town."

If Northwestern is The Quiet Company, Milwaukee is The Quiet City. If Milwaukee is a big small town, Northwestern is a big small company — one that has worked diligently to preserve the simplicity, the attention to detail, the traditional values of its modest beginnings. Both the company and the city are frugal, slow to change, somewhat complacent, somewhat parochial. Quality is more important to both than size. Both pay their bills on time. One keeps the corporate garden free of weeds while the other plants flowers along the boulevards. Northwestern is a national company, a giant in its field, but the roots of its character go deep into the substance of Milwaukee.

There are some final truths. Northwestern operates according to principles established by men long dead. It will, barring catastrophe, some day be managed by men and women not yet born. The challenge of the past and the challenge of the present are identical: to change, and to remain the same.

BIBLIOGRAPHY

Company Materials

Chapin, Edwin K. *The First Fifty Years: A History of the Special Agents Association from 1908 to 1958.* Special Agents Association, 1966.

Jones, Laflin C. *To Have Seen A Century.* Northwestern Mutual Life, 1957.

Kellogg, Amherst W. *History of the Northwestern Mutual Life Insurance Company to 1870.* Unpublished, 1908 (?).

Tyrrell, Henry F. *Semi-Centennial History of the Northwestern Mutual Life Insurance Company.* NML, 1908.

Tyrrell, Henry F. *Testimony of Time.* Unpublished, 1933.

Williamson, Harold F. and Smalley, Orange A. *Northwestern Mutual Life: A Century of Trusteeship.* Northwestern University Press, 1957.

Annual Reports, 1950-82.

Periodicals: *Columns* (1981-83), *Coverage* (1972-83), *Field Notes* (1945-81), *Field-News* (1971-81), *Gazette* (1970-83), *Investor* (1977-83), *Management Bulletin* (1972-83), *New Life News* (1953-83), *Pillar* (1941-83), and *Your Milwaukee Letter* (1954-71).

Proceedings, Association of Agents annual meeting, 1947-77.

Minutes of Board of Trustees, Building Advisory Committee, Centennial Council, Corporate Social Responsibility Committee.

Files of Edward Flitz, Armin Gumerman, George Hardy, Ralph Harkness, Victor Henningsen, David Hingtgen, Laflin Jones, Wilfred Kraegel, James McKeon, Frank Rice, Deal Tompkins, and Donald Schuenke.

Jones Memorial Library. Planning materials.

NML Oral History Archives, Marquette University.

Background Materials

Bernstein, Jeremy. *The Analytical Engine.* Random House, 1963.

Best's Review. Various issues, 1947-83.

Cahn, William H. *A Matter of Life and Death: The Connecticut Mutual Story.* Random House, 1970.

Carr, William H.A. *From Three Cents A Week: A Story of the Prudential Insurance Company of America.* Prentice-Hall, 1975.

Clough, Shepard B. *A Century of American Life Insurance: A History of the Mutual Life Insurance Company of New York.* Columbia University Press, 1946.

Conard, Howard C., ed. *The History of Milwaukee County.* American Biographical Publishing Co., 1895.

Gregory, John G. *History of Milwaukee, Wisconsin.* S.J. Clarke, 1931.

Greider, Janice E. and Beadles, William T. *Principles of Life Insurance.* Richard D. Irwin, 1972.

Guernsey, Orrin G. and Willard, Josiah F. *The History of Rock County.* Janesville, 1856.

Historical Messenger of the Milwaukee County Historical Society. Various issues, 1957-70.

History of Rock County, Wisconsin. Western Historical Co., 1879.

Janesville Gazette. April 14, 1909.

Jones, Landon Y. *Great Expectations: America and the Baby Boom Generation,* Coward, McCann and Geoghagen, 1980.

Kraegel, Wilfred A. and Reiskytl, James F. *Policy Loans and Equity.* Society of Actuaries, 1976.

Leuchtenberg, William E. *A Troubled Feast: American Society since 1945.* Little, Brown and Co., 1979.

Life Insurance Fact Book. Institute of Life Insurance, 1946-75; American Council of Life Insurance, 1976-82.

Milwaukee City Directory. Various issues, 1857-1930.

Milwaukee Sentinel. Various issues, 1859-1880.

Mittra, Sid. *Inside Wall Street.* Dow Jones-Irwin, 1971.

Monitoring Attitudes of the Public. Institute of Life Insurance, 1968-75; American Council of Life Insurance, 1976-82.

The National Underwriter. Various issues, 1947-83.

Nesbit, Robert C. *Wisconsin: A History.* University of Wisconsin Press, 1973.

O'Brien, James A. *Computers in Business Management.* Richard D. Irwin, 1979.

Odiorne, George S. *Management by Objectives.* Pitman Publishing Co., 1965.

Report of the Joint Committee of Senate and Assembly on the Affairs of Life Insurance Companies. State of Wisconsin, 1907.

Sawyer, Elmer W. *Insurance as Interstate Commerce.* McGraw-Hill, 1945.

Shannon, David A. *Twentieth-Century America.* Rand-McNally, 1977.

Stalson, J. Owen. *Marketing Life Insurance.* Richard D. Irwin, 1969.

Still, Bayrd. *Milwaukee: The History of a City.* State Historical Society of Wisconsin, 1948.

Tobias, Andrew. *The Invisible Bankers.* The Linden Press, 1982.

Wall, Joseph F. *Policies and People: The First Hundred Years of The Bankers Life.* Prentice-Hall, 1979.

Wisconsin Magazine of History. State Historical Society of Wisconsin. Various issues, 1945-70.

Wittner, Lawrence S. *Cold War America.* Praeger Publishing Co., 1974.

ACKNOWLEDGEMENTS

The Quiet Company is based largely on formal and informal conversations with Northwestern employees and agents. The author expresses his thanks to the following individuals for their contributions of time and information:

Chester Adamson	Russell Jensen
Ronald Beshear	Laflin Jones
Margaret Bonvicini	Michael Jones
Glenn Buzzard	John Konrad
Robert Carboni	Wilfred Kraegel
Robert Carlson	Kenneth Lafferty
William Cary	Mark Lucius
Thomas Christenson	Dick Matthisen
Catherine Cleary	James McKeon
William Cochran	Rita Micheli
Gordon Davidson	William Minehan
Robert Dineen	Donald Mundt
James Ehrenstrom	Lucille Neff
James Ericson	Robert Ninneman
Francis Ferguson	Will Reimer
Edward Flitz	James Reiskytl
Michael Gorichanaz	Frank Rice
Charles Groeschell	James Ruff
Dale Gustafson	Donald Schuenke
Gerald Haig	Benjamin Snow
Richard Haggman	Jason Stone
Richard Hall	Dennis Tamcsin
George Hardy	Robert Templin
Ralph Harkness	Joe Thompson, Jr.
William Hegge	Deal Tompkins
Victor Henningsen	Stanley Trotman
Clarence Husak	Robert Walker
David Hingtgen	Harvey Wilmeth
Milford Jacobson	Richard Wright

From inception to release, *The Quiet Company* was the responsibility of the History Book Committee. The original members were Ralph Harkness (chair), Robert Carboni, and Frank Rice. The following members joined during the production phase: Daryl Carter, William Drehfal, Patricia Ehr, Patricia Johnson, Nancy LaMonte, Ira Ludwig, and Thomas Towers.

Special thanks to Laflin Jones for his counsel and friendship, to Lorraine Wankowski of Word Processing for her painstaking work on the manuscript and tapes, and to the staff of the Personnel Department for making the author's stay in the home office pleasant and trouble-free.

APPENDIX

BOARD OF TRUSTEES
January 1, 1957 — March 2, 1983

Trustee	On	Off	Profession or Business	State
Charles D. Gelatt	1960 —		Engraving	Wisconsin
William A. Jahn	1960 —	1976	Manufacturing	Wisconsin
Conrad A. Elvehjem	1961 —	1962	University	Wisconsin
H. Stuart Harrison	1961 —	1980	Manufacturing	Ohio
Maxwell H. Herriott	1961 —	1972	Attorney	Wisconsin
John R. Kimberly	1961 —	1975	Paper Products	Wisconsin
Harry C. Moore	1961 —		Manufacturing	Wisconsin
Everett G. Smith	1961 —	1979	Tannery	Wisconsin
Albert L. Butler, Jr.	1963 —		Manufacturing	North Carolina
Oscar G. Mayer, Jr.	1963 —	1983	Food Processing	Wisconsin
Gilbert H. Scribner	1964 —	1968	Real Estate	Illinois
Daniel S. Parker	1965 —	1973	Manufacturing	Wisconsin
George Slade Schuster	1965 —	1978	Health	Minnesota
Robert A. Uihlein, Jr.	1965 —	1976	Brewing	Wisconsin
James O. Wright	1965 —		Manufacturing	Wisconsin
F. Markoe Rivinus	1966 —	1971	Pharmaceutical	Pennsylvania
*Francis E. Ferguson	1967 —		Insurance	Wisconsin
Francis F. Rosenbaum	1967 —	1972	Physician	Wisconsin
Edward C. Wells	1967 —	1972	Aircraft	Washington
A. H. Aymond	1968 —		Utilities	Michigan
Dutton Brookfield	1968 —	1979	Clothing	Missouri
Fletcher L. Byrom	1968 —	1977	Manufacturing	Pennsylvania
*Laflin C. Jones	1968 —	1973	Insurance	Wisconsin
Lynford Lardner, Jr.	1968 —	1973	Attorney	Wisconsin
Judson Bemis	1969 —		Manufacturing	Minnesota
Harold F. Ohlendorf	1969 —	1979	Agriculture	Arkansas
Edmund B. Fitzgerald	1970 —		Manufacturing	Wisconsin
Wayne J. Roper	1971 —		Attorney	Wisconsin
*Robert E. Templin	1971 —	1980	Insurance	Wisconsin
Richard H. Holton	1972 —		University	California
William C. Messinger	1972 —		Manufacturing	Wisconsin
James H. Wilson, Jr.	1972 —		Attorney	Georgia
*Robert B. Barrows	1973 —	1977	Insurance	Wisconsin
Joseph B. Flavin	1973 —		Manufacturing	Connecticut
Harold Byron Smith, Jr.	1973 —		Manufacturing	Illinois
J. Fred Risk	1974 —	1978	Banking	Indiana
Robert M. Hoffer	1976 —		Utilities	Wisconsin
Randolph W. Bromery	1977 —	1979	University	Massachusetts
John V. James	1977 —	1982	Petroleum	Texas
*Donald K. Mundt	1977 —		Insurance	Wisconsin
I. Andrew Rader	1977 —		Manufacturing	Wisconsin
J. Thomas Lewis	1978 —		Attorney	Louisiana
Dan M. McGill	1978 —		University	Pennsylvania
Frank M. Bertsch	1979 —		Manufacturing	Iowa
Leonard W. Cronkhite, Jr.	1979 —		University	Wisconsin
Sidney Epstein	1979 —		Engineering	Illinois
Richard H. Lillie	1979 —		Surgeon	Wisconsin
Patricia Albjerg Graham	1980 —		University	Massachusetts
Walter H. Helmerich, III	1980 —		Petroleum	Oklahoma
*Donald J. Schuenke	1980 —		Insurance	Wisconsin
George M. Chester	1981 —		Attorney	Wisconsin
Laurence A. McNeil	1982 —		Petroleum	Texas

*Executive Officers of NML

FUNCTIONAL TABLE OF ORGANIZATION
1957

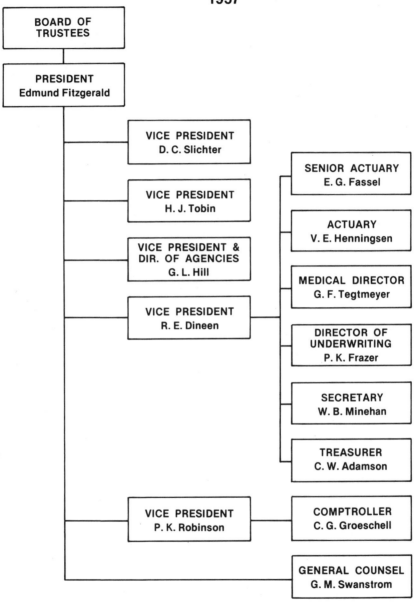

FUNCTIONAL TABLE OF ORGANIZATION

April 1, 1983

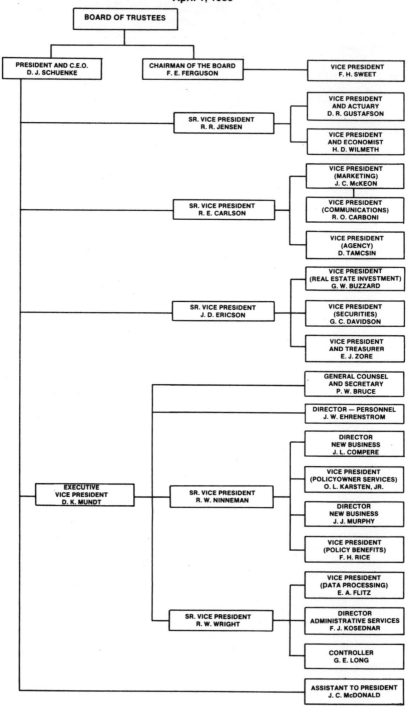

BOARD OF TRUSTEES

PRESIDENT AND C.E.O.
D. J. SCHUENKE

CHAIRMAN OF THE BOARD
F. E. FERGUSON

VICE PRESIDENT
F. H. SWEET

SR. VICE PRESIDENT
R. R. JENSEN

VICE PRESIDENT AND ACTUARY
D. R. GUSTAFSON

VICE PRESIDENT AND ECONOMIST
H. D. WILMETH

SR. VICE PRESIDENT
R. E. CARLSON

VICE PRESIDENT (MARKETING)
J. C. McKEON

VICE PRESIDENT (COMMUNICATIONS)
R. O. CARBONI

VICE PRESIDENT (AGENCY)
D. TAMCSIN

SR. VICE PRESIDENT
J. D. ERICSON

VICE PRESIDENT (REAL ESTATE INVESTMENT)
G. W. BUZZARD

VICE PRESIDENT (SECURITIES)
G. C. DAVIDSON

VICE PRESIDENT AND TREASURER
E. J. ZORE

EXECUTIVE VICE PRESIDENT
D. K. MUNDT

GENERAL COUNSEL AND SECRETARY
P. W. BRUCE

DIRECTOR — PERSONNEL
J. W. EHRENSTROM

SR. VICE PRESIDENT
R. W. NINNEMAN

DIRECTOR NEW BUSINESS
J. L. COMPERE

VICE PRESIDENT (POLICYOWNER SERVICES)
O. L. KARSTEN, JR.

DIRECTOR NEW BUSINESS
J. J. MURPHY

VICE PRESIDENT (POLICY BENEFITS)
F. H. RICE

SR. VICE PRESIDENT
R. W. WRIGHT

VICE PRESIDENT (DATA PROCESSING)
E. A. FLITZ

DIRECTOR ADMINISTRATIVE SERVICES
F. J. KOSEDNAR

CONTROLLER
G. E. LONG

ASSISTANT TO PRESIDENT
J. C. McDONALD

GENERAL AGENTS

General Agency	January, 1957	February, 1983
ALABAMA		
Birmingham	————	Jack Wright, CLU
ARIZONA		
Phoenix	Harold F. Vinson, CLU	Robert W. Kersting, CLU
CALIFORNIA		
Fresno	————	John Paul
Los Angeles	John R. Mage, CLU	Stephen T. Mellinger, CLU
Oakland	Paul E. Demeter, CLU	Thomas E. Bowman, CLU
Sacramento	John S. Kerns	William W. Fobes
San Bernardino	————	R. Keith Guise, CLU
San Diego	Robert W. Stockton, CLU	James E. Whistler, CLU
San Francisco	Richard J. Shipley	J. Edward Tippetts, CLU
San Jose	————	Thomas H. Burkhart, CLU
Santa Ana	————	Tim N. Templin
Woodland Hills	————	Jerome S. Simon, CLU
COLORADO		
Denver	————	C. Michael McKeever, CLU
Denver	Ralph L. Theisen, CLU	Thomas R. Richards, CLU
CONNECTICUT		
Hartford	Glenn B. Dorr, CLU	Glenn B. Dorr, Jr., CLU
Stamford	————	Phillip J. Pierz, CLU
DISTRICT OF COLUMBIA		
Washington	Paul R. Harrison	Warren J. Negri, Jr.
FLORIDA		
Jacksonville	————	Donald R. Wilkinson, CLU
Miami	————	Edwin B. Cole, CLU
Tallahassee	————	Melvin L. Pope, Jr.
Tampa	————.	James L. Erb, CLU
GEORGIA		
Atlanta	John M. Law, CLU	William O. Goodwin, CLU
Atlanta	————	John T. Shanholtz
HAWAII		
Honolulu	————	Joe G. Grant, CLU
IDAHO		
Boise	Ray M. Wagoner	Robert F. Rice, CLU
ILLINOIS		
Aurora	Bernard J. Stumm & William C. Roeder, Sr.	William C. Roeder, Jr.
Belleville	Winfred L. Jacobsen	————
Champaign	————	John W. Wright
Chicago	————	Albert C. Fellinger, CLU
Chicago	John H. Jamison & Nelson D. Phelps, CLU	O. Alfred Granum, CLU

General Agency	January, 1957	February, 1983
Elgin	———	Alvin G. Pofahl, CLU
Evanston	Dan A. Kaufman, CLU	Harry P. Hoopis, CLU
Peoria	Clifford R. Garrett	Taylor French, CLU
Springfield	Charles V. Durr	Joseph P. McCormick, CLU
INDIANA		
Evansville	Burwell A. Million	Marvin L. Smith, CLU
Indianapolis	Guy E. Morrison, CLU	Gene G. Koch, CLU
South Bend	Herbert L. Cramer	John M. Hazlitt, CLU
IOWA		
Cedar Rapids	Lowell P. Schwinger	Thomas S. Redford
Davenport	James H. Copeland	Richard J. Hines
Des Moines	Thomas W. Hyland	Rex C. Teigen, CLU
Sioux City	Dean M. Kerl, CLU	Willard D. Thompson
KANSAS		
Kansas City	Joseph D. McTigue	Joseph D. McTigue
Wichita	Russell L. Law, Jr.	Willard L. Momsen, Jr., CLU
KENTUCKY		
Lexington	Wendell H. Honeycutt	Frank A. Fisher, Jr., CLU
Louisville	Henry M. Johnson, Jr., CLU	David L. Corrie
LOUISIANA		
Lafayette	———	Donald J. Romero
New Orleans	———	Will S. Hornsby, III, CLU
MAINE		
Portland	W. Bradford Cushman, CLU	Richard L. Rawlings, CLU
MARYLAND		
Baltimore	Paul E. Burke, Jr.	Donald R. Iodice, CLU (effective March 1, 1983)
MASSACHUSETTS		
Boston	Jason E. Stone, Jr.	Jason C. Stone, CLU
Springfield	G. Brady Buckley	Richard G. McKenney, CLU
MICHIGAN		
Detroit	Charles R. Eckert	James A. Edwards, CLU
Detroit	———	Larry L. Herb
Flint	Albert I. Roeder	Gary C. Holvick, CLU
Grand Rapids	Bruce W. Gilmore, CLU	John H. Myaard, CLU
Kalamazoo	Ralph W. Emerson, CLU	Byron J. Crosse, CLU
Marquette	J. Rex DeHaas	———
MINNESOTA		
Duluth	William C. Dunbar, CLU	Robert W. Chapman
Mankato	Robert J. McTigue	Russell L. Keller, Jr.
Minneapolis	Francis R. Olsen	Jack G. Brown, CLU
St. Paul	Warren W. Lundgren, CLU	Larry L. Kuhlman, CLU

General Agency	January, 1957	February, 1983
MISSISSIPPI		
Jackson	———	Trenton H. Shelton
MISSOURI		
Kansas City	Samuel C. Pearson, Jr.	Dan J. Ertz
St. Louis	J. Harry Veatch	Robert B. Qualy, CLU
MONTANA		
Billings	Howard F. Hoene, CLU	———
Bozeman	———	Michael M. Anderson, CLU
NEBRASKA		
Lincoln	Richard T. Seckinger	Charles F. Scanlon, CLU
Omaha	Kenneth M. Snyder, CLU	Hal W. Walter
NEW HAMPSHIRE		
Manchester	Vaughn D. Griffin	Craig D. Potter, CLU
NEW JERSEY		
Burlington	———	David P. Cecco, CLU
Newark	J. Vincent Talbot	———
Springfield	———	Robert E. Stone, CLU
Trenton	Paul R. Comegys, CLU	Joseph M. Savino, CLU
NEW MEXICO		
Albuquerque	Jack Dunn	William E. Ebel, CLU
NEW YORK		
Albany	Edward R. Gettings	William E. Bick, CLU
Buffalo	Peter T. Allen	Michael W. Halloran, CLU
Garden City	———	Melvin A. Gang
New York City	Alfred J. Johannsen, CLU	———
New York City	Harry Krueger, CLU	Gerald N. Gilberg, CLU
New York City	J. Robert Guy, CLU	Peter S. Hearst, CLU
New York City	Joseph V. Buck	———
Poughkeepsie	Elmer R. Dill	Austin E. Hodgkins, Jr., CLU
Rochester	Earl E. Lincoln	Frederick S. Bolyard, CLU
Syracuse	E. Parker Colborn, CLU	Klaude R. Konrad
Utica	Peter A. Karl, Jr.	Don Antonette, CLU
NORTH CAROLINA		
Chapel Hill	———	Arthur S. DeBerry, CLU
Charlotte	———	Richard H. Shober, CLU
Durham	John G. Darling, CLU	———
NORTH DAKOTA		
Fargo	Paul W. Avery	John R. Dobbs, CLU
OHIO		
Akron	Russell E. Werts	Donald E. Kelley, CLU
Cincinnati	Roe Walker, CLU	Ronald W. Beshear, CLU (effective April 1, 1983)
Cleveland	Raymond J. Dolwick	James D. Bonebrake
Columbus	Sterling L. Youngquist	Larry V. Carlson, CLU
Dayton	Herbert E. Whalen, Jr.	Thomas R. Tillander, CLU
Toledo	Elmer V. Gettys, CLU	Gary L. Brown, CLU

General Agency	January, 1957	February, 1983
OKLAHOMA		
Oklahoma City	Arthur W. Miller	Rocco V. Perciavalle
Tulsa	John J. Stoia, CLU	John J. Stoia, CLU
OREGON		
Portland	Lawrence J. Evans	Stephen Konrad, CLU
PENNSYLVANIA		
Greensburg	Donald L. Ford, CLU	John T. Holdorf, CLU
Harrisburg	Richard E. Eckel, CLU	John Pierz, CLU
Lancaster	George K. Reynold, Jr.	Robert W. McEldowney, III, CLU
Philadelphia	Aaron C. F. Finkbiner, CLU	Richard A. Goldman, CLU
Pittsburgh	Roger A. Clark, CLU	Charles I. Ferrara, CLU
Scranton	Charles A. Votaw, CLU	Arthur S. Patterson, CLU
RHODE ISLAND		
Providence	Eugene T. Lothgren, CLU	David McCahan, Jr., CLU
SOUTH CAROLINA		
Columbia	———	James R. Worrell
SOUTH DAKOTA		
Sioux Falls	H. Neal Jones, CLU	Gary H. Barsness, CLU
TENNESSEE		
Memphis	———	Edward A. Burch, CLU
Nashville	Edwin T. Proctor, CLU	William S. Cochran, CLU
TEXAS		
Dallas	———	Austin D. Rinne
Houston	———	Paul M. Nick, CLU
UTAH		
Salt Lake City	Sherman Young	Jerry R. Gerovac, CLU
VIRGINIA		
Richmond	Howard D. Goldman, CLU	Robert E. Pogue, CLU
WASHINGTON		
Seattle	Joe F. Habegger, CLU	Thomas D. O'Brien, CLU
Spokane	Norman K. Bishop	Martin S. Polhemus, CLU
WEST VIRGINIA		
Charleston	Deal H. Tompkins	Thomas D. Wilkerson, CLU
WISCONSIN		
Appleton	Stuart H. Koch, CLU	Peter W. Nordell, CLU
Eau Claire	Clifton L. Egbert	Richard W. Cable, CLU
Madison	Frank R. Horner, CLU	David L. Roeder, CLU
Milwaukee	J. Lowell Craig	Thomas E. Goris, CLU
Milwaukee	Willard L. Momsen, CLU	Dennis W. Laudon, CLU
Oshkosh	Verne W. Huber, CLU	James D. Hepola, CLU

REGIONAL MANAGERS

REAL ESTATE INVESTMENT
(as of June, 1983)

FIELD OFFICES — EASTERN DIVISION

ATLANTA, Georgia .... Richard D. Crossley
CHICAGO, Illinois .... Theodore C. Mesjak
MIAMI, Florida .... Gregory J. Walz
MINNEAPOLIS, Minnesota .... Dale E. Huber
MILWAUKEE, Wisconsin .... John W. Seifert*
TAMPA, Florida .... David A. Roby*
WASHINGTON, D.C. .... Patrick H. McGuire, III

FIELD OFFICES — WESTERN DIVISION

DALLAS, Texas .... Richard W. Graves
DENVER, Colorado .... Theodore C. MacLeod
HOUSTON, Texas .... Michael R. Buchholz*
LOS ANGELES, California .... Donald L. Goodson
MEMPHIS, Tennessee .... John S. Shoaf
SAN FRANCISCO, California .... Everett H. Merriman, Jr.
SEATTLE, Washington .... Clair E. Hugh
VISALIA, California .... Morris A. Arneson

*District Manager

NUMBER OF EMPLOYEES — HOME OFFICE

Year	Full-time Employees	Part-time Employees	Supervisors and Specialists	Officers	Total
1957	1,332	123	120	84	1,659
1958	1,327	126	118	90	1,661
1959	1,354	162	127	88	1,731
1960	1,421	150	133	87	1,791
1961	1,450	136	137	90	1,813
1962	1,371	129	141	92	1,733
1963	1,355	131	145	97	1,728
1964	1,362	116	154	103	1,735
1965	1,337	96	161	108	1,702
1966	1,346	105	166	115	1,732
1967	1,357	119	182	117	1,775
1968	1,388	134	180	122	1,824
1969	1,550	172	206	127	2,055
1970	1,560	184	230	133	2,107
1971	1,452	152	227	138	1,969
1972	1,355	141	235	143	1,874
1973	1,354	152	254	150	1,910
1974	1,392	182	286	159	2,019
1975	1,384	184	303	165	2,036
1976	1,384	182	326	171	2,063
1977	1,372	163	326	179	2,040
1978	1,360	191	344	186	2,081
1979	1,396	245	361	188	2,190
1980	1,416	253	372	200	2,241
1981	1,389	248	380	210	2,227
1982	1,382	306	407	210	2,305

NUMBER OF AGENTS

Year	General Agents	District Agents	Full-Time Agents	Total Full-Time	College Agents	Part-Time & Emeritus	CLUs	Full-Time Appointments
1957	95	245	1,923	2,263	---	1,620	NA	410
1958	97	249	2,038	2,384	---	1,559	NA	516
1959	97	252	2,008	2,357	---	1,619	406	474
1960	98	261	2,067	2,426	---	1,575	426	522
1961	96	256	2,033	2,385	---	1,580	457	489
1962	97	251	2,041	2,389	---	1,539	484	498
1963	98	254	2,142	2,494	---	1,475	515	602
1964	98	254	2,126	2,478	---	1,594	542	614
1965	98	265	2,136	2,499	---	1,533	575	558
1966	98	270	2,122	2,490	71*	1,522	635	507
1967	101	275	2,105	2,481	155	1,471	681	480
1968	102	263	2,170	2,535	224	1,382	758	475
1969	103	263	2,204	2,570	254	1,316	799	503
1970	105	257	2,390	2,752	349	1,278	857	693
1971	107	266	2,566	2,939	340	1,153	904	769
1972	108	263	2,751	3,122	309	1,119	946	813
1973	113	269	2,857	3,239	312	1,052	1,002	794
1974	113	275	3,004	3,392	309	1,003	1,061	853
1975	114	272	3,146	3,532	276	1,011	1,104	950
1976	113	271	3,195	3,579	318	1,012	1,162	827
1977	114	287	3,284	3,685	384	1,006	1,238	849
1978	114	295	3,538	3,947	428	987	1,322	913
1979	114	304	3,802	4,220	459	980	1,401	1,033
1980	115	309	4,008	4,432	464	993	1,481	1,149
1981	116	299	4,156	4,571	415	1,007	1,576	1,177
1982	115	295	4,339	4,749	348	997	1,634	1,340

*Special contracts were first offered in 1966; prior to 1966 college agents were included in full-time agents.

Source: Report to Trustees

AGENTS' ASSOCIATIONS

Presidents

Year Ending In July	Association of Agents	CLU Association	Senior Agents Association
1957	G. Wendell Dygert, CLU	Clifford A. Seys	————
1958	John O. Todd, CLU	C. Rigdon Robb	————
1959	John R. Mage, CLU	John G. Darling	————
1960	D. E. McTigue	Horace H. Mickley	————
1961	Ben S. McGiveran, CLU	Guy E. Morrison	————
1962	Lawrence J. Evans	Francis A. Duggan	————
1963	Leigh T. Prettyman, CLU	Robert J. Habegger	————
1964	Corlett J. Cotton, CLU	Dennis W. Laudon	————
1965	Horace H. Mickley, CLU	David McCahan, Jr.	————
1966	Lowell P. Schwinger	J. Robert Winegardner	————
1967	Robert A. Files, CLU	David H. Hilton	————
1968	M. Luther Hahs, CLU	Jason C. Stone	————
1969	Adon N. Smith, II, CLU	James S. Harding	Frank R. Horner, CLU
1970	Aaron C. F. Finkbiner, Sr., CLU	Jack G. Brown	John O. Todd, CLU
1971	Robert Casey	Robert A. Files	Lowell P. Schwinger
1972	Robert G. Shorey, CLU	Gary R. Froid	C. Rigdon Robb, CLU
1973	Leo T. Tibensky, CLU	Sidney F. Greeley, Jr.	William K. Pierce, CLU
1974	Roe Walker, CLU	Charles T. Morse	Arthur D. Reed, CLU
1975	Jack Paul Fine, CLU	James T. Turner, III	Herbert J. Schwahn, CLU
1976	Dean Sangalis, CLU	Ronald E. Schermacher	Corlett J. Cotton, CLU
1977	Joe Thompson, Jr., CLU	Hans G. Moser	J. Eldon Bailey
1978	John M. Law, CLU	Ronald F. Knox, Jr.	Royall R. Brown, CLU
1979	David H. Hilton, CLU	Martin S. Polhemus	Lee Loventhal, II, CLU
1980	Gary R. Froid, CLU	J. Peter Schma	Hal McIntyre, CLU
1981	Gene J. Gilmore, CLU	Fred M. Goodwin	Leigh T. Prettyman, CLU
1982	Joseph D. McTigue	Howard B. Edelstein	Franklin W. Bowen, CLU

AGENTS' ASSOCIATIONS

Presidents

Year Ending In July	Special Agents	District Agents	General Agents
1957	Leigh T. Prettyman, CLU	John H. Vance	Willard L. Momsen, CLU
1958	Ben S. McGiveran, CLU	Charles K. Zug, CLU	Lawrence J. Evans
1959	Charles A. McCotter, CLU	Merrill Garcelon, CLU	Howard D. Goldman, CLU
1960	Robert A. Files, CLU	Allen F. Moore, CLU	Frank R. Horner, CLU
1961	John P. Propis, CLU	Richard E. Thomas, CLU	Francis R. Olsen
1962	Adon N. Smith, II, CLU	M. Luther Hahs, CLU	Deal H. Tompkins
1963	Robert Casey	Francis B. Donovan, CLU	William C. Roeder
1964	Clarence E. P. Crauer, CLU	Leslie R. Fowler, CLU	Joseph D. McTigue
1965	Leo T. Tibensky, CLU	Dale N. Shutt	John M. Law, CLU
1966	Jack Paul Fine, CLU	H. Jack Stoltz, CLU	J. Lowell Craig, CLU
1967	Joe Thompson, Jr., CLU	Robert G. Shorey, CLU	John S. Stobbelaar
1968	Archie A. Campbell	Charles F. Mead, CLU	Willard H. Griffin, CLU
1969	Francis A. Duggan, CLU	Burtis W. Anderson, CLU	Stuart H. Koch, CLU
1970	David H. Hilton, CLU	Eldon C. Johnson, Jr.	Roswell H. Pickford, Jr., CLU
1971	Robert A. Lauer, CLU	John H. Myaard, CLU	Aaron C. F. Finkbiner, Jr., CLU
1972	Gene J. Gilmore, CLU	Dean Sangalis, CLU	Dan A. Kaufman, CLU
1973	H. Stanley Mansfield, Jr., CLU	Gerald McTigue	Robert J. McTigue, CLU
1974	Fred M. Goodwin, Jr., CLU	Jack H. Thompson	Edgar D. Coffman, CLU
1975	Gordon Farrar, CLU	Milton D. Mussehl	Roe Walker, CLU
1976	Richard H. Love, CLU	Gary R. Froid, CLU	John J. Stoia, CLU
1977	Charles T. Morse, CLU	Charles E. Pike	Michael P. Goodrich, CLU
1978	Alan H. Maltenfort, CLU	John Poort, Jr.	Robert B. Qualy, CLU
1979	James H. Anderson, CLU	Donald T. Patrick Steele	O. Alfred Granum, CLU
1980	Jack D. Minner, CLU	Stephen J. Plank, CLU	James S. Harding, CLU
1981	Edward R. Frantz, CLU	David L. Shumate, CLU	Jason C. Stone, CLU
1982	Frederic R. Marschner, CLU	Bernard E. Archbold, CLU	Robert E. Pogue, CLU

TOP 20 GENERAL AGENTS
New Sales
(Volume in Millions)

1957

John R. Mage, CLU	Los Angeles, CA	$24
Bernard J. Stumm & William C. Roeder, Sr.	Aurora, IL	23
John H. Jamison & Nelson D. Phelps, CLU	Chicago, IL	22
Frank R. Horner, CLU	Madison, WI	20
Willard L. Momsen, CLU	Milwaukee, WI	20
J. Lowell Craig	Milwaukee, WI	19
Dan A. Kaufman, CLU	Evanston, IL	18
Aaron C.F. Finkbiner, Sr., CLU	Philadelphia, PA	16
Lowell P. Schwinger	Cedar Rapids, IA	15
Charles R. Eckert	Detroit, MI	15
Roger A. Clark, CLU	Pittsburgh, PA	14
Guy E. Morrison, CLU	Indianapolis, IN	14
Raymond J. Dolwick	Cleveland, OH	13
Jason E. Stone, Jr.	Boston, MA	13
Deal H. Tompkins	Charleston, WV	13
Francis R. Olsen	Minneapolis, MN	12
Bruce W. Gilmore, CLU	Grand Rapids, MI	12
John M. Law, CLU	Atlanta, GA	12
Peter T. Allen	Buffalo, NY	12
J. Vincent Talbot	Newark, NJ	11

1982

Austin D. Rinne	Dallas, TX	$331
Gerald N. Gilberg, CLU	New York, NY	321
O. Alfred Granum, CLU	Chicago, IL	256
Glenn B. Dorr, Jr., CLU	Hartford, CT	230
Martin S. Polhemus, CLU	Spokane, WA	207
Dennis W. Laudon, CLU	Milwaukee, WI	202
Gene G. Koch, CLU	Indianapolis, IN	199
Melvin A. Gang	Garden City, NY	198
Harry P. Hoopis, CLU	Evanston, IL	198
Robert B. Qualy, CLU	St. Louis, MO	192
John H. Myaard, CLU	Grand Rapids, MI	190
Peter S. Hearst, CLU	New York, NY	179
Robert W. Kersting, CLU	Phoenix, AZ	176
James L. Erb, CLU	Tampa, FL	174
William S. Cochran, CLU	Nashville, TN	174
Robert E. Pogue, CLU	Richmond, VA	173
Jason C. Stone, CLU	Boston, MA	162
Donald J. Romero	Lafayette, LA	162
Phillip J. Pierz, CLU	Darien, CT	161
Jack G. Brown, CLU	Minneapolis, MN	157

TOP 20 DISTRICT AGENTS
New Sales
(Volume in Millions)

1957

Robert E. Castelo, CLU	Illinois	$4
G. Wendell Dygert, CLU	Indiana	4
Cornelius J. Ryan, CLU	Ohio	3
William K. Pierce, CLU	Illinois	3
Royall R. Brown, CLU	North Carolina	3
Thomas A. Lauer, CLU	Illinois	3
J. Kenneth Roberts	Wisconsin	3
Charles F. Mead, CLU	Wisconsin	3
Richard E. Thomas, CLU	California	3
Byron J. Crosse, CLU	Wisconsin	3
Howard E. Blair, CLU	New York	3
John J. Lansing	Iowa	3
Donald T. P. Steele	Iowa	3
Clifford A. Seys	Michigan	3
Dale N. Shutt	Ohio	3
Richard E. Cormier	Massachusetts	3
Kenneth L. Bragdon	Iowa	3
H. Jack Stoltz, CLU	Illinois	3
R. Merle Palmer, CLU	Washington	2
J. Burton Cardiff	Wisconsin	2

1982

R. Allen Angell, CLU	Texas	$92
Gary R. Froid, CLU	Florida	80
Bruce Davidoff	New York	67
Richard A. De Vita	New York	66
A. B. Hemberger, CLU	Connecticut	55
C. Don Davis, CLU	Texas	53
James D. Shanley, CLU	Washington	52
Hans G. Moser, CLU	Wisconsin	51
Edmond M. Dorman, CLU	Florida	51
Henry S. Meyers	New York	49
William A. Fochi, CLU	Connecticut	46
David P. Cecco, CLU	New Jersey	45
Harold B. Hunt	Colorado	45
Donald R. Iodice, CLU	Connecticut	38
Don M. Henderson, CLU	Texas	37
John C. Wise	Kentucky	37
Dean Sangalis, CLU	Indiana	36
Peter M. Andel, CLU	New York	36
James M. Oravec	Connecticut	36
Roger L. Merrill	Utah	34

TOP 20 AGENTS
New Sales
(Volume in Millions)
Agents Year

June 1, 1956 through May 31, 1957

Jack N. Meeks	Ohio	$4.8
John O. Todd, CLU	Illinois	3.9
Clyde Fuller	Wisconsin	3.3
Franklin A. Morse	Indiana	2.9
Lewis T. Stearn	Minnesota	2.4
H. Ben Ruhl, CLU	Michigan	2.3
H. Karl Schuetter	Wisconsin	2.1
Royall R. Brown, CLU	North Carolina	2.1
Aaron C. F. Finkbiner, Jr., CLU	Pennsylvania	2.0
Sidney Weisman	Michigan	1.9
Frederick D. Leete, Jr., CLU	Indiana	1.9
Adolph E. Gillman	Maryland	1.9
Clarence E. P. Crauer, CLU	New York	1.8
Alden H. Smith, CLU	Tennessee	1.7
Clifford A. Seys, CLU	Michigan	1.5
Conant M. Ohl, CLU	Ohio	1.5
R. G. Littell	Washington	1.5
Donald T. P. Steele	Iowa	1.5
Albert A. Simpler, Jr.	Delaware	1.5
Edward Russo	Maryland	1.4

June 1, 1981 through May 31, 1982

Daniel E. Brunette, CLU	Indiana	$32.9
John H. Ellerman, CLU	Illinois	29.3
H. Stanley Mansfield, Jr., CLU	New York	28.7
Val K. Mayers	Louisiana	25.3
David G. Hast, CLU	Pennsylvania	25.2
Joseph J. Israel	New York	23.9
Edward R. Van Vliet, CLU	Washington	22.6
Paul G. Krasnow	California	21.9
David A. Stinnett	Indiana	20.5
Edward E. Packel, CLU	Oklahoma	20.0
Gaylord E. Davis, CLU	Oregon	18.9
James R. Fruge, CLU	Louisiana	17.9
Thomas A. Otteson, CLU	Minnesota	17.5
Gene J. Gilmore, CLU	Michigan	17.3
Ronald F. Knox, Jr., CLU	Tennessee	16.7
Gary R. Froid, CLU	Florida	16.6
Alan Nero	Rhode Island	16.3
Ann Spinazzola	Texas	16.2
James T. Turner, III, CLU	California	15.3
Blaine P. Swint, CLU	California	15.2

CAREER PRODUCTION
Over $100,000,000 by Dec. 31, 1982

Agent	State	Amount
David G. Hast, CLU	Pennsylvania	$216,002,259
John H. Ellerman, CLU	Illinois	210,475,957
H. Stanley Mansfield, Jr., CLU	New York	200,076,752
John O. Todd, CLU	Illinois	188,229,707
Joseph J. Israel	New York	175,805,739
Alfred J. Ostheimer	New Mexico	175,106,760
Val K. Mayers	Louisiana	165,596,873
David Hale Hilton, CLU	Illinois	156,060,485
Lyle L. Blessman	Colorado	155,450,956
Jack Paul Fine, CLU	Virginia	151,818,939
Hugh G. Thompson, Jr., CLU	Florida	151,801,340
Gene J. Gilmore, CLU	Michigan	151,117,289
Alden H. Smith, CLU	Tennessee	140,600,499
Thomas A. Otteson, CLU	Minnesota	139,738,043
James T. Turner, III, CLU	California	135,874,235
Robert A. Lauer, CLU	Ohio	131,831,812
Norman H. Winer, CLU	Minnesota	129,341,219
Stephen K. Lieberman, CLU	Minnesota	126,350,797
Daniel E. Brunette, CLU	Indiana	119,449,161
Lawrence D. Christie	Minnesota	119,139,041
Ronald F. Knox, Jr., CLU	Tennessee	118,884,639
J. Peter Schma, CLU	Michigan	112,976,905
Hans G. Moser, CLU	Wisconsin	112,550,776
Joe Thompson, Jr., CLU	Tennessee	111,531,870
Royall R. Brown, CLU	N. Carolina	110,933,554
Gary Robert Froid, CLU	Florida	106,553,206
Peter M. Peck, CLU	New York	103,451,222
G. Fred Smith, CLU	Wisconsin	102,615,036
George C. Turner, CLU	Connecticut	101,512,099
Charles T. Morse, CLU	Indiana	101,435,281

LIFE INSURANCE

New Business & Insurance In Force

(Millions of Dollars)

Year	Northwestern Mutual New Business	Northwestern Mutual In Force	Ordinary Insurance All Companies New Business	Ordinary Insurance All Companies In Force	Total Life Insurance All Companies New Business	Total Life Insurance All Companies In Force
1957	$ 748	$ 8,896	$ 48,937	$ 276,043	$ 71,748	$ 482,437
1958	730	9,336	50,839	300,559	72,918	521,925
1959	861	9,898	55,138	328,597	75,107	570,759
1960	865	10,411	56,183	355,608	78,417	618,189
1961	857	10,878	58,888	381,061	85,317	665,628
1962	862	11,336	61,259	407,777	84,624	715,435
1963	1,005	11,946	68,862	439,147	95,882	775,265
1964	1,129	12,707	79,430	478,334	111,899	850,090
1965	1,238	13,559	89,643	522,694	149,812	958,623
1966	1,347	14,524	95,987	568,025	130,659	1,051,701
1967	1,435	15,547	103,823	615,671	154,070	1,155,619
1968	1,709	16,778	112,820	667,532	162,091	1,266,151
1969	1,954	18,154	124,124	721,236	172,811	1,381,101
1970	2,050	19,477	134,802	777,163	206,795	1,506,472
1971	2,440	21,136	145,496	839,767	208,579	1,620,343
1972	2,845	23,139	159,063	906,255	228,377	1,760,350
1973	3,509	25,615	175,629	983,388	250,556	1,922,311
1974	4,148	28,554	198,981	1,071,369	323,451	2,144,580
1975	4,490	31,629	207,052	1,153,160	316,452	2,312,283
1976	4,974	35,088	233,583	1,257,738	352,197	2,530,767
1977	5,983	39,382	277,310	1,382,356	407,658	2,788,679
1978	7,690	45,188	304,136	1,535,982	437,886	3,107,513
1979	8,622	51,462	359,147	1,722,106	526,825	3,507,495
1980	10,336	61,079	461,553	2,086,569	654,720	4,055,933
1981	11,375	69,842	555,246	2,571,344	906,874	4,977,804
1982	14,213	79,027	671,433	2,861,783	925,967	5,459,975

Source: Annual Statement   Source: Life Insurance Fact Book

ASSETS

(Millions)

Year	BONDS					STOCKS	
	U.S. Government	State, Municipal & Provincial	Railroads	Public Utility	Industrial and Miscellaneous	Preferred	Common
1957	$177	$211	$146	$744	$ 832	$ 32	$ 18
1958	181	210	142	746	861	34	38
1959	152	224	137	744	894	32	55
1960	144	221	129	744	942	31	70
1961	162	235	124	697	963	29	103
1962	177	227	121	675	1,008	35	113
1963	176	216	116	643	1,069	62	152
1964	165	212	139	502	1,134	130	190
1965	158	206	140	455	1,187	187	209
1966	196	202	137	447	1,204	189	107
1967	165	178	134	508	1,287	186	181
1968	115	164	130	544	1,318	197	265
1969	88	148	124	553	1,292	200	252
1970	95	143	99	554	1,289	214	272
1971	83	130	97	589	1,430	238	376
1972	63	129	89	643	1,507	300	510
1973	47	113	77	570	1,487	340	433
1974	64	112	69	536	1,501	344	298
1975	209	135	66	517	1,615	354	362
1976	186	184	63	522	1,944	362	392
1977	196	194	62	529	2,099	411	389
1978	171	199	45	513	2,223	411	409
1979	178	166	42	481	2,206	434	390
1980	202	136	35	412	2,298	430	295
1981	254	149	34	379	2,258	398	229
1982	610	158	24	363	2,293	384	389

Source: Annual Report to Policyowners

ASSETS

(Millions)

| Year | MORTGAGE LOAN | | | INVESTMENT | |
	Commercial	Residence	Farm	Real Estate	Other
1957	$ 429	$698	$ 99	$ 82	$ 12
1958	467	706	119	90	27
1959	499	730	149	100	26
1960	520	752	177	106	26
1961	573	762	202	119	26
1962	600	765	227	121	26
1963	626	785	257	121	25
1964	646	822	322	130	24
1965	676	839	379	140	24
1966	720	855	406	148	21
1967	730	798	431	189	21
1968	747	774	443	221	25
1969	849	762	394	215	28
1970	870	755	380	241	31
1971	848	689	359	233	38
1972	896	641	349	230	55
1973	1,043	624	320	248	134
1974	1,170	614	302	275	163
1975	1,289	581	286	299	170
1976	1,344	522	299	309	195
1977	1,446	464	338	314	211
1978	1,684	433	347	313	289
1979	2,012	418	415	286	354
1980	2,251	401	408	298	388
1981	2,382	364	389	358	478
1982	2,407	346	353	455	520

Source: Annual Report to Policyowners

ASSETS

(Millions)

Year	Loans on Policies	ISA Loans	Bank Balances and Cash	Other Assets	Separate Account Business	Total
1957	$ 153	----	$24	$ 70	----	$ 3,727
1958	167	----	31	74	----	3,893
1959	190	----	32	77	----	4,041
1960	226	----	27	83	----	4,198
1961	250	----	29	90	----	4,364
1962	273	$ 2	33	91	----	4,494
1963	291	6	23	89	----	4,657
1964	312	11	24	89	----	4,852
1965	339	16	25	91	----	5,071
1966	452	22	26	97	----	5,229
1967	512	29	23	104	----	5,476
1968	610	35	21	111	----	5,720
1969	827	41	18	118	$ 1	5,910
1970	983	46	22	127	4	6,125
1971	1,032	46	25	140	100	6,453
1972	1,093	54	27	146	124	6,856
1973	1,291	63	22	153	131	7,096
1974	1,499	73	25	169	130	7,344
1975	1,599	85	21	173	157	7,918
1976	1,701	98	33	194	196	8,544
1977	1,839	114	30	211	215	9,062
1978	2,069	134	32	234	230	9,736
1979	2,480	155	23	262	252	10,554
1980	3,048	176	19	286	268	11,351
1981	3,672	195	26	314	275	12,154
1982	4,087	215	15	361	397	13,377*

*Includes the subsidiaries: Northwestern Retirement Insurance and Annuity Company and Standard of America Life Insurance Company

Source: Annual Report to Policyowners

NORTHWESTERN MUTUAL: SOURCE OF INCOME

(Millions)

Year	From Premiums	Net* From Investments	Other	Total
1957	$ 307	$148	$52	$ 507
1958	317	159	54	530
1959	326	171	50	547
1960	336	180	46	562
1961	344	195	58	597
1962	363	208	54	625
1963	378	204	53	635
1964	394	218	58	670
1965	413	232	54	699
1966	442	248	56	746
1967	467	261	50	778
1968	499	279	51	829
1969	533	299	46	878
1970	558	317	48	923
1971	599	338	46	983
1972	639	367	51	1,057
1973	689	398	68	1,155
1974	751	423	70	1,244
1975	817	451	81	1,349
1976	894	497	78	1,469
1977	1,003	550	84	1,637
1978	1,121	617	77	1,815
1979	1,244	703	74	2,021
1980	1,406	790	85	2,281
1981	1,559	841	88	2,488
1982	1,719	921	81	2,721

*Before Federal income taxes

Source: Report to Trustees

PAYMENTS TO POLICYOWNERS
(Millions)

Year	Death Claims	Matured Endowments & Annuities	Surrenders	Disability Benefits	Interest and Payments on Policy or Supplementary Contract Funds	Dividends	Total
1957	$ 82	$26	$ 54	$ 1	$ 68	$ 75	$ 306
1958	83	27	62	1	61	82	316
1959	88*	27	62	1	65	89	332
1960	87	27	72	1	63	94	344
1961	95	33	78	1	62	99	368
1962	95	32	98	1	67	106	399
1963	101	33	104	1	70	121	430
1964	103	33	82	1	69	122	410
1965	110	24	100	1	71	137	443
1966	110	29	80	2	77	142	440
1967	114	25	87	2	76	164	468
1968	128	27	99	2	76	169	501
1969	126	26	108	2	78	179	519
1970	128	32	118	3**	77	197	555
1971	133	29	105	3	70	209	549
1972	143	27	109	3	70	234	586
1973	144	29	134	4	80	246	637
1974	152	31	133	5	85	264	670
1975	142	35	134	6	86	293	696
1976	166	34	147	7	86	323	763
1977	163	40	151	8	88	366	816
1978	174	39	149	9	99	416	886
1979	188	40	190	12	109	489	1,028
1980	216	41	232	12	138	543	1,182
1981	231	44	270	16	130	597	1,288
1982	251	39	345	17	137	695	1,484

*Accidental Death Benefits start
**Disability Income payments start

Source: Report to Trustees

LIFE INSURANCE

| Year | LIFE INSURANCE Average Size Policy | | INVESTMENT YIELD | |
	New	In Force	Before Income Tax	After Income Tax
1957	$ 9,981	$ 5,494	3.90%	3.61%
1958	10,148	5,716	4.01	3.52
1959	11,342	5,978	4.14	3.68
1960	11,655	6,235	4.27	3.78
1961	11,798	6,478	4.41	3.88
1962	12,112	6,749	4.57	4.00
1963	12,774	7,078	4.62	4.00
1964	13,428	7,424	4.74	4.10
1965	13,911	7,837	4.83	4.18
1966	14,730	8,224	4.98	4.27
1967	15,590	8,631	5.04	4.33
1968	17,335	9,124	5.15	4.34
1969	19,950	9,712	5.32	4.46
1970	19,233	10,227	5.46	4.59
1971	20,685	10,841	5.60	4.70
1972	22,370	11,573	5.81	4.85
1973	24,866	12,448	6.02	5.03
1974	27,452	13,443	6.19	5.18
1975	28,691	14,409	6.26	5.29
1976	30,082	15,474	6.42	5.32
1977	33,215	16,706	6.66	5.61
1978	38,202	18,319	7.00	5.79
1979	41,352	20,031	7.41	6.08
1980	45,930	22,857	7.72	6.69
1981	49,770	25,256	7.66	6.93
1982	67,737	28,169	7.80	7.39

Source: Annual Statement

INDEX

Numbers in italics indicate illustrations